GLEIM®

2022 EDITION

EA REVIEW

PART 3: REPRESENTATION, PRACTICES & PROCEDURES

by

Irvin N. Gleim, Ph.D., CPA, CIA, CMA, CFM

and

James R. Hasselback, Ph.D.

THE GOLD STANDARD IN EA REVIEW
GLEIM
TRUSTED BY TAX PROFESSIONALS SINCE 1974
4 DECADES OF SERVICE

Gleim EA Review for the IRS Special Enrollment Exam 5/1/2022 - 2/28/2023

Gleim Publications, Inc.
PO Box 12848
Gainesville, Florida 32604
(800) 87-GLEIM or (800) 874-5346
(352) 375-0772
www.gleimEA.com
GleimEA@gleim.com

For updates to this 2022 edition of ***EA Review: Part 3, Representation, Practices & Procedures***

Go To: www.gleim.com/EAupdate

Or: Email update@gleim.com with **EA 3 2022-1** in the subject line. You will receive our current update as a reply.

Updates are available until the next edition is published.

ISSN: 2168-3883

ISBN: 978-1-61854-493-3 *EA 1: Individuals*
ISBN: 978-1-61854-494-0 *EA 2: Businesses*
ISBN: 978-1-61854-495-7 *EA 3: Representation, Practices & Procedures*
ISBN: 978-1-61854-503-9 *Enrolled Agent Exam Guide: A System for Success*

First Printing: February 2022

ACKNOWLEDGMENTS

The authors appreciate and thank the Internal Revenue Service and Prometric for their cooperation. Questions have been used from the 1978-2021 Special Enrollment Examinations.

ABOUT THE AUTHORS

Irvin N. Gleim, who authored the first edition of Gleim EA Review over 20 years ago, was Professor Emeritus in the Fisher School of Accounting at the University of Florida and a member of the American Accounting Association, Academy of Legal Studies in Business, American Institute of Certified Public Accountants, Association of Government Accountants, Florida Institute of Certified Public Accountants, The Institute of Internal Auditors, and the Institute of Management Accountants. The late Dr. Gleim published articles in the *Journal of Accountancy*, *The Accounting Review*, and the *American Business Law Journal* and authored numerous accounting books, aviation books, and CPE courses.

James R. Hasselback is an Adjunct Professor at Louisiana State University. He has previously taught at Florida State University, Eastern Michigan University, the University of Florida, and Texas A&M University. A member of the American Accounting Association and the American Taxation Association, he has published over 160 papers in professional and academic journals, including *The Accounting Review*, *The Tax Adviser*, *Financial Management*, *Journal of Real Estate Taxation*, and the *American Business Law Journal*. Dr. Hasselback has presented papers at many national and regional professional meetings and has served as chairman at tax sessions of professional conferences. He regularly presents continuing education seminars for certified public accountants. In addition, he has been coauthor and technical editor of a two-volume introductory taxation series published by CCH, Inc., for the past 30 years and has served as technical editor of several publications by CCH and Harper-Collins. Dr. Hasselback has compiled over 40 editions of the *Accounting Faculty Directory*.

A PERSONAL THANKS

This manual would not have been possible without the extraordinary effort and dedication of Jedidiah Arnold, Jacob Bennett, Julie Cutlip, Ethan Good, Doug Green, Fernanda Martinez, Bree Rodriguez, Veronica Rodriguez, Joanne Strong, Elmer Tucker, and Ryan Van Tress, who typed the entire manuscript and all revisions and drafted and laid out the diagrams, illustrations, and cover for this book.

The authors also appreciate the production and editorial assistance of Brianna Barnett, Michaela Giampaolo, Jessica Hatker, Sonora Hospital-Medina, Katie Larson, Bryce Owen, David Sox, and Alyssa Thomas.

The authors also appreciate the critical reading assistance of Amanda Allen, Andrew Johnson, Melissa Leonard, Andrew Schreiber, and Maris Silvestri.

The authors also appreciate the video production expertise of Gary Brook, Philip Brubaker, and Matthew Church, who helped produce and edit our Gleim Instruct Video Series.

Finally, we appreciate the encouragement, support, and tolerance of our families throughout this project.

REVIEWERS AND CONTRIBUTORS

Garrett W. Gleim, CPA, CGMA, leads production of the Gleim CPA, CMA, CIA, and EA exam review systems. He is a member of the American Institute of Certified Public Accountants and the Florida Institute of Certified Public Accountants and holds a Bachelor of Science in Economics with a Concentration in Accounting from The Wharton School, University of Pennsylvania. Mr. Gleim is coauthor of numerous accounting and aviation books and the inventor of multiple patents with educational applications. He is also an avid pilot who holds a commercial pilot rating and is a certified flight instructor. In addition, as an active supporter of the local business community, Mr. Gleim serves as an advisor to several start-ups.

D. Scott Lawton, B.S., EA, is a graduate of Brigham Young University-Idaho and Utah Valley University. Previously, he was an auditor for the Utah State Tax Commission. Mr. Lawton provided substantial editorial assistance throughout the project.

LouAnn M. Lutter, M.S. Acc., CPA, received a Master of Science in Accounting from the University of Colorado, Boulder. Previously, she was an Accounting Manager in Corporate Accounting and Shared Business Services at Caesars Entertainment. Ms. Lutter provided substantial editorial assistance throughout the project.

Mark S. Modas, M.S.T., CPA, holds a Bachelor of Arts in Accounting from Florida Atlantic University and a Master of Science in Taxation from Nova Southeastern University. Prior to joining Gleim, he worked in internal auditing, accounting and financial reporting, and corporate tax compliance in the public and private sectors. Mr. Modas provided substantial editorial assistance throughout the project.

Nate Wadlinger, J.D., LL.M., EA, CPA, is a Lecturer of Accounting at the University of Central Florida, where he teaches tax and accounting courses in the Bachelor and Master of Accounting programs. Mr. Wadlinger received his Bachelor of Science in Accounting, Master of Accounting, and Juris Doctor from the University of Florida and his LL.M. in Taxation from Boston University. In addition, he is an EA, a CPA licensed by the State of Florida, and a member of the Florida Bar. Mr. Wadlinger is the EA Gleim Instruct lecturer.

Returns of books purchased from bookstores and other resellers should be made to the respective bookstore or reseller. For more information regarding the Gleim Return Policy, please contact our offices at (800) 874-5346 or visit www.gleim.com/returnpolicy.

TABLE OF CONTENTS

DETAILED TABLE OF CONTENTS

A MESSAGE FROM OUR AUTHORS

The purpose of this book is to help **you** prepare to pass Part 3, Representation, Practices and Procedures, of the IRS Special Enrollment Exam, which is commonly referred to as the EA (enrolled agent) exam. Our goal is to provide an affordable, effective, and easy-to-use study program. Our course

1. Explains how to maximize your score through learning strategies and exam-taking techniques perfected by Gleim EA.
2. Outlines all of the content topics described in the IRS Exam Content Outlines and tested on Part 3 of the EA exam.
3. Organizes all of the subject matter tested on Part 3 in 7 easy-to-use study units, reflecting 2021 tax law (which is what will be tested on the 2022 EA exam).
4. Presents multiple-choice questions taken or modeled from past EA examinations to prepare you for the types of questions you will find on your EA exams.
   a. In our book, the answer explanations are presented to the immediate right of each question for your convenience. Use a piece of paper to cover our detailed answer explanations as you answer the question and then review all answer choices to learn why the correct one is correct and why the other choices are incorrect.
   b. You should also practice answering these questions through our online platform, which mimics Prometric's user interface, so you are comfortable answering questions online like you will do on test day. Our adaptive course will focus and target your weak areas.

The outline format, spacing, and question and answer formats in this book are designed to increase readability, learning, understanding, and success on the EA exam. Our most successful candidates use the Gleim Premium EA Review System, which includes Gleim Instruct videos; our Access Until You Pass Guarantee; our innovative SmartAdapt technology; expertly authored books; the largest test bank of multiple-choice questions; audio lectures; flashcards; and the support of our team of accounting experts. To maximize the efficiency and effectiveness of your EA exam preparations, start by reviewing the *Enrolled Agent Exam Guide: A System for Success*.

Thank you for trusting us with your EA studies. We appreciate any and all feedback. Immediately after you take the exam and receive your exam score, please go to www.gleim.com/feedbackEA3 to share suggestions on how we can improve this edition. The EA exam is a **nondisclosed** exam, which means you must maintain the confidentiality of the exam by not divulging the nature or content of any EA question or answer under any circumstances. We ask only for information about our materials and any improvements that can be made regarding topics that need to be added or expanded or need more emphasis.

On behalf of our entire team, we want to thank every EA candidate who has trusted us to help them pass the EA exam and achieve career success.

Good Luck on the Exam,

Irvin N. Gleim
James R. Hasselback

ACCOUNTING TITLES FROM GLEIM PUBLICATIONS

EA Review:

- Part 1: Individuals
- Part 2: Businesses
- Part 3: Representation, Practices and Procedures

CIA Review:

- Part 1: Essentials of Internal Auditing
- Part 2: Practice of Internal Auditing
- Part 3: Business Knowledge for Internal Auditing
- CIA Challenge Exam

CMA Review:

- Part 1: Financial Planning, Performance, and Analytics
- Part 2: Strategic Financial Management

CPA Review:

- Auditing & Attestation (AUD)
- Business Environment & Concepts (BEC)
- Financial Accounting & Reporting (FAR)
- Regulation (REG)

Exam Questions and Explanations (EQE) Series:

- Auditing & Systems
- Business Law & Legal Studies
- Cost/Managerial Accounting
- Federal Tax
- Financial Accounting

Gleim Publications also publishes aviation training materials. Go to www.GleimAviation.com for a complete listing of our aviation titles.

PREPARING FOR AND TAKING THE IRS ENROLLED AGENT EXAMINATION

READ THE *ENROLLED AGENT EXAM GUIDE: A SYSTEM FOR SUCCESS*

Access the free copy of the Gleim ***Enrolled Agent Exam Guide*** by visiting www.gleim.com/PassEA and reference it throughout your studies for a deeper understanding of the EA exam. This booklet is your system for success.

OVERVIEW OF THE EA EXAMINATION

The **exam consists of three parts, with 3.5 hours for each part** (4 hours total seat time to include tutorial, survey, and optional 15-minute break). The total exam for all three parts is 10.5 hours of testing (12 hours total seat time to include tutorials, surveys, and optional 15-minute breaks). It covers **federal taxation; tax accounting; and the use of tax return forms for individuals, partnerships, corporations, trusts, estates, and gifts**. It also covers **ethical considerations and procedural requirements**.

The questions on the examination are directed toward the tasks that enrolled agents must perform to complete and file forms and tax returns and to represent taxpayers before the Internal Revenue Service. Each part of the examination consists of **100 multiple-choice questions** and covers the following tax topics:

Part 1 - Individuals
Part 2 - Businesses
Part 3 - Representation, Practices and Procedures

Based on the experience of our customers who have taken all three parts of the exam, Gleim recommends that candidates sit for Parts 1 and 2 before taking Part 3. Feedback indicates that Part 3 candidates should be knowledgeable about topics covered in Parts 1 and 2 as they relate to the topics that Part 3 tests.

IRS's NONDISCLOSURE AGREEMENT

The EA exam is nondisclosed. The following is taken from the IRS's *Candidate Information Bulletin*. It is reproduced here to remind all EA candidates about the IRS's strict policy of nondisclosure, which Gleim consistently supports and upholds.

> *This exam is confidential and proprietary. It is made available to you, the examinee, solely for the purpose of assessing your proficiency level in the skill area referenced in the title of this exam. You are expressly prohibited from disclosing, publishing, reproducing, or transmitting this exam, in whole or in part, in any form or by any means, verbal or written, electronic or mechanical, for any purpose, without the prior express written permission of the IRS.*

DATES OF THE EXAMINATION/TAX LAW COVERED

The 2022 examination test window will begin May 1, 2022, and examinations will be offered continuously through February 28, 2023.

Each testing year's EA exam (through February of the following year) covers the tax law in effect the previous December 31. For example, the May 1, 2022-February 28, 2023, testing window will test tax law in effect December 31, 2021.

Gleim consistently monitors any changes the IRS makes to the exam. Stay up to date on any EA exam changes at www.gleim.com/EAexamchanges.

GLEIM PREMIUM EA REVIEW WITH SMARTADAPT

Gleim Premium EA Review features the most comprehensive coverage of exam content and employs the most efficient learning techniques to help you study smarter and most effectively. The Gleim Premium EA Review System is powered by SmartAdapt technology, an innovative platform that identifies where you should focus (and where you should not) as you move through the following steps for optimized EA review:

Step 1:

Complete a Diagnostic Study Quiz. As you work through this quiz, you will get immediate feedback on your answer choices. This allows you to learn as you study the detailed answer explanations. Meanwhile, your quiz results set a baseline that our SmartAdapt technology will use to create a custom learning track for each bite-sized module.

Step 2:

Solidify your knowledge by studying the suggested Knowledge Transfer Outline(s) or watching the suggested Gleim Instruct video(s). You will also be able to take notes within your online course while reviewing either of these learning tools.

Step 3:

Focus on weak areas and perfect your question-answering techniques by taking the adaptive quizzes that SmartAdapt directs you to.

Final Review:

After completing all study units, take the first full-length Mock Exam. Then, SmartAdapt will guide you through a Final Review based on your results, which will help pinpoint where you need to focus. Finally, a few days before your exam date, take the second full-length Mock Exam. SmartAdapt will tell you when you are ready to pass with confidence.

To facilitate your studies, the Gleim Premium EA Review System uses the largest bank of multiple-choice questions on the market. Our system's content and presentation precisely mimic the whole exam environment so you feel completely at ease on test day.

TIME-BUDGETING AND QUESTION-ANSWERING TECHNIQUES FOR THE EXAM

The following suggestions are to assist you in maximizing your score on Part 3 of the EA exam. Remember, knowing how to take the exam and how to answer individual questions is as important as studying/reviewing the subject matter tested on the exam.

1. **Budget your time.** We make this point with emphasis–**finish your exam before time expires**.
    a. You will have 3 hours and 30 minutes (210 minutes) to answer 100 multiple-choice questions. On your Prometric computer screen, the time remaining (starting with 03:30:00) appears in the top middle of the screen.
    b. As you work through the individual multiple-choice questions, monitor your time. If you allocate 1.5-2 minutes per question, you will require 150-200 minutes to finish all 100 questions, leaving 10-60 minutes to review your answers and "flagged" questions (see item 2.b. below). Spending 2 minutes should be reserved for only the most difficult questions. You should complete 10 questions every 15-20 minutes. If you pace yourself during the exam, you will have adequate time.
    c. The exam is broken into two halves of 50 questions each with an optional 15-minute break. The first half should take 75-100 minutes. You should finish answering and reviewing by the time you are 105 minutes through your exam. The remaining time will be spent on the second half.
2. **Answer the questions in consecutive order.**
    a. Do **not** agonize over any one question. Stay within your time budget: 1.5-2 minutes per question.
    b. Note any items you are unsure of by clicking the button with the flag icon and return to them later if time allows. Plan on going back to all flagged questions.
    c. Never leave a question unanswered. Make your best guess within your budgeted time. Your score is based on the number of correct responses. You will not be penalized for guessing incorrectly. You can always flag the question and return to it later.
3. **For each multiple-choice question,**
    a. **Try to ignore the answer choices as you determine the answer.** Do not allow the answer choices to affect your reading of the question.
        1) If four answer choices are presented, three of them are incorrect. These incorrect answers are called **distractors** for good reason. Often, distractors are written to appear correct at first glance until further analysis.
        2) In computational items, distractors are carefully calculated so that they are the result of making common mistakes. Be careful, and double-check your computations if time permits.
    b. **Read the question** carefully to determine the precise requirement.
        1) Focusing on what is required enables you to ignore extraneous information and proceed directly to determining the correct answer. This will save you valuable time.
            a) Be especially careful to note when the requirement is an **exception**; e.g., "Which of the following is **not** includible in gross income?"

c. **Determine the correct answer** before looking at the answer choices.

   1) However, some multiple-choice items are structured so that the answer cannot be determined from the stem alone. See the stem in 3.b.1)a) on the previous page.

d. **Then read the answer choices carefully.**

   1) Even if the first answer appears to be the correct choice, do not skip the remaining answer choices. Questions often ask for the "best" of the choices provided. Thus, each choice requires your consideration.

   2) Treat each answer choice as a true/false question as you analyze it.

e. **Click on the best answer.**

   1) If you are uncertain, you have a 25% chance of answering the question correctly by guessing blindly. Improve your odds with educated guessing.

   2) For many of the multiple-choice questions, two answer choices can be eliminated with minimal effort, thereby increasing your educated guess to a 50-50 proposition.

4. After you have answered the 50 questions in each exam section, return to the questions you flagged. Make sure to stay within your time budget. Then, verify that all questions have been answered.

5. **If you don't know the answer:**

   a. Again, guess but make it an educated guess. First, rule out answers you think are incorrect. Second, speculate on what the IRS is looking for and/or the rationale behind the question. Third, select the best answer or guess between equally appealing answers. Your first guess is usually the most intuitive. If you cannot make an educated guess, read the stem and each answer, and pick the most intuitive answer.

   b. Make sure you accomplish this step within the predetermined time budget.

LEARNING FROM YOUR MISTAKES

Learning from questions you answer incorrectly is very important. Each question you answer incorrectly is an **opportunity** to avoid missing actual test questions on your EA exam. Thus, you should carefully study the answer explanations provided until you understand why the original answer you chose is wrong, as well as why the correct answer indicated is correct. This learning technique is clearly the difference between passing and failing for many EA candidates.

Also, you must determine why you answered questions incorrectly and learn how to avoid the same error in the future. Reasons for missing questions include

1. Misreading the requirement (stem)
2. Not understanding what is required
3. Making a mathematical error
4. Applying the wrong rule or concept
5. Being distracted by one or more of the answers
6. Incorrectly eliminating answers from consideration
7. Not having knowledge of the topic tested
8. Employing poor intuition when guessing

HOW TO BE IN CONTROL WHILE TAKING THE EXAM

You have to be in control to be successful during exam preparation and execution. Control can also contribute greatly to your personal and other professional goals. Control is a process whereby you

1. Develop expectations, standards, budgets, and plans.
2. Undertake activity, production, study, and learning.
3. Measure the activity, production, output, and knowledge.
4. Compare actual activity with expected and budgeted activity.
5. Modify the activity to better achieve the desired outcome.
6. Revise expectations and standards in light of actual experience.
7. Continue the process or restart the process in the future.

Exercising control will ultimately develop the confidence you need to outperform most other EA candidates and PASS the EA exam!

> Learn more about these strategies and other helpful tips in our free *Enrolled Agent Exam Guide: A System for Success*. You can view this booklet online at www.gleim.com/PassEA.

IF YOU HAVE QUESTIONS ABOUT GLEIM MATERIALS

Gleim has an efficient and effective way for candidates who have purchased the Premium EA Review System to submit an inquiry and receive a response regarding Gleim materials directly through their course. This system also allows you to view your Q&A session in your Gleim Personal Classroom.

Questions regarding the information in this introduction and/or the *Enrolled Agent Exam Guide* (study suggestions, studying plans, exam specifics) should be emailed to personalcounselor@gleim.com.

Questions concerning orders, prices, shipments, or payments should be sent via email to customerservice@gleim.com and will be promptly handled by our competent and courteous customer service staff.

For technical support, you may use our automated technical support service at www.gleim.com/support, email us at support@gleim.com, or call us at (800) 874-5346.

FEEDBACK

Please fill out our online feedback form www.gleim.com/feedbackEA immediately after you take the EA exam so we can adapt to changes on the exam. Our approach has been approved by the IRS.

STUDY UNIT ONE

PRACTICE BEFORE THE IRS

(19 pages of outline)

When a dispute or disagreement over tax issues arises, a taxpayer may have to appear before the IRS. Enrolled agents, CPAs, attorneys, and other individuals authorized to practice before the IRS may represent taxpayers. This study unit discusses the various individuals who may practice before the IRS, their standards of conduct, and other requirements of enrolled agents.

1.1 AUTHORITY TO PRACTICE

Rules of Practice

1. The rules governing practice before the Internal Revenue Service (IRS) appear in Treasury Department Circular 230, *Regulations Governing Practice before the Internal Revenue Service*.
   a. We have reproduced Circular 230 as Appendix A.

Practice before the IRS

2. Practice before the IRS is the presentation to the IRS, or any of its officers or employees, of any matter relating to a taxpayer's rights, privileges, or liabilities under laws or regulations administered by the IRS.
3. Practicing before the IRS includes
   a. Communicating with the IRS for a taxpayer
   b. Representing a taxpayer at conferences, hearings, or meetings with the IRS
   c. Preparing necessary documents and filing them with the IRS for a taxpayer
   d. Rendering written advice with respect to any entity, transaction, plan, or arrangement, or other plan or arrangement having a potential for tax avoidance or evasion
4. The following do **not** constitute practicing before the IRS:
   a. Preparing a tax return, an amended return, or a claim for refund
   b. Furnishing information upon request of the IRS
   c. Appearing as a witness for the taxpayer

Who May Practice

5. Only authorized persons may practice before the IRS (i.e., practitioners).
   a. The following persons may practice before the IRS:
      1) Attorneys
         a) An attorney is a member in good standing of the bar of the highest court of any state, possession, territory, commonwealth, or the District of Columbia.
      2) CPAs
         a) A CPA who is not suspended from practice by the Office of Professional Responsibility and who is currently qualified to practice as a CPA in any state
      3) Enrolled agents
      4) Enrolled actuaries, for limited purposes listed under Sec. 10.3(d) of Circular 230
      5) Enrolled retirement plan agents, for limited purposes listed under Sec. 10.3(e) of Circular 230
      6) Annual Filing Season Program participants
         a) The limited right to represent clients before the IRS is accorded to non-credentialed preparers only if they participate in the IRS Annual Filing Season Program (AFSP) and they must have prepared the return.
      7) Unenrolled individuals, if specifically permitted
      8) Appraisers

	Types of Practitioners	Attorney, CPA, EA	AFSP Participants/ Others Specifically Allowed to Practice
	Allowed Practice before the IRS	Unlimited	Limited
Type of Practice before the IRS	Preparation of Return or Claim for Refund	Sign returns and refunds when completed "all or substantially all" of a return or refund	Sign returns and refunds when completed "all or substantially all" of a return or refund
Type of Practice before the IRS	Representation	1) Before anyone at the IRS 2) Examination and appeals 3) Any return or refund	1) Before IRS revenue agents, customer service representatives, and employees 2) During examination only 3) Return that tax return preparer signed him- or herself for the period under examination 4) Must participate in AFSP or be specifically permitted to practice
Type of Practice before the IRS	Tax Advice	Unlimited including tax planning	Limited to return or refund preparation

Attorney or CPA Requirements to Practice

   b. To practice before the IRS, an attorney or a CPA must
      1) File a written declaration, for each party (s)he represents, that (s)he
         a) Is qualified currently
         b) Has been authorized to represent the party
      2) Not be suspended or disbarred

Enrolled Agent

c. An enrolled agent is an individual, other than an attorney or a CPA, who is eligible, qualified, and certified as authorized to represent another in practice before the IRS.

1) An enrolled agent may not appear in a representative capacity on behalf of any taxpayer unless the enrolled agent

a) Is recognized to practice before the IRS and
b) Presents satisfactory identification.

2) Recognition must be evidenced when the enrolled agent appears for the initial meeting in the first office of the IRS in which (s)he represents the taxpayer.

a) A person will be recognized to practice before the IRS if (s)he meets the requirements set forth in Circular 230. Under Circular 230, an enrolled agent may represent a particular party upon filing a written declaration that (s)he

i) Is qualified currently and
ii) Has been authorized to represent the party.

d. Only natural persons may be enrolled agents.

1) U.S. citizenship is not required.

2) Enrollment is available to, but not required of, attorneys and CPAs. They are automatically entitled to practice before the IRS.

Eligibility to Become Enrolled

e. Eligible individuals must meet certain requirements for enrollment.

1) **Conduct.** Enrollment is precluded by conduct that justifies suspension or disbarment from practice.

2) **Exam.** A person who passes the IRS Special Enrollment Exam (also known as the Enrolled Agent or EA exam) may be enrolled.

3) **IRS experience.** Past service in the IRS and technical experience are a basis for enrollment.

a) Factors considered are

i) Length (minimum of 5 continuous years), scope, and extent of employment

ii) Recommendation of the employing division's superior officer

Application to Become Enrolled

f. A properly executed application for enrollment is necessary.

1) **Temporary recognition** to practice may be granted to an applicant in unusual circumstances. The application must be regular on its face and properly executed.

a) It does not constitute a finding of eligibility or enrollment.
b) It may be withdrawn at any time.

2) Consideration of the application may be conditioned on both

a) Filing additional information and
b) Submitting to written or oral examination under oath.

3) An applicant may file a written appeal to the Secretary of the Treasury within 30 days after the receipt of a notice of denial.

4) Enrollment card. Each approved applicant is issued an enrollment card.

Eligibility of Non-Form 1040 Series Preparers to Represent Clients

g. Non-Form 1040 series preparers are individuals who certify that they do not prepare, or assist in the preparation of, any Form 1040 series tax return or claim for refund, except Form 1040-PR or Form 1040-SS, for compensation. Non-Form 1040 series preparers may

1) Sign any tax return they prepare or assist in preparing
2) Represent taxpayers before revenue agents, customer service representatives, or similar officers and employees of the IRS (including the Taxpayer Advocate Service) during an examination if the individual signed the tax return or claim for refund for the taxable year under examination

Other Persons who may Practice before the IRS on a Limited Basis (AKA "limited practice")

h. The IRS may authorize any person to represent another without enrollment. Individuals who are under suspension or disbarment from practice before the IRS may not engage in limited practice before the IRS. Listed below are situations in which representation by an individual without enrollment has been authorized:

1) **Family.** An individual may represent, without compensation, an immediate family member.
2) **Employee.** An employee may represent his or her regular, full-time employer.
3) **Partnership.** A general partner or full-time partnership employee may represent the partnership.
4) **Corporation.** An officer or a regular, full-time corporate employee may represent the corporation.
5) **Fiduciary.** A trustee, a receiver, a guardian, an administrator, or an executor may represent the trust, receivership, guardianship, or estate.
6) **Overseas.** An individual may provide representation to any individual or entity if the representation takes place outside the U.S.
7) **Student Attorney/Student CPA.** A student can apply for permission to practice before the IRS by virtue of his or her status as a law student or CPA student under Sec. 10.7(d) of Circular 230.
8) **Others.** An individual may be authorized by the Commissioner of the IRS to represent others in a particular matter.

Who Is Subject to Regulations in Circular 230

6. Any practitioner who for compensation prepares or assists with the preparation of all or substantially all of a tax return or claim for refund is subject to the duties and restrictions relating to practice, as well as subject to the sanctions for violation of the regulations in Circular 230.

Who May Not Practice

7. Unauthorized persons may not practice before the IRS.
   a. A member of Congress may not practice before the IRS in connection with any matter for which (s)he directly or indirectly receives, agrees to receive, or seeks any compensation.
   b. An officer or employee of the U.S. (legislative, executive, or judicial branch) or its agencies may not practice before the IRS, except as
      1) The representative of an immediate family member
      2) A personal fiduciary, such as trustee, receiver, guardian, administrator, or executor, representing the fiduciary entity or beneficiary
   c. A state employee who investigates, passes upon, or otherwise deals with state tax matters may not practice before the IRS if (s)he may disclose information applicable to federal tax matters.
   d. An individual convicted of any offense involving dishonesty or breach of trust may not practice before the IRS.

Limited Practice (ICBU)

8. Any practitioner who is an unenrolled return preparer (i.e., not a CPA, attorney, or EA) may only represent clients before revenue agents and customer service representatives (not appeals officers, revenue officers, or counsel) and may only represent clients for the tax return (s)he signed/prepared.

Oversight of Practice

9. The Commissioner of Internal Revenue or his or her delegate
   a. Acts on applications for enrollment
   b. Makes inquiries respecting matters under the commissioner's jurisdiction
   c. Institutes and provides for the conduct of disciplinary proceedings relating to practitioners
   d. Performs duties prescribed by the Secretary of the Treasury

PTIN

10. Any individual who for compensation prepares or assists with the preparation of all or substantially all of a federal tax return or claim for refund must have a Preparer Tax Identification Number (PTIN). Tax preparers can sign up for a PTIN online or by paper application.
    a. The PTIN must be renewed annually.

***STOP AND REVIEW!* You have completed the outline for this subunit. Study multiple-choice questions 1 through 4 beginning on page 26.**

1.2 CONDUCT OF PRACTICE

Rules for conduct of an attorney, a CPA, or an enrolled agent in practice before the IRS are provided in the applicable sections of Part 10 of Circular 230. Examples follow. Unless otherwise indicated, “practitioner” includes anyone preparing a tax return, e.g., an attorney, a CPA, or an EA.

Qualified

1. The person representing a taxpayer before the IRS must be qualified, e.g., an EA.
   a. The duty may not be delegated to an employee of the qualified practitioner.
   b. A power of attorney or written authorization from the taxpayer is insufficient.

Declaration

2. A written declaration that the representative is both qualified and authorized to represent the particular principal must be filed with the IRS.

Relying on Information Furnished by Clients

3. A practitioner advising a client to take a position on a tax return, document, affidavit, or other paper submitted to the IRS, or preparing or signing a tax return as a preparer, generally may rely in good faith without verification upon information furnished by the client.
   a. However, the preparer may not ignore the implications of the information.
   b. The preparer must make **reasonable inquiries** if the information appears inaccurate or incomplete.
   c. The preparer should make appropriate inquiries of the taxpayer about the existence of documentation for deductions.

Conflict of Interest

4. According to Sec. 10.29 of Circular 230, a conflict of interest exists if
   a. The representation of one client will adversely impact another client or
   b. There is a significant risk that the representation of one or more clients will be materially limited by the practitioner’s responsibilities
      1) To another client,
      2) To a former client or a third person, or
      3) By a personal interest of the practitioner.
5. A practitioner may represent conflicting interests before the IRS only if
   a. All directly affected parties provide informed, written consent at the time the existence of the conflict is known by the agent
      1) Written consent must be within 30 days of informed consent.
   b. The representation is not prohibited by law
   c. The practitioner reasonably believes that (s)he can provide competent and diligent representation to each client
6. Copies of the written consents must be retained by the practitioner for at least 36 months from the date of the conclusion of the representation of the affected clients, and the written consents must be provided to any officer or employee of the IRS on request.

7. The following are additional rules for conflict of interest:
   a. A former government employee who participated in a transaction may not represent or knowingly assist any party who is or was a specific party to that transaction.
   b. A former IRS employee who participated in a matter administered by the IRS may not represent or assist anyone in the matter.
   c. No agent may knowingly accept direct or indirect assistance from a former government employee such that 5.a. or 5.b. on the previous page would be violated.
   d. Members of a former IRS employee's current firm, however, may represent or assist a specific party to such a matter if the former IRS employee is screened (isolated) such that (s)he does not assist in the representation.
   e. A practitioner may not administer oaths or certify papers as a notary public in connection with matters in which (s)he is employed as agent for the taxpayer or in which (s)he may be in any way interested before the IRS.

Diligence

8. Diligence must be exercised in preparing and in assisting in preparing, approving, and filing returns, documents, and other papers relating to IRS matters.
   a. Due diligence must also be exercised in determining the correctness of oral or written representations made by the practitioner to the Department of the Treasury and to clients.
   b. Diligence is presumed if the practitioner
      1) Relies upon the work product of another person and
      2) Uses reasonable care in engaging, supervising, training, and evaluating the person.
   c. If the practitioner engages a specialist, the focus is on engaging the specialist; when delegating to an employee, the focus is on training, supervising, and evaluating the employee.
   d. A practitioner may not unreasonably delay the prompt disposition of any matter before the IRS.

Information

9. Information or records properly and lawfully requested by a duly authorized officer or employee of the IRS must be promptly submitted.
   a. If reasonable basis exists for a good-faith belief that the information is privileged or that the request is not proper and lawful, the practitioner is excused from submitting the requested information.
   b. A practitioner also is required to provide information about the identity of persons that (s)he reasonably believes may have possession or control of the requested information if the practitioner does not.
      1) This only requires that the practitioner make a reasonable inquiry of his or her client to determine this information and does not require independent verification of the client's statement.

Assistance from a Suspended or Disbarred Practitioner

10. A practitioner may not knowingly accept assistance (in practice before the IRS) from or give assistance to a person suspended or disbarred from practice before the IRS.

Negotiating Client Refunds

11. A practitioner must not negotiate, including by endorsement, any income tax refund check issued to a client.

Client Noncompliance

12. A practitioner who knows that a client has not complied with the revenue laws of the U.S. is required to promptly advise the client of noncompliance as well as the consequences of noncompliance under the Code and regulations.
    a. Circular 230 does not require the practitioner to notify the IRS or to advise the client to correct the error.

Fees

13. A practitioner may not charge an unconscionable fee in connection with any practice before the IRS.
    a. Published fees. If an agent publishes a fee schedule, (s)he must abide by it for the longer of a reasonable time or 30 days.
    b. A practitioner may not charge a **contingent fee** in relation to any matter before the IRS except
        1) Examination of returns,
        2) Claim for credit or refund (interest and penalties), and
        3) Judicial proceedings.

Return of Client Records

14. A practitioner must return a client's records on request, regardless of any fee dispute.
    a. Records deemed returnable for purposes of this requirement are those records necessary for a client to comply with his or her federal tax obligations.
    b. However, returns or other documents prepared by the practitioner that the practitioner is withholding pending payment of a fee are not included.

Advertising

15. Circular 230 allows advertising and solicitation.
    a. An enrolled agent may use the phrases
        1) "enrolled to practice before the Internal Revenue Service,"
        2) "enrolled to represent taxpayers before the Internal Revenue Service,"
        3) "admitted to practice before the Internal Revenue Service."
            a) A temporarily recognized person may not use the phrase.
            b) An applicant is granted temporary recognition pending approval of application.
    b. Enrolled agents may not indicate an employer-employee relationship with the IRS or use the term "certified" while describing their professional designation.
    c. False, fraudulent, misleading, deceptive, or coercive statements or claims are not allowed. Claims must be subject to factual verification.
        1) A practitioner may advertise that practice is limited to certain areas, if true.
    d. Radio or television advertising must be recorded.
        1) A recording of the audio transmission must be retained.
    e. Copies of communications must be retained by the practitioner for at least 36 months from the date of the last transmission or use.
    f. Uninvited solicitation, direct or indirect, of employment in matters related to the IRS is not allowed if the solicitation violates federal or state law or other applicable rule.
        1) Mail solicitation designed for the general public is permissible.
        2) Mail solicitation for non-tax return services based on specific tax return circumstances unique to the recipient is not permissible.
        3) Making the availability of professional services known to other practitioners is allowed as long as the person or firm contacted is not a potential client.
    g. Fees. Each of the following may be advertised:
        1) Fixed fees for specific routine services
        2) A range of fees for particular services
        3) The fee for an initial consultation
        4) Hourly rates
        5) Availability of a written fee schedule
            a) Refer to item 13.a. on the previous page.
    h. A practitioner may not assist or accept assistance from any person or entity that the practitioner knows has obtained clients in violation of Circular 230's advertising and solicitation rules.

STOP AND REVIEW! **You have completed the outline for this subunit. Study multiple-choice questions 5 through 9 beginning on page 27.**

1.3 BEST PRACTICES FOR TAX ADVISORS

1. Tax advisors should provide clients with the highest quality representation concerning tax issues by adhering to best practices in providing advice and in preparing or assisting in the preparation of a submission to the IRS.
2. Best practices include four general elements:
   a. Performing the steps needed to support the facts for a tax filing:
      1) Establish the facts, determine which facts are relevant, evaluate the reasonableness of any assumptions or representations, relate applicable law to the relevant facts, and arrive at a conclusion supported by the law and the facts.
   b. Communicating clearly with the client about the terms of the engagement
   c. Advising the client regarding the importance of the conclusions reached, including, for example, whether a taxpayer may avoid accuracy-related penalties under the Internal Revenue Code (IRC) if a taxpayer acts in reliance on the advice
   d. Acting fairly and with integrity in practice before the IRS
3. Tax advisors must communicate the nature of any known errors or omissions, including any potential consequences under the Code or regulations.
4. Tax advisors with responsibility for overseeing a firm's practice of providing advice concerning federal tax issues or of preparing or assisting in the preparation of submissions to the IRS should take reasonable steps to ensure that the firm's procedures for all members, associates, and employees are consistent with the best practices.
5. If a representative is acting on behalf of an employer or any firm or other entity in connection with conduct subject to sanction, the Secretary of the Treasury may impose a monetary penalty on such employer, firm, or entity if it knew, or reasonably should have known, of such conduct. Such penalty shall not exceed the gross income derived (or to be derived) from the conduct giving rise to the penalty and may be in addition to, or in lieu of, any suspension, disbarment, or censure of the representative.

STOP AND REVIEW! **You have completed the outline for this subunit.** **Study multiple-choice question 10 on page 29.**

1.4 SUPERVISOR RESPONSIBILITY

Procedures to Ensure Compliance with Circular 230

1. Any practitioner who has or shares principal authority and responsibility for overseeing a firm's practice of preparing tax returns, claims for refunds, or other documents for submission to the IRS must take reasonable steps to ensure that the firm has adequate procedures in effect for all members, associates, and employees for purposes of complying with Circular 230.
2. Any practitioner who has or shares this principal authority will be subject to discipline for failing to comply in certain circumstances.
   a. The practitioner does not take reasonable steps to ensure that the firm has adequate procedures to comply with Circular 230, and one or more members, employees, or associates of the firm engage in a pattern or practice of noncompliance.
   b. The practitioner knows or should know of a pattern or practice of noncompliance, and the practitioner fails to take prompt corrective action.
   c. The practitioner is liable for such inaction if it is willful, reckless, or grossly incompetent.

Requirements for Written Tax Advice

3. A practitioner may give written advice (including by means of electronic communication) concerning one or more federal tax matters subject to the requirements below:
   a. When providing written advice about any federal tax matter, a practitioner must
      1) Base the advice on reasonable assumptions,
      2) Reasonably consider all relevant facts that are known or should be known, and
      3) Use reasonable efforts to identify and determine the relevant facts.
   b. The advice cannot rely upon representations, statements, findings, or agreements that are unreasonable, i.e., are known to be incorrect, inconsistent, or incomplete.
   c. The advice must not consider the possibility that a tax return will not be audited or a matter will not be raised during the audit in evaluating a federal tax matter.
   d. When providing written advice, a practitioner may rely in good faith on the advice of another practitioner only if that advice is reasonable given all the facts and circumstances.
   e. The practitioner cannot rely on the advice of a person who the practitioner knows or should know is not competent to provide the advice or has an unresolved conflict of interest.

STOP AND REVIEW! **You have completed the outline for this subunit. Study multiple-choice question 11 on page 30.**

1.5 SANCTIONS AND DISCIPLINARY PROCEEDINGS

Any practitioner, e.g., an attorney, a CPA, or an EA, may be censured (given public reprimand), suspended, or disbarred from practice before the IRS for willful violations of any of the regulations contained in Circular 230.

Censure, Suspend, Disbar

1. The Secretary of the Treasury may censure, suspend, or disbar from practice before the IRS any practitioner, e.g., attorney, CPA, or enrolled agent, who
    a. Is shown to be incompetent or disreputable
    b. Refuses to comply with the rules and regulations relating to practice before the IRS
    c. Willfully and knowingly, with intent to defraud, deceives, misleads, or threatens any client
2. The following is a brief list of incompetence and disreputable conduct for which a practitioner may be sanctioned under Circular 230 Sec. 10.50 that includes, but is not limited to
    a. Conviction of any criminal offense under the federal tax laws.
    b. Conviction of any criminal offense involving dishonesty or breach of trust.
    c. Conviction of any felony under federal or state law for which the conduct involved renders the practitioner unfit to practice before the IRS.
    d. Giving false or misleading information, or participating in any way in the giving of false or misleading information to the Department of the Treasury or any office or employee thereof, or to any tribunal authorized to pass upon federal tax matters, in connection with any matter pending or likely to be pending before them, knowing the information to be false or misleading.
    e. Solicitation of employment as prohibited under Sec. 10.30, the use of false or misleading representations with intent to deceive a client or prospective client in order to procure employment, or intimating that the practitioner is able improperly to obtain special consideration or action from the IRS or any officer or employee thereof.
    f. Willfully failing to make a federal tax return in violation of the federal tax law or willfully evading, attempting to evade, or participating in any way in evading or attempting to evade any assessment or payment of any federal tax.
    g. Willfully assisting, counseling, encouraging a client or prospective client in violating, or suggesting to a client or prospective client to violate, any federal tax law, or knowingly counseling or suggesting to a client or prospective client an illegal plan to evade federal taxes or payment thereof.
    h. Misappropriation of, or failure properly or promptly to remit, funds received from a client for the purpose of payment of taxes or other obligations due the United States.
    i. Directly or indirectly attempting to influence, or offering or agreeing to attempt to influence, the official action of any officer or employee of the IRS by the use of threats, false accusations, duress, or coercion, by the offer of any special inducement or promise of an advantage or by the bestowing of any gift, favor, or thing of value.
    j. Disbarment or suspension from practice as an attorney, certified public accountant, public accountant, or actuary by any duly constituted authority of any state, territory, or possession of the United States, including a commonwealth, or the District of Columbia, any federal court of record or any federal agency, body, or board.
    k. Knowingly aiding and abetting another person to practice before the IRS during a period of suspension, disbarment, or ineligibility of such other person.

l. Contemptuous conduct in connection with practice before the IRS, including the use of abusive language, making false accusations or statements, knowing them to be false, or circulating or publishing malicious or libelous matter.

m. Giving a false opinion, knowingly, recklessly, or through gross incompetence, including an opinion which is intentionally or recklessly misleading, or engaging in a pattern of providing incompetent opinions on questions arising under the federal tax laws.

n. Willfully failing to sign a tax return prepared by the practitioner when the practitioner's signature is required by federal tax laws unless the failure is due to reasonable cause and not due to willful neglect.

o. Willfully disclosing or otherwise using a tax return or tax return information in a manner not authorized by the Internal Revenue Code, contrary to the order of a court of competent jurisdiction, or contrary to the order of an administrative law judge in a proceeding instituted under Sec. 10.60.

p. Willfully failing to file, on magnetic or other electronic media, a tax return prepared by the practitioner when the practitioner is required to do so by the federal tax laws unless the failure is due to reasonable cause and not due to willful neglect.

q. Willfully preparing all or substantially all of, or signing, a tax return or claim for refund when the practitioner does not possess a current or otherwise valid PTIN or other prescribed identifying number.

r. Willfully representing a taxpayer before an officer or employee of the IRS unless the practitioner is authorized to do so pursuant to this part.

3. **Circular 230** lists conduct that may result in suspension or disbarment. A brief list of examples follows:

   a. Being convicted of an offense involving dishonesty or breach of trust
   b. Providing false or misleading information to the Treasury Department, including the IRS
   c. Negotiating a client's refund check or not promptly remitting a refund check
   d. Circulating or publishing matter, related to practice before the IRS, deemed libelous or malicious; using abusive language
   e. Forming or maintaining a partnership to practice tax law or accounting with a person suspended or disbarred from practice before the IRS
   f. Violating a Circular 230 rule
   g. Filing a complaint against IRS personnel if the practitioner knows the complaint to be false
   h. Advancing an argument or claim that the practitioner knows is frivolous
   i. Conviction of any felony involving conduct that renders the practitioner unfit to practice before the IRS
   j. Attempting to influence the official action of any IRS employee by bestowing a gift, favor, or thing of value
   k. Failing to electronically file when required to do so
   l. Preparing all or substantially all of, or signing, a tax return without a PTIN
   m. Unauthorized representation of a taxpayer before the IRS
   n. Failing to remit funds from a client to the IRS for payment of tax or other obligations
   o. Failing to make a federal tax return in violation of the federal tax laws
   p. Intimating ability to obtain special consideration from the IRS
   q. Instituting or maintaining proceedings primarily for delay

4. The commissioner may confer with a practitioner on allegations of misconduct whether or not a proceeding for suspension or disbarment has been instituted.

A Complaint Begins a Proceeding

5. A proceeding is begun by filing a complaint that names the respondent and is signed by an authorized representative of the IRS.
    a. The complaint should contain a clear and concise statement of the allegations that constitute the basis of the proceeding.
        1) It is sufficient if it fairly informs the respondent of the charges, such that (s)he can prepare a defense.
        2) It should also contain any recommended sanctions and a demand for an answer.

Service of Complaint

    b. The complaint must be served on the practitioner by means of one of the following:
        1) Delivery in person
        2) Private delivery service
        3) Certified mail
        4) First-class mail, if the certified letter is not accepted by the practitioner

Compliance Opportunity

6. A proceeding is not instituted until the complaint is received and until the practitioner is provided the opportunity to show or achieve compliance with all lawful requirements.

Consent to Suspension

7. A practitioner may offer to consent to suspension to avoid institution of a suspension or disbarment proceeding. However, the IRS is not bound to accept the offer.

Complaint Response

8. The practitioner must file an answer to the complaint in writing within the time specified.
    a. The practitioner must have at least 30 days from the date of service to file the answer.
    b. An extension may be granted if application is made to the Administrative Law Judge (ALJ).
    c. If an answer to the complaint is not filed, the ALJ may
        1) Treat the respondent as if (s)he
            a) Admitted each allegation and
            b) Waived a hearing
        2) Not require proof by evidence at a hearing
        3) Decide against the respondent practitioner by default
    d. The answer to the complaint must
        1) Contain a statement of facts that constitute the grounds for defense
        2) Admit or deny each allegation set forth in the complaint or state (s)he lacks sufficient information to form a belief
    e. The practitioner may not
        1) Deny a material allegation that (s)he knows to be true
        2) State that (s)he lacks sufficient information to form a belief when (s)he has such information

f. Special matters of defense must be affirmatively stated.

g. Each allegation not denied is treated as

1) Admitted and
2) Proved.

Information Request

9. The IRS may request, for suspension or disbarment, any person to provide information concerning violation of the rules and to testify at a proceeding.

a. A practitioner is required to honor the request unless, with a reasonable basis, (s)he believes in good faith and on reasonable grounds that the information is privileged.

Hearing

10. An ALJ presides at hearings on complaints for sanctions. If either party, after due notice of a hearing has been sent, fails to appear, (s)he is treated as having waived the right to a hearing and the ALJ may enter a decision against him or her by default.

a. The hearing should occur within 180 days after the time for filing the answer.

b. Unless otherwise ordered by the ALJ, each party shall file and serve on the opposing party a prehearing memorandum identifying, in general,

1) Exhibits,
2) Witnesses,
3) Depositions,
4) Expert witnesses, and
5) Undisputed facts.

c. A respondent may appear in person, be represented by a practitioner, or be represented by an attorney who has not filed a declaration to practice before the IRS.

1) The representative need not be an enrolled agent.

d. Hearings must be stenographically recorded and transcribed.

e. Testimony of witnesses must be taken under oath or affirmation.

f. An ALJ does not necessarily follow rules of evidence applied in courts of law and equity.

1) Evidence may be admitted in the form of depositions, exhibits, and proof of documents.

2) The ALJ may exclude evidence that is irrelevant, immaterial, or repetitious.

g. If the sanction sought is censure or a suspension of less than 6 months, the standard of proof for Circular 230 proceedings is preponderance of the evidence. If the sanction sought is (1) a monetary penalty, (2) a suspension of 6 months or more, or (3) disbarment, the standard of proof is clear and convincing evidence.

h. The ALJ must allow the parties reasonable opportunity to submit proposed findings and conclusions and reasons supporting them.

Appeal

11. Either party may appeal the ALJ's decision to the Secretary of the Treasury within 30 days of its date.

Notice of Censure, Suspension, or Disbarment

12. The list of those receiving the issuance of a notice of censure, suspension, or disbarment from practice before the IRS includes
    a. IRS employees,
    b. Interested departments,
    c. Agencies of the federal government, and
    d. Appropriate state authorities.

Censure

13. Censure is a public reprimand to practitioners who violate the rules of practice. Censured practitioners may be subject to conditions imposed for a reasonable period in light of the gravity of the violation.

Suspension

14. A suspended practitioner is not allowed to practice before the IRS while the suspension is in effect.

Reinstatement

15. Five years after a practitioner's disbarment, the IRS may consider a petition for reinstatement.
    a. The IRS must be satisfied that the petitioner's conduct will comply with rules and regulations governing practice before the IRS.

Records Disclosure

16. The IRS will make available for public inspection the roster of
    a. Persons enrolled to practice;
    b. Persons censured, suspended, or disbarred from practice before the IRS; and
    c. Persons on the roster of all disqualified appraisers.
17. Other records of the Director of the Office of Professional Responsibility may be disclosed upon specific request, in accordance with the applicable disclosure rules of the IRS and the Treasury Department (Circular 230).

STOP AND REVIEW! **You have completed the outline for this subunit. Study multiple-choice questions 12 through 20 beginning on page 30.**

1.6 RENEWAL

To maintain active enrollment to practice before the IRS, enrolled agents must renew enrollment every third year after initial enrollment is granted. An enrolled agent's renewal schedule is determined by the last digit of the individual's Social Security or tax identification number as provided in Section 10.6(d) of Circular 230. The renewal schedules are staggered, with approximately one-third of enrolled agents renewing every year. To apply for renewal, individuals file Form 8554, *Application for Renewal of Enrollment to Practice Before the Internal Revenue Service*.

1. Application for renewal is based on the last digit of the enrolled agent's Social Security number or tax identification number.
   a. Enrolled agents whose Social Security number or tax identification number ends in 0, 1, 2, or 3, except those who receive their initial enrollment after November 1, 2021, must apply for renewal between November 1, 2021, and January 31, 2022. The renewal is effective April 1, 2022.
   b. Enrolled agents whose Social Security number or tax identification number ends in 4, 5, or 6, except those who receive their initial enrollment after November 1, 2022, must apply for renewal between November 1, 2022, and January 31, 2023. The renewal is effective April 1, 2023.
   c. Enrolled agents whose Social Security number or tax identification number ends in 7, 8, or 9, except those who receive their initial enrollment after November 1, 2023, must apply for renewal between November 1, 2023, and January 31, 2024. The renewal is effective April 1, 2024.
   d. Enrolled agents must renew between November 1 and January 31 of every third year. Enrolled agents who received their initial enrollment after November 1 and before April 2 of their renewal period do not have to renew until the next full renewal period after they received their initial enrollment.
2. Application for renewal is required to maintain active renewal status.
   a. Failure to receive notice of the renewal requirement from the IRS does not justify circumventing the requirement.
   b. A noncomplying enrolled agent will be given an opportunity to state the basis for the noncompliance with the possible consequence of being placed on the roster of inactive enrolled agents for a 3-year enrollment period.

Continuing Education

3. Renewal is conditioned on completing a minimum of 72 hours continuing education (CE) credits during the 3-year enrollment cycle, including at least 16 hours in each of the 3 enrollment years (each enrollment year runs from January 1 to December 31).
   a. All programs are measured in contact hours. A contact hour is 50 minutes of continuous participation.
   b. Two hours per month of CE credit is required of an individual whose initial enrollment begins during a cycle.
   c. An individual who receives initial enrollment during an enrollment cycle must complete 2 hours of ethics or professional conduct for each enrollment year during the enrollment cycle. Enrollment for any part of an enrollment year is considered enrollment for the entire year.
   d. Qualified CE program. A course of learning may qualify for CE credit if it is a program designed to enhance professional knowledge in federal tax law, federal tax-related matters, qualified retirement plan matters, or federal tax-related ethics.
   e. Teaching. For each contact hour of a qualifying program, the following CE credit is awarded:
      1) Two hours for actual subject preparation time, substantiated
      2) One hour as instructor, discussion leader, or speaker

      NOTE: The maximum credit for instruction and preparation may not exceed 6 hours annually.

   NOTE: The maximum credit for publication preparation may not exceed 25% of the CE requirement of an enrollment cycle.

   f. Each individual applying for renewal must retain for a period of 4 years following the date of renewal of enrollment the documentation required with regard to qualifying CE credit hours.

STOP AND REVIEW! **You have completed the outline for this subunit. Study multiple-choice questions 21 through 25 beginning on page 33.**

1.7 IDENTITY THEFT

1. Identity theft occurs when someone uses another person's personal information such as name, Social Security number (SSN), or other identifying information, without permission, to commit fraud or other crimes.
2. Usually, an identity thief uses a legitimate taxpayer's identity to fraudulently file a tax return and claim a refund. Generally, the identity thief will use a stolen SSN to file a forged tax return and attempt to get a fraudulent refund early in the filing season.
3. A taxpayer may be unaware that this has happened until (s)he files his or her return later in the filing season and discovers that two returns have been filed using the same SSN. A taxpayer should be alert to possible identity theft if (s)he receives an IRS notice or letter that states:
   a. More than one tax return for the taxpayer was filed,
   b. The taxpayer has a balance due, has a refund offset, or has had collection actions taken against him or her for a year (s)he did not file a tax return, or
   c. IRS records indicate that the taxpayer received wages from an employer unknown to the taxpayer.
4. Taxpayers subject to identity theft will need to fill out Form 14039, *Identity Theft Affidavit*. Taxpayers should be aware that the IRS does not initiate contact with taxpayers by email to request personal or financial information. This includes any type of electronic communication, such as text messages and social media channels.

STOP AND REVIEW! **You have completed the outline for this subunit. Study multiple-choice question 26 on page 35.**

QUESTIONS

1.1 Authority to Practice

1. Identify the item below that is NOT considered practice before the IRS.

A. Corresponding with the Internal Revenue Service on behalf of a client.

B. Appearing as a witness for the taxpayer.

C. Representing a client at an audit.

D. Calling the IRS to discuss a letter received by a client.

Answer (B) is correct.

REQUIRED: The activity that is not considered practicing before the IRS.

DISCUSSION: Circular 230 states that practice before the Internal Revenue Service comprises all matters connected with a presentation to the Internal Revenue Service or any of its officers or employees relating to a client's rights, privileges, or liabilities under laws or regulations administered by the Internal Revenue Service. Such presentations include preparing and filing necessary documents; corresponding and communicating with the Internal Revenue Service; and representing a client at conferences, hearings, and meetings. Preparing all or substantially all of a tax return, furnishing information at the request of the IRS, or appearing as a witness for the taxpayer is not practice before the IRS. These acts can be performed by anyone.

2. The following persons are authorized to represent a taxpayer before the IRS:

A. An individual representing a member of his or her immediate family.

B. A regular full-time employee of an individual employer representing the employer.

C. An officer or full-time employee of a corporation representing the corporation.

D. All of the answers are correct.

Answer (D) is correct.

REQUIRED: The individuals authorized to represent a taxpayer before the IRS.

DISCUSSION: Circular 230 states that attorneys, CPAs, enrolled agents, and other individuals who qualify under Sec. 10.7 for limited practice may practice before the IRS. The individuals who qualify are a taxpayer representing himself or herself; an individual representing a family member; a full-time employee of a company; a partner; a bona fide officer of a corporation, an association, or an organized group that represents the corporation or association; and a trustee, an administrator, or an executor of a trust or an estate.

3. Which of the following statements is true with respect to the limited practice of an unenrolled return preparer who completed the IRS AFSP?

A. An unenrolled return preparer may represent the taxpayer for any year the taxpayer provides authorization, whether or not the unenrolled preparer prepared the return in question.

B. An unenrolled return preparer who completed the IRS AFSP is only permitted to represent taxpayers before the examination and collection functions of the Internal Revenue Service.

C. If authorized by the taxpayer, an unenrolled return preparer who completed the IRS AFSP can sign consents to extend the statutory period for assessment or collection of tax.

D. An unenrolled preparer who completed the IRS AFSP cannot receive refund checks.

Answer (D) is correct.

REQUIRED: The true statement regarding unenrolled tax preparers.

DISCUSSION: A practitioner, properly authorized by the taxpayer, who signed a return as having prepared it for the taxpayer or who prepares a return but is not required (by the instructions on the return or regulations) to sign the return, may represent the taxpayer with respect to tax liability for the period covered by the return. This applies to representation by individuals other than attorneys, CPAs, and enrolled agents and before revenue agents and the Examination Division, but not before the Collection Division. In addition, an unenrolled agent cannot receive refund checks.

Answer (A) is incorrect. An unenrolled agent who completed the IRS AFSP may only represent the taxpayer in the year in which (s)he prepared the tax return, and for returns signed beginning in 2016, representation is allowed only if (s)he meets the requirements of the Annual Filing Season Program. **Answer (B) is incorrect.** An unenrolled agent cannot represent the taxpayer before the collection division. **Answer (C) is incorrect.** The unenrolled agent has no authority over matters regarding the collection of the tax from the taxpayer.

4. For taxpayers who want someone to represent them in their absence at an examination or an appeal within the IRS, all of the following statements are true EXCEPT

A. The taxpayer must furnish that representative with written authorization on Form 2848, *Power of Attorney and Declaration of Representative*, or any other properly written authorization.

B. The representative can be an attorney, a certified public accountant, or an enrolled agent.

C. The representative can be anyone who helped the taxpayer prepare the return.

D. Even if the taxpayer appointed a representative, the taxpayer may attend the examination or appeals conference and may act on his or her own behalf.

Answer (C) is correct.

REQUIRED: The false statement regarding taxpayers who want someone to represent them in their absence before the IRS.

DISCUSSION: Only attorneys, CPAs, and enrolled agents may represent a taxpayer before anyone at the IRS. Annual Filing Season Program participants may appear as the taxpayer's representative before revenue agents or customer service representatives during an examination, but not before appeals officers, revenue officers, or counsel at an appeal. Tax preparers without a certification may not practice before anyone at the IRS.

1.2 Conduct of Practice

5. Rich, an enrolled agent, is currently representing Dana before the Internal Revenue Service. Mike, Dana's former business partner, asks Rich to represent him before the Internal Revenue Service. Notwithstanding the existence of a conflict of interest between Dana and Mike, Rich may still represent Mike before the Internal Revenue Service if certain requirements are met. Which of the following statements is NOT a requirement that Rich has to satisfy before he can represent Mike?

A. Dana and Mike must each give informed consent, confirmed in writing, to Rich.

B. Rich must reasonably believe that he will be able to provide competent and diligent representation to both Dana and Mike.

C. Rich must immediately notify the commissioner in writing that he is representing both Dana and Mike.

D. The representation of Dana must not be prohibited by law.

Answer (C) is correct.

REQUIRED: The statement which is not a requirement when an enrolled agent faces a conflict of interest among clients.

DISCUSSION: Circular 230 prohibits a practitioner from representing a client before the IRS if the representation involves a conflict of interest. According to Sec. 10.29 of Circular 230, a conflict of interest is present if representation of one client will be directly adverse to another client, or if a significant risk exists that representation of the client will be materially limited by the practitioner's responsibilities to others.

Even if a conflict of interest exists, a practitioner may still represent a client if the following three elements are met:

1. The practitioner reasonably believes that (s)he can provide competent and diligent representation to each client,
2. The representation is not prohibited by law, and
3. Each affected client gives informed, written consent.

Answer (A) is incorrect. Dana and Mike must each give informed consent, confirmed in writing, to Rich. However, Rich is not required to notify the commissioner in writing that he is representing both Dana and Mike. **Answer (B) is incorrect.** Rich must reasonably believe that he will be able to provide competent and diligent representation to both Dana and Mike. However, Rich is not required to notify the commissioner in writing that he is representing both Dana and Mike. **Answer (D) is incorrect.** The representation must not be prohibited by law. However, Rich is not required to notify the commissioner in writing that he is representing both Dana and Mike.

6. Which of the following acts performed by an attorney, a CPA, or an enrolled agent is NOT prohibited by Sec. 10.24 (Assistance from or to disbarred or suspended persons and former IRS employees) of Circular 230?

A. Assisting a person disbarred from practice before the IRS.

B. Preparing the tax return for an individual suspended or disbarred from practice before the IRS.

C. Accepting assistance from a former government employee when the provisions of Sec. 10.25 (Practice by former government employees, their partners, and their associates) of Circular 230 would be violated.

D. Accepting assistance from a person disbarred from practice before the IRS.

Answer (B) is correct.

REQUIRED: The act not prohibited by Sec. 10.24 of Circular 230.

DISCUSSION: Circular 230, Sec. 10.24, states that no practitioner shall, in practice before the Internal Revenue Service, knowingly and directly or indirectly

1. Assist or accept assistance (related to matters constituting practice) from any person who is under disbarment or suspension from practice before the Internal Revenue Service
2. Accept assistance from any former government employee where the provisions of Sec. 10.25 or any federal law would be violated

Preparing a return for a suspended or disbarred individual is permissible.

Answer (A) is incorrect. Assisting a person disbarred from practice before the IRS is specifically prohibited by Sec. 10.24 of Circular 230. **Answer (C) is incorrect.** Accepting assistance from a former government employee when the provisions of Sec. 10.25 (Practice by former government employees, their partners, and their associates) of Circular 230 would be violated is specifically prohibited by Sec. 10.24 of Circular 230. **Answer (D) is incorrect.** Accepting assistance from a person disbarred from practice before the IRS is specifically prohibited by Sec. 10.24 of Circular 230.

7. Sandy is an enrolled agent. He is preparing a brochure to hand to prospective clients and would like to explain the designation "enrolled agent." Which of the following language is Sandy NOT permitted to use?

A. "I am permitted to practice before the IRS."

B. "I am enrolled to represent taxpayers before the IRS."

C. "I am certified by the IRS."

D. "I am admitted to practice before the IRS."

Answer (C) is correct.

REQUIRED: The language that is not permitted when explaining the designation of "enrolled agent."

DISCUSSION: Circular 230 allows advertising and solicitation. An enrolled agent may use the phrase "enrolled to practice before the IRS." The variations of this phrase are acceptable as long as the enrolled agent does not claim to be "certified by the IRS."

8. Which of the following statements regarding Circular 230 is true?

A. A practitioner may charge a contingent fee for providing tax planning services.

B. A practitioner may never charge a contingent fee for any tax related service.

C. A practitioner may never charge an unconscionable fee in any practice before the IRS.

D. All of the answers are correct.

Answer (C) is correct.

REQUIRED: The true statement(s) regarding a practitioner's fees.

DISCUSSION: A practitioner may not charge an unconscionable fee in connection with practice before the IRS. Practice before the IRS includes tax planning and advice, representation before the IRS, etc.

9. Mike is an enrolled agent. Widget, Inc., is an accrual-basis taxpayer. In Year 3, while preparing Widget's Year 2 return, Mike discovered that Widget failed to include income on its Year 1 return that Widget received in Year 2 but which should have been included in income in Year 1 under the accrual method of accounting. What must Mike do?

A. Advise Widget of the error and the consequences of the error.

B. Include the income on the Year 2 return.

C. Refuse to prepare Widget's Year 2 return until Widget agrees to amend its Year 1 return to include the amount of income.

D. Change Widget to the cash method of accounting.

Answer (A) is correct.

REQUIRED: The action required by an enrolled agent who knows that a client has not complied with the revenue laws.

DISCUSSION: An agent who knows that a client has not complied with the revenue laws of the U.S. is required to promptly advise the client of noncompliance, as well as the consequences of noncompliance under the Code and regulations. Under Circular 230, the agent is not required to notify the IRS.

Answer (B) is incorrect. An amended return would need to be filed and the agent would file an amended return at the request of the taxpayer. **Answer (C) is incorrect.** It is the client's responsibility to request for the amended return to be filed for Year 1. **Answer (D) is incorrect.** Widget, Inc., may be required to maintain an accrual method of accounting due to the Code and regulations. Also, amending the Year 1 return would be the only way to properly correct the understatement of income.

1.3 Best Practices for Tax Advisors

10. Tax advisors should adhere to "best practices" in providing advice and in preparing a submission to the IRS. Best practices include all of the following EXCEPT

A. Clearly communicating the terms of the engagement with the client.

B. Establishing the facts, their relevancy, and arriving at a conclusion supported solely by the facts.

C. Advising the client regarding the importance of the conclusions reached.

D. Acting fairly with integrity in practice before the IRS.

Answer (B) is correct.

REQUIRED: The choice that is not considered among "best practices."

DISCUSSION: According to Sec. 10.33 of Circular 230, best practices should include the following:

1. Communicating clearly with the client regarding the terms of the engagement;
2. Establishing the facts, determining which facts are relevant, evaluating the reasonableness of any assumptions or representations, relating applicable law to the relevant facts, and arriving at a conclusion supported by the law and the facts;
3. Advising the client regarding the importance of the conclusions reached; and
4. Acting fairly and with integrity in practice before the IRS.

The correct answer failed to include the law as a basis of support for a conclusion.

Answer (A) is incorrect. Clearly communicating the terms of the engagement with the client is included in the best practices. **Answer (C) is incorrect.** Advising the client regarding the importance of the conclusions reached is included in the best practices. **Answer (D) is incorrect.** Acting fairly with integrity in practice before the IRS is included in the best practices.

1.4 Supervisor Responsibility

11. Under Treasury Circular 230, in which of the following situations is a CPA prohibited from giving written advice concerning one or more federal tax issues?

A. The CPA takes into account the possibility that a tax return will not be audited.

B. The CPA reasonably relies upon representations of the client.

C. The CPA considers all relevant facts that are known.

D. The CPA takes into consideration assumptions about future events related to the relevant facts.

Answer (A) is correct.

REQUIRED: The situation in which a CPA is prohibited from issuing written advice.

DISCUSSION: A CPA is prohibited from giving written advice concerning a federal tax issue in which the CPA takes into account the possibility that a tax return will not be audited.

Answer (B) is incorrect. A CPA is permitted to give written advice concerning a federal tax issue in which the CPA reasonably relies upon representation of the client. **Answer (C) is incorrect.** A CPA is permitted to give written advice concerning a federal tax issue in which the CPA considers all relevant facts that are known. **Answer (D) is incorrect.** A CPA is permitted to give written advice concerning a federal tax issue in which the CPA takes into consideration assumptions about future events related to the relevant facts.

1.5 Sanctions and Disciplinary Proceedings

12. Which of the following is NOT an example of disreputable conduct (as described in Sec. 10.51 of Circular 230) for which an enrolled agent may be suspended or disbarred from practice before the IRS?

A. Knowingly giving false or misleading information to the Treasury Department.

B. Willful failure to make a federal tax return in violation of federal revenue laws.

C. Failure to respond to a request by the Commissioner of Internal Revenue to provide information.

D. Misappropriation of funds received from a client for the purpose of payment of federal tax.

Answer (C) is correct.

REQUIRED: The action for which an enrolled agent may not be disbarred or suspended from practice.

DISCUSSION: Section 10.51 of Circular 230 lists several examples of disreputable conduct for which an enrolled agent may be disbarred or suspended from practice before the Internal Revenue Service. Failure to respond to a request by the commissioner to provide information is not disreputable conduct under Sec. 10.51 of Circular 230.

Answer (A) is incorrect. Knowingly giving false or misleading information to the Treasury Department is prohibited by Circular 230. **Answer (B) is incorrect.** Willful failure to make a federal tax return in violation of federal revenue laws is prohibited by Circular 230. **Answer (D) is incorrect.** Misappropriation of funds received from a client for the purpose of payment of federal tax is prohibited by Circular 230.

13. An appeal from the initial decision ordering disbarment is made to which of the following?

A. The Secretary of the Treasury.

B. The administrative law judge.

C. The United States District Court for the District of Columbia.

D. The United States Tax Court.

Answer (A) is correct.

REQUIRED: The official to whom an appeal from the initial decision ordering disbarment is made.

DISCUSSION: The initial decision for disbarment of an enrolled agent, made by an administrative law judge, is appealed to the Secretary of the Treasury (Circular 230).

Answer (B) is incorrect. The initial decision is made by the administrative law judge. **Answer (C) is incorrect.** The United States District Court for the District of Columbia is a forum for taxpayer appeals, not enrolled agent disbarment appeals. **Answer (D) is incorrect.** The United States Tax Court is a court that hears taxpayers' cases, not enrolled agent disbarment cases.

14. All of the following are considered examples of disreputable conduct for which an enrolled agent can be disbarred or suspended EXCEPT

A. Directly or indirectly attempting to influence the official action of any employee of the Internal Revenue Service by use of threats or false accusations or by bestowing any gift, favor, or thing of value.

B. Misappropriation or failure to remit funds received from a client for the purpose of payment of taxes or other obligations due the United States.

C. Knowingly aiding and abetting another person to practice before the Internal Revenue Service during a period of suspension or disbarment.

D. Failure to timely pay personal income taxes.

Answer (D) is correct.

REQUIRED: The statement that does not describe disreputable conduct for which an enrolled agent can be disbarred or suspended.

DISCUSSION: Section 10.51 of Circular 230 lists several examples of disreputable conduct for which an enrolled agent may be disbarred or suspended from practice before the Internal Revenue Service. Failure to timely pay personal income taxes is not disreputable conduct under Sec. 10.51 of Circular 230.

15. Ray was suspended from practice for 4 months by the IRS. Which of the following is Ray permitted to do during the period of suspension?

A. Appear as a witness before the IRS.

B. Sign closing agreements regarding tax liabilities.

C. Represent taxpayers before the IRS with respect to returns Ray did not prepare.

D. Sign a consent to extend the statute of limitations for the assessment and collection of tax.

Answer (A) is correct.

REQUIRED: The action permitted by a person who is suspended from practice.

DISCUSSION: A person who is suspended from practice for 4 months by the IRS may still appear as a witness before the IRS. However, a suspended agent is not allowed to practice before the IRS while the suspension is in effect.

Answer (B) is incorrect. Signing closing agreements regarding tax liabilities is considered practicing before the IRS and is prohibited during suspension. **Answer (C) is incorrect.** The agent is prohibited from representing taxpayers before the IRS while the agent is suspended. It is irrelevant whether the agent prepared the tax return. **Answer (D) is incorrect.** Signing a consent to extend the statute of limitations for the assessment and collection of tax is considered practice before the IRS.

16. The IRS has documentation that an enrolled agent has violated the law or regulations governing practice before the IRS. It may

A. Reprimand such person.

B. Institute proceedings for disbarment.

C. Institute proceedings for suspension.

D. All of the answers are correct.

Answer (D) is correct.

REQUIRED: The actions permitted the Director of Practice when an enrolled agent violates the law or regulations.

DISCUSSION: Section 10.60 of Circular 230 provides that, whenever the IRS has reason to believe any enrolled agent has violated any of the laws or regulations governing practice before the IRS, the IRS may reprimand such person or institute a proceeding for disbarment or suspension. The proceeding is instituted by a complaint naming the respondent and signed by an authorized representative of the IRS.

17. After a decision has been made on a complaint filed by the IRS, the practitioner or IRS may appeal the decision. Which statement is true with respect to filing an appeal of the decision?

A. Within 30 days from the date of the District Court judge's decision, either party may appeal to the Secretary of the Treasury or his or her delegate.

B. Within 30 days from the date of the District Court judge's decision, either party may appeal to the Supreme Court.

C. Within 30 days from the date of the administrative law judge's decision, either party may appeal to the Secretary of the Treasury or his or her delegate.

D. Within 45 days from the date of the administrative law judge's decision, either party may appeal to the Secretary of the Treasury or his or her delegate.

Answer (C) is correct.

REQUIRED: The period of time to submit an appeal and the person to whom it must be submitted.

DISCUSSION: Either the Office of Professional Responsibility or the respondent may appeal the administrative law judge's decision to the Secretary of the Treasury within 30 days of its date.

Answer (A) is incorrect. The decision is made by the administrative law judge. **Answer (B) is incorrect.** If either party appeals, (s)he must appeal to the Secretary of the Treasury. **Answer (D) is incorrect.** If either party wishes to appeal, (s)he must appeal within 30 days of the decision, and (s)he must appeal to the Secretary of Treasury.

18. A practitioner may seek reinstatement after

A. 1 year.

B. 2 years.

C. 4 years.

D. 5 years.

Answer (D) is correct.

REQUIRED: The number of years after disbarment that reinstatement may be considered.

DISCUSSION: Under Sec. 10.81 of Circular 230, 5 years after an agent's disbarment, the IRS may entertain a petition for reinstatement. The IRS must be satisfied that the petitioner's conduct will comply with rules and regulations governing practice before the IRS.

19. Which of the following statements regarding proceedings for disbarment or suspension of an attorney, a certified public accountant, or an enrolled agent from practice before the Internal Revenue Service is false?

A. A complaint shall contain a clear and concise description of the allegations that constitute the basis for the proceedings.

B. Failure to answer the complaint as required will render a decision by default against the respondent.

C. Every allegation in the complaint that is not denied will be deemed to be admitted by the respondent and may be considered as proved.

D. The respondent to the complaint must file his or her answer with the IRS within 30 days from the date the complaint is served.

Answer (D) is correct.

REQUIRED: The false statement about disbarment or suspension proceedings.

DISCUSSION: Section 10.64 of Circular 230 provides that the respondent's answer shall be filed in writing within the time specified in the complaint, unless an application is made and the time is extended by the administrative law judge. The respondent must have at least 30 days to file [Sec. 10.62(c) of Circular 230].

Answer (A) is incorrect. A complaint is sufficient if it fairly informs the respondent of the charges so that (s)he can prepare a defense (Sec. 10.62). **Answer (B) is incorrect.** Failure to answer constitutes an admission of allegations and a waiver of a hearing (Sec. 10.64). **Answer (C) is incorrect.** No further evidence in respect of such an allegation need be proved at a hearing if the respondent does not deny it (Sec. 10.64).

20. Failure to file an answer to a complaint instituting a proceeding for disbarment by the original or extended deadline constitutes

A. An admission of the allegations in the complaint and a waiver of a hearing.

B. An error that can be corrected by filing the answer with the administrative law judge within one year of the original (or extended) deadline.

C. Grounds for criminal sanctions.

D. Equitable estoppel against the practitioner.

Answer (A) is correct.

REQUIRED: The consequence of failing to file an answer to a complaint instituting a proceeding for disbarment by the original or extended deadline.

DISCUSSION: If a respondent fails to answer a complaint filed by the IRS for disbarment, the IRS and/or the administrative law judge may treat the respondent as if (s)he had admitted all allegations and waived a hearing (Circular 230).

Answer (B) is incorrect. Circular 230 does not contain any provisions for correcting the failure of a respondent to timely file an answer to a complaint for disbarment. **Answer (C) is incorrect.** The consequences for failing to timely file an answer to a disbarment complaint do not include criminal sanctions. **Answer (D) is incorrect.** Equitable estoppel, which is a doctrine preventing a person from asserting a right (s)he otherwise would have had because of the effect his or her conduct will have on another, does not apply in this situation. Because Circular 230 lays out the consequences within the regulation itself, no equitable remedy against the practitioner is required.

1.6 Renewal

21. The period of renewal for the next enrollment cycle for enrolled agents whose Social Security numbers end in 0, 1, 2, or 3 will be

A. February 1, 2021, through March 31, 2022.

B. November 1, 2021, through January 31, 2022.

C. February 1, 2022, through March 31, 2022.

D. November 1, 2022, through January 31, 2023.

Answer (B) is correct.

REQUIRED: The period of renewal for the next enrollment cycle.

DISCUSSION: Circular 230 states that enrolled agents whose Social Security number or tax identification number ends in 0, 1, 2, or 3, except those who received their initial enrollment after November 1, 2021, must apply for renewal between November 1, 2021, and January 31, 2022. The renewal is effective April 1, 2022.

22. Enrolled agents generally must complete continuing education credits for renewed enrollment. Which of the following describes the credit requirements?

A. A minimum of 72 hours must be completed in each year of an enrollment cycle.

B. A minimum of 24 hours must be completed in each year of an enrollment cycle.

C. A minimum of 80 hours must be completed, overall, for the entire enrollment cycle.

D. A minimum of 16 hours must be completed in each year of the enrollment cycle.

Answer (D) is correct.

REQUIRED: The continuing education requirements for enrolled agents.

DISCUSSION: Circular 230, Sec. 10.6(e) states a minimum of 16 hours of continuing education credit must be completed each year of the enrollment cycle.

Answer (A) is incorrect. A minimum of 16, not 72, hours must be completed each year of the enrollment cycle. **Answer (B) is incorrect.** A minimum of 16, not 24, hours must be completed in each year. **Answer (C) is incorrect.** The minimum hours are 16, not 80, and are required each year of the cycle, not collectively over the entire cycle.

23. How long must each practitioner maintain records of his or her completed CE credits?

A. CE credit information does not have to be retained by the enrolled agent since the qualifying organization provides the IRS a list of each participant that completed CE credits.

B. CE credit information must be maintained for a period of 4 years from the date they are completed.

C. CE credit information must be retained for a period of 4 years following the date of renewal of enrollment.

D. CE credit information must be retained for a period of 1 year following the year they are completed.

Answer (C) is correct.

REQUIRED: The retention period for records of completed CE credits.

DISCUSSION: Renewal is conditioned on completing a minimum of 72 hours continuing education credits during the 3-year enrollment cycle, including at least 16 hours in each of the 3 years. Each individual applying for renewal must retain, for a period of 4 years following the date of renewal of enrollment, the information required with regard to qualifying continuing education credit hours.

24. Janice has been enrolled to practice before the IRS since 1997. Her Social Security number ends in 2. When may she destroy records documenting her continuing education from January 2021?

A. April 1, 2024.

B. April 1, 2026.

C. April 1, 2025.

D. April 1, 2027.

Answer (B) is correct.

REQUIRED: The suggested time frame to retain records for continuing education.

DISCUSSION: Circular 230 states that a minimum of 72 hours of continuing education credit must be completed each 3-year period. Each such 3-year period is known as an enrollment cycle. Each enrollment year is from January 1 through December 31. The cycle including January 2020 will end April 1, 2022, for enrolled agents whose Social Security numbers end in 2. The next enrollment cycle will end on April 1, 2025. The records for January 2020 should be kept for 4 years after the end of the enrollment cycle.

25. Which of the following statements concerning continuing education (CE) requirements for enrolled agents is false?

A. An enrolled agent must complete a minimum of 72 hours of CE credits if enrolled for the entire enrollment cycle with the minimum being 16 hours per year.

B. The current enrollment cycle, the period during which enrolled agents must meet their minimum continuing education requirements, is determined by the enrolled agent's Social Security number.

C. An enrolled agent who does not meet the renewal requirements for one enrollment cycle will be required to take and pass all three parts of the Special Enrollment Examination in order to retain enrolled agent status.

D. An individual who becomes enrolled during an enrollment cycle must complete 2 hours of CE for each month enrolled during the cycle, beginning with the month enrolled.

Answer (C) is correct.

REQUIRED: The false statement regarding CE for enrolled agents.

DISCUSSION: Although a noncomplying enrolled agent will not be required to take an examination, (s)he will be given an opportunity to state the basis for the noncompliance with the possible consequence of being placed on the roster of inactive enrolled agents for a 3-year period.

Answer (A) is incorrect. Enrolled agents must complete 72 hours of CE credit for the enrollment cycle, with 16 hours being the minimum per year. **Answer (B) is incorrect.** The enrollment cycle is determined by the enrolled agent's Social Security number. **Answer (D) is incorrect.** Two hours of CE credit per month is required for individuals who become enrolled during a cycle.

1.7 Identity Theft

26. Which of the following statements concerning identity theft and the IRS is true?

A. Taxpayers subject to identity theft need to fill out Form 1040.

B. Taxpayers must always respond promptly to an IRS email initiating contact.

C. Initial contact by the IRS may occur via a text message or social media channels.

D. Victims of identity theft need to complete the IRS Identity Theft Affidavit.

Answer (D) is correct.

REQUIRED: The true statement about identity theft and the IRS.

DISCUSSION: Taxpayers subject to identity theft will need to fill out the IRS Identity Theft Affidavit, Form 14039. The taxpayers should be aware that the IRS does not initiate contact with taxpayers by email to request personal or financial information. This includes any type of electronic communication, e.g., text messages and social media channels.

Answer (A) is incorrect. Form 1040 is the individual tax return, not the Identity Theft Affidavit. **Answer (B) is incorrect.** The IRS does not initiate contact via email. **Answer (C) is incorrect.** The IRS does not initiate contact via text messaging or social media channels.

STUDY UNIT TWO

TAX PREPARERS AND PENALTIES

(21 pages of outline)

A tax return preparer does **not** have to be a practitioner (i.e., an enrolled agent, a CPA, an attorney, or any other person authorized to practice before the IRS) in order to prepare tax returns. Additionally, a tax return preparer is subject to Circular 230 **only if** (s)he is also a practitioner.

However, **all** tax return preparers are subject to preparer penalties. Preparer penalties include penalties for understatement of a taxpayer's liability due to unreasonable positions or willful or reckless conduct, for disclosing taxpayer information, and for promoting abusive tax shelters.

2.1 TAX PREPARERS

Defining Tax Return Preparer

1. A tax return preparer is any person who prepares for compensation, or employs one or more persons to prepare for compensation, all or a substantial portion of any return of tax or claim for refund under the IRC (Title 26).
   a. Preparation of certain information returns is also within the scope of the tax return preparer rules.
   b. Unless stated otherwise, tax return preparers include the following persons:
      1) A person who furnishes to a taxpayer or other preparer sufficient information and advice so that completion of the return is simply a mechanical matter is considered a tax return preparer.
      2) **Substantial portion.** A tax return preparer is a person who prepares for compensation, or employs another who prepares for compensation, a substantial portion of an applicable return.
         a) Preparation outside the U.S. is included.
         b) Length and complexity of the portion (or a schedule) are compared to the return as a whole.
      3) **Insubstantial Portion**
         a) A portion or a schedule of a return is not considered substantial if it involves gross income, deductions, or amounts on the basis of which credits are determined of less than either
            i) $10,000 or
            ii) $400,000 and less than 20% of the AGI (or GI if not an individual) shown in the return.
         b) A person who gives advice only on specific issues is generally not considered to be a tax return preparer.

c) A tax return preparer of one return is not considered a preparer of another return because an entry or entries reported on the first may affect an entry reported on the second, unless the entries

i) Are directly reflected on the other return, e.g., a partnership and partner return, and

ii) Represent a substantial portion of the second return. A substantial portion of the return includes gross income over $400,000 or greater than 20% of the gross income of the return.

4) **Primary responsibility.** If more than one tax return preparer is involved in preparing a return or claim for refund, the one with primary responsibility for the overall substantive accuracy is considered the (only) preparer for purposes of the signing requirement.

a) The tax preparer with primary responsibility cannot be relieved of that responsibility by sharing any of the following functional tasks:

i) Acquiring needed information
ii) Applying tax law
iii) Completing the return
iv) Reviewing the information, the application of tax law, and the return
v) Applying taxpayer policy
vi) Advising a position regarding the law
vii) Obtaining final determination or approval

5) **Compensation.** If no compensation is provided for a person (or for his or her employee) to prepare a return or claim for refund, the person is not a tax return preparer.

a) Absent an explicit or implicit agreement for compensation, a person is not a tax return preparer, even if (s)he receives a gift, return service, or favor.

6) **The following are not tax return preparers:**

a) An employee who prepares a return for the employer by whom (s)he is regularly and continuously employed

b) A fiduciary who prepares a return or refund claim for any person (the trust)

c) A person who prepares a refund claim in response to a notice of deficiency issued to another

d) A person who furnishes typing, reproducing, or other mechanical assistance

e) A person who merely gives an opinion about events that have not happened, i.e., planning

7) **A person can be a tax return preparer without regard to educational qualifications or professional status.**

Mechanics of Preparing a Return

2. Significant aspects of tax return preparation are making factual inquiries and taking a position relative to tax law.

Inquiry of Client Financials

a. A tax return preparer may rely, if in good faith, upon information furnished by the taxpayer without having to obtain third-party verification.

1) The preparer may not ignore the implications of the information furnished.

2) The preparer must make reasonable inquiries if the information appears inaccurate or incomplete.

3) **Deductions.** The preparer should make appropriate inquiries of the taxpayer to determine the existence of facts and circumstances required by an IRC section or regulations incidental to a deduction, including, e.g., substantiating documentary evidence, even if for a minimal amount.

Preparer's Position on Law

b. A tax return preparer may not adopt a position without **substantial authority** for the position.

1) There is substantial authority for the tax treatment of an item only if the weight of the authorities supporting the treatment is substantial in relation to the weight of authorities supporting contrary treatment.

a) What constitutes substantial authority is defined by statute and IRS statements.

i) A revenue ruling, for example, constitutes legal authority that, together with other authority, may be found substantial.

b) All authorities relevant to the tax treatment of an item, including the authorities contrary to the treatment, are taken into account in determining whether substantial authority exists.

c) The weight of authorities is determined in light of the pertinent facts and circumstances.

d) A tax return preparer may not rely on unreasonable assumptions.

e) There may be substantial authority for more than one position with respect to the same item.

f) A taxpayer's belief that there is a substantial authority for the tax treatment of an item is a subjective determination. It is important to note that the IRS definition of the substantial authority standard is an objective standard and this objective standard is the one the IRS holds tax return preparers to.

2) A penalty will not apply if the position was disclosed and there is a reasonable basis for the position.

Substantial and Reasonable Belief

3) For tax shelters, tax preparers are required to have both substantial authority and a reasonable belief for their position and this belief must be "more likely than not" the proper treatment.

4) The penalty for unreasonable undisclosed positions is an amount equal to the greater of $1,000 or 50% of the income derived from the position.

Errors and Omissions

c. Circular 230 addresses the possibility of an omission from a taxpayer's tax return in Sec. 10.21.

1) It states that, when a practitioner discovers that a client has made an error or omission from any document filed with the IRS, (s)he must notify the client of the error or omission immediately.

2) In addition, the practitioner must advise the client on the consequences of such an omission as provided by the IRC and regulations.

3. **Procedural Requirements**

Signature

a. A tax return preparer is required to sign the return or claim for refund after it has been completed and before it is presented to the taxpayer.

1) If the preparer is unavailable for signature, another preparer must review the entire preparation of the return (or claim) and then must sign it.

2) If more than one preparer is involved, the preparer with primary responsibility for the overall accuracy of the return or claim is considered the preparer for purposes of the signing requirement.

3) A valid signature is defined by state law and may be anything that clearly indicates the intent to sign.

4) Requirements exist for the use of alternative methods when signing as a tax return preparer and not on behalf of the taxpayer.

a) Original returns, amended returns, or requests for filing extensions that include a separate signature line for a paid tax preparer may be signed via computer software programs, mechanical devices, or rubber stamps.

5) Preparers physically unable to manually sign returns must indicate "unable to sign" as the signature.

6) In a situation in which one or more persons are employed as tax return preparers, only the employer is considered to be a tax return preparer.

Identifying Number

b. A return or refund claim prepared by a tax return preparer and filed with the IRS must include the preparer's identifying number.

1) The identifying number of an individual is his or her preparer tax identification number (PTIN).
2) The identifying number of the partnership or employer [employer identification number (EIN)], if applicable, also must be included.
3) The address of the preparer's place of business where the return was prepared also must be included.
4) The preparer is not required to sign or affix an identification number to the taxpayer's copy of a tax return.

Copy to Taxpayer

c. A tax return preparer is required to furnish a completed copy of the return or refund claim to the taxpayer no later than the time it is presented for the taxpayer's signature.

Employer of Preparers

d. A person who employs one or more tax return preparers is required to file a return setting forth the name, identifying number, and principal place of work of each employed tax return preparer.

1) The IRS may approve an alternative reporting method.
2) The requirements are satisfied if the tax return preparer
   a) Retains a record of the information and
   b) Makes it available for inspection upon request by the commissioner for the 3-year period following the relevant return period.
3) A partnership is treated as the employer of the partners and shall retain and make available a record with respect to the employees (e.g., partners, others).
4) A sole proprietor shall retain and make available a record with respect to himself or herself.

Records

e. A tax return preparer is required to retain a completed copy of each return or claim prepared for 3 years after the close of the return period.

1) Records relating to employment taxes and federal withholding taxes must be maintained for at least 4 years after the later of (a) the due date of the tax or (b) the date such tax was paid.
2) Alternatively, a list may be kept that includes, for the returns and claims prepared, the following information:
   a) The taxpayers' names
   b) Taxpayer identification numbers
   c) Their tax years
   d) Types of returns or claims prepared
3) The return period means the 12-month period beginning July 1 each year.

Accuracy

4. While software is largely effective, users are advised to trust the software but verify all data inputs and outputs. For example, a complication stemming from the way brokerages keep stock transaction records means that software might import incomplete data, leading to possibly costly calculation errors. It is a taxpayer's responsibility to verify all tax information.
   a. Some items to consider when checking for accuracy include inconsistencies with the source data, miscalculations, the recognition of duplicate entries, a need to read diagnostics, the matching of inputs and outputs across forms, etc.
   b. The IRS provides two forms for correcting erroneous information provided in an information return.
      1) The IRS will send the taxpayer a Form 4852, *Substitute for Form W-2, Wage and Tax Statement, or Form 1099-R, Distributions From Pensions, Annuities, Retirement or Profit-Sharing Plans, IRAs, Insurance Contracts, etc.*
         a) Form 4852 may also be used to report income when a W-2, 1099, or other reporting document is not received.
         b) Form 4852 is designed to be used by a taxpayer to report disputed amounts reported in a W-2 or 1099.
      2) Form 8082, *Notice of Inconsistent Treatment or Administrative Adjustment Request (AAR)*, is used to report situations where an S corporation shareholder's return was going to be inconsistent with the corporate return, or a partner's return inconsistent with the partnership return.
         a) When a difference between K-1 information and a Form 1040 has not been reported, the IRS can issue a correction notice without going through normal deficiency procedures, as though the taxpayer had made a math error on the return.
         b) There is no administrative procedure to appeal the correction of an error in a return, so failure to properly report inconsistent treatment can lead to serious administrative difficulty that only the courts can fix.

Free File Software

5. Everyone can use Free File, the free way to prepare and e-file federal taxes either through brand-name software or online fillable forms.
   a. Individuals or families with 2021 adjusted gross incomes of $72,000 or less can use Free File software. Free File Fillable Forms, the electronic version of IRS paper forms, has no income restrictions.
   b. Free File software is a product of a public-private partnership between the IRS and the Free File Alliance, LLC. The Alliance is a consortium of approximately 20 tax software providers who make versions of their products available exclusively at www.irs.gov/freefile.
      1) All Free File members must meet certain security requirements and use the latest in encryption technology to protect taxpayers' information.

Data Security

6. In an effort to thwart criminals from fraudulently preparing taxpayers' returns, the IRS is asking all practitioners to be aware of data security.
   a. Cybercriminals are targeting client data, so it is important to
      1) Ensure the computer network has a firewall
      2) Set all electronic devices to update automatically
      3) Install anti-malware and antivirus security on all electronic devices
      4) Encrypt all files and emails
      5) Back up sensitive data to secure external sources not connected to the main network
      6) Limit access to taxpayer information to only the employees who need it to complete their work
   b. Practitioners should not ignore evidence of a cybercrime, such as the following:
      1) Clients receive letters, refunds, or notices from the IRS when they are not expecting correspondence
      2) Clients responding to emails that the practitioner never sent
      3) Computers or networks locking out practitioners
      4) Computers or networks acting slower than usual
      5) The number of returns filed with the tax practitioner's Electronic Filing Identification Number (EFIN) exceeds the number of clients
   c. Report any data theft or data loss to your local IRS Stakeholder Liaison.

***STOP AND REVIEW!* You have completed the outline for this subunit. Study multiple-choice questions 1 through 12 beginning on page 58.**

2.2 DISCLOSURE OF TAXPAYER INFORMATION

1. A **penalty** is imposed on any tax return preparer who discloses or uses any tax return information without the consent of the taxpayer other than for the specific purpose of preparing, assisting in preparing, or providing services in connection with the preparation of any tax return of the taxpayer.
   a. The penalty is $250 per disclosure, with a maximum of $10,000 per year.
   b. If convicted of knowingly or recklessly disclosing the information, a preparer would be guilty of a misdemeanor and subject to up to $1,000 in fines and up to a year in prison.
2. **Exceptions.** The penalty for disclosure is not imposed if the disclosure was made
   a. Pursuant to other provisions of the Code
   b. To a related taxpayer, provided the taxpayer had not expressly prohibited the disclosure
   c. Pursuant to a court order
   d. Pursuant to a subpoena issued by a federal or state grand jury or by the United States Congress
   e. By one officer, employee, or partner to another officer, employee, shareholder, or partner
   f. To provide information for educational purposes
   g. To solicit tax return preparation services
   h. For the purpose of a conflict, quality, or peer review
3. The **taxpayer's consent** must be a written, formal consent authorizing the disclosure for a specific purpose. The taxpayer must authorize a preparer to
   a. Use the taxpayer's information to solicit additional current business in matters not related to the IRS from the taxpayer
   b. Disclose the information to additional third parties
   c. Disclose the information in connection with another person's return
4. The **confidentiality privilege** is extended to certain nonattorneys.
   a. In noncriminal tax proceedings before the IRS, a taxpayer is entitled to the same common-law protections of confidentiality, with respect to the tax advice given by any "federally authorized tax practitioner," as a taxpayer would have if the advising individual were an attorney.
   b. The privilege also applies in any noncriminal tax proceeding in federal court brought by or against the United States.
   c. The privilege may not be asserted to prevent the disclosure of information to any regulatory body other than the IRS.
   d. A "federally authorized tax practitioner" includes any nonattorney who is authorized to practice before the IRS, such as an enrolled agent, an enrolled actuary, or a CPA.
   e. "Tax advice" is defined as advice given by an individual with respect to matters that are within the scope of the individual's authority to practice before the IRS.
   f. The privilege does not apply to any written communication between a federally authorized tax practitioner and a director, shareholder, officer, employee, agent, or representative of a corporation in connection with the promotion of any tax shelter in which the corporation is a direct or indirect participant.

STOP AND REVIEW! **You have completed the outline for this subunit. Study multiple-choice questions 13 through 15 beginning on page 63.**

2.3 TAX SHELTERS

1. A tax shelter is a legal method of minimizing or decreasing an investor's taxable income and, therefore, tax liability.
   a. A tax benefit includes deductions, exclusions from gross income, nonrecognition of gain, tax credits, adjustments (or the absence of adjustment) to the basis of property, status as an entity exempt from federal income taxation, and any other tax consequences that may reduce a taxpayer's federal tax liability by affecting the amount, timing, character, or source of any item of income, gain, expense, loss, or credit.
2. The IRS considers certain tax shelters potentially improper tax shelter activity. Taxpayers are required to disclose reportable transactions. Disclosures are reported to the IRS on Form 8886. A copy of Form 8886 must be attached to each year's tax return that includes the transaction, and a copy must be filed with the Office of Tax Shelter Analysis in the first year of the transaction.
   a. There are five major categories of reportable transactions:
      1) Listed transactions. These are tax avoidance transactions the IRS has identified by notice, regulation, or other forms of published guidance, or transactions that are expected to obtain the same or substantially similar types of tax consequences.
      2) Confidential transactions. These are transactions offered under conditions of confidentiality, such as where the disclosure of a transaction is limited in any manner by express or implied understanding or agreement whether or not such understanding or agreement is legally binding.
         a) Regulations include a minimum fee requirement of $250,000 for corporations (excluding S corporations) and $50,000 for most other transactions.
      3) Transactions with contractual protection. These are transactions when the taxpayer has the right to a full or partial refund of fees paid to any person who makes or provides an oral or written statement about the potential tax consequences of a transaction if it is not sustained, or if fees are contingent on the taxpayer's realization of tax benefits from the transaction.

4) Loss transactions. These are transactions when taxpayers claim losses under Sec. 165 exceeding certain thresholds for

a) Corporations (excluding S corporations) and partnerships having only corporations (excluding S corporations) as partners, exceeding $10 million in a single year or $20 million in any combination of taxable years.

b) All other partnerships, individuals, S corporations, or trusts, exceeding $2 million in any single year or $4 million in any combination of taxable years.

c) Individuals or trusts involved in certain foreign currency transactions, exceeding $50,000 in any single taxable year.

i) Revenue Procedure 2003-24, known as the "Angel List," provides that certain losses are exceptions to the reporting requirements. Exceptions include, but are not limited to, loss from an asset sold or exchanged with a qualifying basis; fire, storm, or shipwreck; mark-to-market treatment; hedging transactions; basis treatment; abandonment of property; and the bulk sale of inventory.

5) Transactions of interest. These are transactions identified by the IRS via notice, regulation, or other published guidance as having the potential for tax avoidance or evasion, but which lack sufficient information to determine if they should be identified as tax avoidance transactions.

b. Generally, a penalty will be imposed if a person required to register a tax shelter fails to register the shelter timely.

1) No penalty will be imposed on a person for failure to register a tax shelter if the failure is due to reasonable cause.

c. The fact that a transaction must be reported on Form 8886 does not mean the tax benefits from the transaction will be disallowed.

3. Tax return preparers are subject to a penalty for promoting abusive tax shelters equal to the lesser of

a. $1,000 for each sale or organization of an abusive arrangement or plan, or
b. 100% of the income derived from the activity.

***Stop and Review!* You have completed the outline for this subunit. Study multiple-choice question 16 on page 64.**

2.4 PENALTIES

Tax return preparers are subject to penalties for violations [Sec. 6696(a)]. The degree of severity varies among the penalties. Also subject to penalties are individuals with overall supervisory responsibility for advice given by a firm.

1. **Compliance**
   a. A penalty of up to $27,000 per year may be imposed on a tax return preparer at $50 for each failure to comply with each procedural requirement.
   b. Applicable procedural requirements with respect to returns, claims, and employees are
      1) Signing a return or claim
      2) Affixing an identifying number
      3) Furnishing a copy to the taxpayer
      4) Filing a correct information return
      5) Retaining records by copies or a list
   c. Reasonable cause precludes the imposition of penalties if willful neglect was not a cause.
2. **Misconduct**
   a. A court may issue an injunction upon finding that a tax return preparer has engaged in one of the following:
      1) Misrepresenting eligibility to practice before the IRS
      2) Guaranteeing a tax refund or allowance of a credit
      3) Substantially interfering with Internal Revenue laws through deceptive or fraudulent conduct
      4) Understating tax liability
   b. In the case of an **injunction**, the court might enjoin the person from
      1) Engaging in such conduct or
      2) Acting as a tax return preparer if the court finds a pattern of continual or repeated conduct.

<u>**Accuracy-Related Penalty**</u>

3. Generally, the accuracy-related penalty is 20% of any portion of a tax underpayment attributable to (a) negligence or disregard of rules or regulations, (b) any substantial understatement of income tax, (c) any substantial valuation misstatement under Chapter 1 of the Internal Revenue Code, (d) any substantial overstatement of pension liabilities, (e) any substantial estate or gift tax valuation understatement, or (f) any claim of tax benefits from a transaction lacking economic substance [as defined by Sec. 7701(o)] or failing to meet the requirements of any similar rule of law.
   a. The penalty is 40% of any portion of a tax underpayment attributable to one or more gross valuation misstatements in (c), (d), or (e) above if the applicable dollar limitation under Sec. 6662(h)(2) is met.
      1) The penalty also increases to 40% for failing to adequately disclose a transaction that lacks economic substance in (f) above.
      2) The penalty is 40% of any portion of an underpayment that is attributable to any undisclosed foreign financial asset understatement.

b. **Reasonable basis.** Generally, the taxpayer can avoid the disregard of regulations and substantial understatement portions of the accuracy-related penalty if the position is adequately disclosed and has at least a reasonable basis. To avoid the disregard of regulations portion of the accuracy-related penalty, the position taken must also represent a good-faith challenge to the validity of the regulation.

   1) Reasonable basis is a relatively high standard of tax reporting that is significantly higher than not frivolous or not patently improper. The reasonable basis standard is not satisfied by a return position that is merely arguable.

   2) The penalty will not be imposed on any part of an underpayment if there was reasonable cause for the taxpayer's position and (s)he acted in good faith in taking that position.

c. While some taxpayers choose to use tax software to prepare their tax returns, the Tax Court does not find reliance on tax preparation software justifiable to avoid an accuracy-related penalty.

   1) According to the Taxpayer Advocate Service, the Tax Court has observed that "the misuse of tax preparation software, even if unintentional or accidental, is no defense to accuracy-related penalties under section 6662." Examples of such rulings include *Bartlett v. Commissioner* and *Anyika v. Commissioner*.

Negligence

d. The term "negligence" includes any failure to make a reasonable attempt to comply with the provisions of the internal revenue laws or to exercise ordinary and reasonable care in the preparation of a return.

Substantial Understatement

e. An understatement is the excess of the amount of tax required to be shown on the return for the tax year, over the amount of tax shown on the return for the tax year, reduced by any rebates.

   1) There is a substantial understatement of income tax if the amount of the understatement for any year exceeds the greater of

      a) 10% of the tax required to be shown on the return for the tax year or
      b) $5,000.

   2) An understatement of a corporation (other than an S corporation or a personal holding company) is substantial if it exceeds in any year the lesser of

      a) 10% of the tax required to be shown on the return for the tax year (or, if greater, $10,000) or
      b) $10,000,000.

Substantial Valuation Misstatement

f. In general, a taxpayer is liable for a 20% penalty for a substantial valuation misstatement if all the following are true:

1) The value or adjusted basis of any property claimed on the return is 150% or more of the correct amount (i.e., overvaluation).

2) The taxpayer underpaid the tax by more than $5,000 because of the misstatement.

3) The taxpayer cannot establish reasonable cause for the underpayment and that (s)he acted in good faith.

g. The taxpayer may be assessed a penalty of 40% for a gross valuation misstatement. If the value is misstated or the adjusted basis of property is 200% or more of the amount determined to be correct, the taxpayer will be assessed a penalty of 40%, instead of 20%, of the amount the taxpayer underpaid because of the gross valuation misstatement. The penalty rate is also 40% if the property's correct value or adjusted basis is zero.

Transaction Lacking Economic Substance

h. The economic substance doctrine only applies to an individual that entered into a transaction in connection with a trade or business or an activity engaged in for the production of income.

i. A transaction has economic substance for an individual taxpayer only if the transaction changes his or her economic position in a meaningful way (apart from federal income tax effects), or the taxpayer must have a substantial purpose (apart from federal income tax effects) for entering into the transaction.

1) For purposes of determining whether economic substance exists, a transaction's profit potential will only be taken into account if the present value of the reasonably expected pre-tax profit from the transaction is substantial compared to the present value of the expected net tax benefits that would be allowed if the transaction were respected.

2) If any part of an underpayment is due to any disallowance of claimed tax benefits by reason of a transaction lacking economic substance or failing to meet the requirements of any similar rule of law, that part of the underpayment will be subject to the 20% accuracy-related penalty even if the taxpayer had a reasonable cause and acted in good faith concerning that part.

3) Additionally, the penalty increases to 40% if the taxpayer does not adequately disclose on the return or in a statement attached to the return the relevant facts affecting the tax treatment of a transaction that lacks economic substance. Relevant facts include any facts affecting the tax treatment of the transaction.

Negotiating Refunds

4. A penalty of $545 is imposed on a tax return preparer for each taxpayer refund check (s)he negotiates, e.g., by endorsement.

a. Taxpayers may authorize the representative to receive a refund check.

1) They must specifically authorize this on the Power of Attorney form.

2) However, if the representative is a tax preparer, (s)he cannot be authorized to endorse or otherwise cash the check related to taxes.

3) A tax return preparer will not be considered to have endorsed or otherwise negotiated a check solely as a result of having affixed the taxpayer's name to a refund check for the purpose of depositing the check into an account in the name of the taxpayer or in the joint names of the taxpayer and one or more other persons (excluding the tax return preparer) if authorized by the taxpayer or the taxpayer's recognized representative.

Due Diligence Requirements

5. Section 6695(g) imposes a $545 penalty with respect to any return or claim for refund for each failure to comply with the four due diligence requirements imposed by regulations with respect to determining a taxpayer's eligibility for the Earned Income Credit, American Opportunity Tax Credit, Child Tax Credit, and Head of Household filing status.
   a. New expanded regulations clarify these requirements and set a performance standard for the "knowledge" requirement (i.e., what a reasonable and well informed tax return preparer, knowledgeable in the law, would do). The following are the four due diligence requirements:

Completion of Form 8867

1) Complete Form 8867, *Paid Preparer's Due Diligence Checklist*, truthfully and accurately and perform any actions described on Form 8867 for any applicable credit(s) claimed and HOH filing status.
   a) If credits are claimed on the return, complete the applicable worksheet(s) associated with Form 1040, 1040-SR, 1040-SS, 1040-PR, or 1040-NR or equivalents and all related forms and schedules.
2) Submit Form 8867 in the manner required.

Knowledge

3) Interview the taxpayer, ask questions, and document the taxpayer's responses and review the information to determine that the taxpayer is eligible to claim the credit(s) or file as HOH.
   a) Do not ignore the implications of information furnished or known.
   b) Make reasonable inquiries to conclude that the information furnished appears to be correct, consistent, and complete.
   c) Document any additional inquiries made and the client's responses.

Record Retention

4) Satisfy the document retention requirement by retaining the following five records:
   a) Form 8867;
   b) The applicable worksheet(s) or the preparer's own worksheet(s) for any credits claimed;
   c) Copies of any taxpayer documents relied on to determine eligibility for any credits or HOH filing status;
   d) A record of how, when, and from whom the information used to prepare the form and worksheet(s) was obtained; and
   e) A record of any additional questions the preparer asked and the client's answers.

   b. These records must be kept for 3 years from the latest of the following due dates:
      1) The due date of the tax return (not including extensions)
      2) The date the return was filed (if a signing tax return preparer electronically filed the return)
      3) The date the return was presented to the taxpayer for signature (if the signing tax preparer is not electronically filing the return)
      4) The date a preparer submitted the part of the return for which they were responsible to the signing tax return preparer (if that preparer is a nonsigning tax return preparer)
   c. The retention of a copy of the Social Security cards of the taxpayer and each qualifying child is not required.

Underpayment Penalty

6. The IRC imposes penalties on tax return preparers for understating a taxpayer's liability due to unreasonable positions and willful or reckless conduct.
   a. The tax return preparer who is subject to the penalties is the one who is primarily responsible for the position(s) on the return or claim for refund giving rise to an understatement. Generally, this is the signing tax return preparer.
7. Section 6694(a) imposes a penalty (the greater of $1,000 or 50% of income derived by the preparer as to the return) on a tax return preparer for taking a position known (or which reasonably should be known) to have no reasonable belief of being sustained on the merits.
   a. Four elements must be present for the penalty to apply:
      1) Understatement of tax liability. Under the IRC, understatement of liability means either
         a) Understating net tax payable or
         b) Overstating the net amount creditable or refundable.

Reasonable Belief

      2) A position with no reasonable belief of success. The penalty is imposed for taking a position with no reasonable belief that the tax treatment of the position would more likely than not be sustained on its merits.
         a) Regulations indicate the position must have a more likely than not possibility of being sustained by a court.
         b) Disclosure of a position may shield a preparer from liability for a nonfrivolous position without a more likely than not chance of success.

Frivolous Position

      3) Knowledge, or a frivolous position. For the penalty to apply, the tax return preparer must know that the position has no reasonable belief of a more likely than not chance of success, or the position must be frivolous.
         a) The standard for determining knowledge is applied objectively. It is what a competent practitioner
            i) Should have known or
            ii) Actually knew.
      4) Nondisclosure, or a frivolous position. The understatement penalty is not imposed if the relevant facts affecting the item's tax treatment are adequately disclosed in the return or in a statement attached to the return, unless the position is frivolous.
   b. A tax return preparer may be excused from the penalty if (s)he
      1) Shows there was reasonable cause for the understatement and
      2) Acted in good faith.

Willfulness

   c. Section 6694(b) imposes a penalty of the greater of $5,000 or 75% of income derived by the tax return preparer as to the return if an understatement of liability is willful or caused by intentional disregard of IRS rules and regulations.
      1) The burden is on the tax return preparer to prove that (s)he neither intentionally nor recklessly disregarded rules and regulations.
      2) Willfulness is implied from disregarding information furnished by the taxpayer or other persons or ignoring its implications by failing to make further inquiry.

Abatement

d. Section 6694(d) allows abatement of the penalty if it is established in final administrative determination or judicial decision that there was no understatement, even if there was a willful attempt to understate.

e. When the IRS examines a return for negligence or intentionally disregarded rules, the tax return preparer has the burden of proving his or her innocence.

Avoidance vs. Evasion

8. **Tax avoidance** is the minimization of tax liability through legal arrangements and transactions. The goal of a business is to maximize profits, and tax avoidance is a key element in obtaining this goal. Avoidance maneuvers take place prior to incurring a tax liability.

9. **Tax evasion** takes place once a tax liability has already been incurred (i.e., taxable actions have been completed). A key distinction between avoidance and evasion is taxpayer "intent." A taxpayer's intent is called into question when one of the "badges" of fraud is identified. These indicators include understatement of income, improper allocation of income, claiming of fictitious deductions, questionable conduct of the taxpayer, and accounting irregularities.

10. Concerning evasion, Sec. 7201 reads as follows: "Any person who willfully attempts in any manner to evade or defeat any tax imposed by this title or the payment thereof shall, in addition to other penalties provided by law, be guilty of a felony and, upon conviction thereof, shall be fined not more than $250,000 ($500,000 in the case of a corporation), or imprisoned not more than five years, or both, together with the costs of prosecution."

Liability and Assessment

11. The IRC has an integrated penalty structure for tax return preparers. But generally applicable sanctions, such as the one mentioned below, may also apply to a tax return preparer.

    a. Section 6701 imposes a $1,000 penalty for aiding or assisting in the preparation of any document if the person knows or has reason to believe

        1) That the document will be used in connection with any material (federal) tax matter and

        2) If it is so used, it will result in an understatement of tax liability.

            a) The penalty is $10,000 if the document relates to a corporate taxpayer's liability.

            b) The burden of proof is on the government.

        3) A tax return preparer is not subject to penalty for failure to follow a rule or regulation if the preparer in good faith and with a reasonable basis takes the position that the rule or regulation does not accurately reflect the Code.

    b. The Sec. 6701 penalty may not be imposed if a penalty is imposed under either of Secs. 6694(a) or (b) for the same violation.

        1) Furthermore, a penalty under Sec. 6694(a) would be offset against a Sec. 6694(b) penalty if it were also imposed for the same violation.

    c. Repeated violations of Sec. 6694(a), or one violation of either of Secs. 6694(b) or 6701, may result in disciplinary action by the Director of the Office of Professional Responsibility (DP).

        1) Thus, a tax return preparer may jeopardize his or her ability to practice his or her profession in representing clients in matters before the IRS.

Liability to Clients

d. A client may not be able to avoid liability for penalties by relying on a professional opinion. Furthermore, a tax return preparer may incur liability to a client who is dissatisfied with the tax liability that results from following the advice of the preparer; e.g., the preparer fails to inform the client that mortgage interest on the client's third (vacation) home is not deductible.

   1) Preparer negligence may be alleged in various forms, such as

      a) Making computational errors
      b) Filing of a tax return late
      c) Providing inaccurate information

   2) Damages may include client losses, such as increased tax liability and penalties.

Statute of Limitations

e. A 3-year limit applies to assessing the penalties for the procedural penalties and the understatement penalty.

   1) No period of limitation applies to assessing penalties for understatement due to willfulness or reckless conduct.

Assessment

f. A tax return preparer who pays 15% or more of an assessed preparer penalty after receipt of notice and demand may file a claim for a refund within 30 days of the notice. The preparer also may request a conference with the IRS agent and present additional information and explanations showing that the penalty is not warranted.

12. Frivolous submission (returns and documents). In addition to other penalties that may be imposed, there is a penalty for filing a frivolous return.

   a. A frivolous return is one that

      1) Omits information necessary to determine the taxpayer's tax liability,
      2) Shows a substantially incorrect tax,
      3) Is based upon a frivolous position (e.g., that wages are not income), or
      4) Is based upon the taxpayer's desire to impede the collection of tax.

   b. A return based on the taxpayer's altering or striking out the "penalty of perjury" language above the signature line also constitutes a frivolous return.

   c. Section 6702 imposes a $5,000 penalty on any person who submits a "specified frivolous submission." A specified frivolous submission is defined as a specified submission that is based on a position that the IRS has identified as frivolous or that reflects a desire to delay or impede the administration of Federal tax laws. A specified submission means a request for a collection due process hearing under Sec. 6320 or 6330 or an application for an installment agreement under Sec. 6159, an offer-in-compromise under Sec. 7122, or a taxpayer assistance order under Sec. 7811.

Fraud

13. Fraudulent transactions. Such transactions ordinarily involve a willful or deliberate action with the intent to obtain an unauthorized benefit.

    a. Per Sec. 7206, a tax return preparer who willfully aids or assists in fraud or false statements shall be fined not more than $250,000 ($500,000 in the case of a corporation) or imprisoned not more than 3 years.

Income

    b. Indicators of Fraud -- Income

        1) Omissions of specific items where similar items are included
        2) Omissions of entire sources of income
        3) Unexplained failure to report substantial amounts of income determined to have been received
        4) Substantial unexplained increases in net worth, especially over a period of years
        5) Substantial excess of personal expenditures over available resources
        6) Bank deposits from unexplained sources substantially exceeding reported income
        7) Concealment of bank accounts, brokerage accounts, and other property
        8) Inadequate explanation for dealing in large sums of currency or the unexplained expenditure of currency
        9) Consistent concealment of unexplained currency, especially in a business not calling for large amounts of cash
        10) Failure to deposit receipts to business account, contrary to normal practices
        11) Failure to file a return, especially for a period of several years although substantial amounts of taxable income were received
        12) Cashing checks representing income at check cashing services and banks other than the taxpayer's
        13) Covering up sources of receipts by false description of source of disclosed income and/or nontaxable receipts

Expenses/Deductions

    c. Indicators of Fraud -- Expenses or Deductions

        1) Substantial overstatement of deductions
        2) Substantial amounts of personal expenditures deducted as business expenses
        3) Claiming fictitious deductions
        4) Dependency exemption claimed for nonexistent, deceased, or self-supporting persons
        5) Loans of trust funds disguised as purchases or deductions

Books/Records

    d. Indicators of Fraud -- Books and Records

        1) Keeping two sets of books or no books
        2) False entries or alterations made on the books and records, backdated or postdated documents, false invoices, false applications, statements, other false documents, or applications
        3) Invoices that are irregularly numbered, unnumbered, or altered
        4) Checks made payable to third parties that are endorsed back to the taxpayer

5) Checks made payable to vendors and other business payees that are cashed by the taxpayer
6) Failure to keep adequate records, concealment of records, or refusal to make certain records available
7) Variances between treatment of questionable items on the return as compared with books
8) Intentional under- or overfooting of columns in journal or ledger
9) Amounts on return not in agreement with amounts in books
10) Amounts posted to ledger accounts not in agreement with source books or records
11) Journalizing of questionable items out of correct account
12) Recording income items in suspense or asset accounts
13) False receipts to donors by exempt organizations

Allocations of Income

e. Indicators of Fraud -- Allocations of Income

1) Distribution of profits to fictitious partners
2) Inclusion of income or deductions in the return of a related taxpayer when difference in tax rates is a factor

Conduct of Taxpayer

f. Indicators of Fraud -- Conduct of Taxpayer

1) False statement about a material fact involved in the examination
2) Attempts to hinder the examination, for example, failure to answer pertinent questions; repeated cancellations of appointments; refusal to provide records; threatening potential witnesses, including the examiner; or assaulting the examiner
3) Failure to follow the advice of accountant or attorney
4) Failure to make full disclosure of relevant facts to the accountant
5) The taxpayer's knowledge of taxes and business practices where numerous questionable items appear on the returns
6) Testimony of employees concerning irregular business practices by the taxpayer
7) Destruction of books and records, especially if just after examination was started
8) Transfer of assets for purposes of concealment, or diversion of funds and/or assets by officials or trustees
9) Patterns of consistent failure over several years to report income fully
10) Proof that the return was incorrect to such an extent and in respect to items of such character and magnitude as to compel the conclusion that the falsity was known and deliberate
11) Payment of improper expenses by or for officials or trustees
12) Willful and intentional failure to execute pension plan amendments
13) Backdating of applications and related documents
14) Making false statements on TEGE (Tax Exempt/Government Entities) determination letter applications
15) Use of false Social Security numbers
16) Submission of false Form W-4
17) Submitting a false affidavit
18) Attempts to bribe the examiner

Methods of Concealment

g. Indicators of Fraud -- Methods of Concealment

1) Inadequacy of consideration
2) Insolvency of transferor
3) Assets placed in other's names
4) Transfer of all or nearly all of debtors' property
5) Close relationship between parties to the transfer
6) Transfer made in anticipation of a tax assessment or while the investigation of a deficiency is pending
7) Reservation of any interest in the property transferred
8) Transaction not in the usual course of business
9) Retention of possession
10) Transactions surrounded by secrecy
11) False entries in books of transferor or transferee
12) Unusual disposition of the consideration received for the property
13) Use of secret bank accounts for income
14) Deposits into bank accounts under nominee names
15) Conduct of business transactions in false names

Badges

14. Badges of fraud are facts that suggest fraud but that, standing alone, do not establish its existence. For example, failure to keep adequate records may be a badge of fraud.

Tax Return Disclosure Statements

15. Form 8275 is used by taxpayers and tax return preparers to disclose items or positions that are not otherwise adequately disclosed on a tax return to avoid certain penalties. Form 8275-R is used to disclose a position taken contrary to a regulation.

a. The form is filed to avoid the portions of the accuracy-related penalty due to a disregarding of rules or to a substantial understatement of income tax or non-tax shelter items if the return position has a reasonable basis.

1) It can also be used for disclosures relating to preparer penalties for understatements due to unreasonable position or a disregarding of rules and the economic substance penalty.

b. The portion of the accuracy-related penalty attributable to the following types of misconduct cannot be avoided by disclosure on Form 8275:

1) Negligence
2) Disregard of regulations
3) Any substantial understatement of income tax
4) Any substantial valuation misstatement
5) Any substantial overstatement of pension liabilities
6) Any substantial estate or gift tax valuation understatements
7) Any claim of tax benefits from a transaction lacking economic substance
8) Any otherwise undisclosed foreign financial asset understatement

c. Form 8275 is filed by individuals, corporations, pass-through entities, and tax return preparers. For items attributable to a pass-through entity, disclosure should be made on the tax return of the entity. If the entity does not make disclosure, the partner, shareholder, etc., can make adequate disclosure of these items.

16. The penalties in the following table may be imposed on tax return preparers:

Act	Fine	Imprisonment
Understatement:		
Due to unreasonable positions	Greater of a) $1,000 or b) 50% of income to be derived	N/A
Due to willful or reckless conduct	Greater of a) $5,000 or b) 75% of income to be derived	N/A
Preparing tax returns for other persons:		
Failure to furnish copy to taxpayer	$50 each, limited to $27,000 per year	N/A
Failure to sign return	$50 each, limited to $27,000 per year	N/A
Failure to furnish identifying number	$50 each, limited to $27,000 per year	N/A
Failure to retain copy or list	$50 each, limited to $27,000 per year	N/A
Failure to file correct information returns	$50 each, limited to $27,000 per year	N/A
Endorses or negotiates checks made to taxpayer in respect of taxes imposed	$545 each, unlimited	N/A
Failure to be diligent in determining credits and head of household status (for the best benefit of taxpayer)	$545 each, unlimited	N/A
Others:		
Promoting abusive tax shelters	Lesser of a) $1,000 for each organization or sale of promotion plan b) Income to be derived	N/A
Aiding and abetting understatement of tax liability	$1,000 each year (noncorporate clients) $10,000 each year (corporate clients)	N/A
Disclosure or use of information	$250 per unauthorized disclosure, limited to $10,000 per year	N/A
Convicted of knowingly or recklessly disclosing information (misdemeanor)	$1,000	Up to 1 year
Fraud and false statements	$250,000 (individual clients) $500,000 (corporate clients)	Up to 3 years
Fraudulent returns, statements, or other documents	$10,000 (individual clients) $50,000 (corporate clients)	Up to 1 year

***STOP AND REVIEW!* You have completed the outline for this subunit. Study multiple-choice questions 17 through 24 beginning on page 65.**

QUESTIONS

2.1 Tax Preparers

1. When must a tax return preparer provide a copy of a tax return to a taxpayer?

A. Within 45 days after the return is filed, including extensions.

B. Within 48 hours after the taxpayer requests a copy of the tax return.

C. Not later than the time the original return is presented to the taxpayer for signature.

D. None of the answers are correct.

Answer (C) is correct.

REQUIRED: The time when a preparer must provide a copy of the return to the taxpayer.

DISCUSSION: Section 6107(a) requires all tax return preparers to furnish a completed copy of the return to the taxpayer not later than the time such return or claim for refund is presented for the taxpayer's signature.

Answer (A) is incorrect. The taxpayer must receive a copy no later than the time the original return is presented for a signature. **Answer (B) is incorrect.** The taxpayer must receive a copy no later than the time the original return is presented for a signature. **Answer (D) is incorrect.** A correct answer choice is provided.

2. Which of the following statements is false regarding tax return preparers?

A. Only a person who signs a return as the preparer may be considered the preparer of the return.

B. Unpaid preparers, such as volunteers who assist low-income individuals, are not considered to be preparers for purposes of preparer penalties.

C. An employee who prepares the return of his or her employer does not meet the definition of a tax preparer.

D. The preparation of a substantial portion of a return for compensation is treated as the preparation of that return.

Answer (A) is correct.

REQUIRED: The false statement about tax return preparers.

DISCUSSION: Under Sec. 7701(a)(36), a tax return preparer is any person who prepares for compensation, or employs others to prepare for compensation, any tax return or claim for refund under Title 26. A person who prepares a substantial portion of a return is considered a preparer even though someone else may be required to sign the return.

3. Which of the following is considered a tax return preparer?

A. A neighbor who assists with preparation of depreciation schedule.

B. A son who enters tax return information into a computer program and prints a return.

C. A woman who prepares tax returns in her home during filing season and accepts payment for her services.

D. A volunteer at a local church who prepares tax returns but accepts no payment.

Answer (C) is correct.

REQUIRED: The person who is a tax return preparer.

DISCUSSION: Under Sec. 7701(a)(36), a tax return preparer is any person who prepares for compensation, or employs others to prepare for compensation, all or a substantial portion of any tax return or claim for refund under the IRC.

Answer (A) is incorrect. A neighbor who assists with the preparation of a depreciation schedule is not a preparer. **Answer (B) is incorrect.** A person who merely furnishes typing, reproducing, or mechanical assistance is not a preparer. **Answer (D) is incorrect.** If no compensation is provided for a person to prepare a return or claim for refund, the person is not subject to the return preparer rules.

4. Ernie is a principal of an international CPA firm. One of the firm's clients owns seven businesses and is a member of over 100 flow-through entities. Several members of Ernie's firm assist in the preparation of the client's individual income tax return. Which one of the following is true with regard to the member of the firm who qualifies as the return preparer?

A. The signatory is the individual preparer who has the primary responsibility for the overall substantive accuracy of the reporting positions on the return.

B. A photocopy of a manually signed copy of the return satisfies the manual signature requirement.

C. If the individual preparer is physically unable to sign the return due to a disability, (s)he can indicate "unable to sign" as the signature.

D. All of the answers are correct.

Answer (D) is correct.

REQUIRED: The true statement regarding the member of the firm who qualifies as the return preparer.

DISCUSSION: A return preparer is required to manually sign the return or claim for refund after it has been completed and before it is presented to the taxpayer. If more than one preparer is involved, the signatory is the preparer with primary responsibility for the overall accuracy of the return or claim for purposes of the signing requirement. The signing requirement may be satisfied with a photocopy of the manually signed return. A valid signature is defined by state law and may be anything that clearly indicates the intent to sign.

5. Mike is an enrolled agent. For the past 5 years, the information that Anne provided Mike to prepare her return included a Schedule K-1 from a partnership showing significant income. However, Mike did not see a Schedule K-1 from the partnership among the information Anne provided to him this year. What does due diligence require Mike to do?

A. Without talking to Anne, Mike should estimate the amount that would be reported as income on the Schedule K-1 based on last year's Schedule K-1 and include that amount on Anne's return.

B. Call Anne's financial advisor and ask him or her about Anne's investments.

C. Nothing, because Mike is required to rely only on the information provided by his client, even if he has a reason to know the information is not accurate.

D. Ask Anne about the fact that she did not provide him with a Schedule K-1.

Answer (D) is correct.

REQUIRED: The actions required to act in due diligence.

DISCUSSION: A tax return preparer may rely, if in good faith, upon information furnished by the taxpayer without having to obtain third-party verification. However, the preparer may not ignore the implications of the information furnished. The preparer must make reasonable inquiries if the information appears inaccurate or incomplete.

Answer (A) is incorrect. The tax return preparer is not supposed to make up numbers. The tax return preparer is required to use the actual amounts in preparing a tax return. **Answer (B) is incorrect.** The tax return preparer cannot contact Anne's financial advisor without Anne's consent. **Answer (C) is incorrect.** A tax return preparer is required to make reasonable inquiries if information provided by the taxpayer appears inaccurate or incomplete.

6. Arnie is a Certified Public Accountant who prepares income tax returns for his clients. One of his clients submitted a list of expenses to be claimed on Schedule C of the tax return. Arnie qualifies as a return preparer and, as such, is required to comply with which one of the following conditions?

A. Arnie is required to independently verify the client's information.

B. Arnie can ignore implications of information known by him.

C. Inquiry is not required if the information appears to be incorrect or incomplete.

D. Appropriate inquiries are required to determine whether the client has substantiation for travel and entertainment expenses.

Answer (D) is correct.

REQUIRED: The conditions with which a return preparer must comply.

DISCUSSION: A practitioner may rely on information provided by a client without further inquiry or verification. However, if the information so provided appears incorrect, incomplete, or inconsistent, the practitioner must make reasonable inquiries about the information. This requirement includes inquiry about unsubstantiated travel and entertainment expenses (Circular 230).

Answer (A) is incorrect. Arnie may rely in good faith on the client's information. **Answer (B) is incorrect.** Arnie may not ignore implications of information known by him. **Answer (C) is incorrect.** Arnie is required to make reasonable inquiries about information that appears to be incorrect or incomplete.

7. Which of the following is NOT a tax return preparer?

A. Someone who employs one or more persons to prepare for compensation, other than for the employer, all or a substantial portion of any tax return under Title 26 of the Code.

B. Someone who prepares a substantial portion of a return or claim for refund under Title 26 of the Code.

C. The preparer of another return with entries directly related to a substantial portion of this second return.

D. Someone who prepares, as a fiduciary, a return or claim for refund for any person.

Answer (D) is correct.

REQUIRED: The person who is not a tax return preparer.

DISCUSSION: Under Sec. 7701(a)(36), a tax return preparer is any person who prepares for compensation, or employs others to prepare for compensation, any return or refund of tax imposed by the IRC. A fiduciary is specifically excluded from qualifying as a tax return preparer.

8. Sam, an enrolled agent, is representing Fred before the Examination Division of the Internal Revenue Service. The Internal Revenue Service is questioning Fred on his Schedule C gross income that is listed on the 2020 tax return. While reviewing the documentation Fred provided, Sam discovers income that was omitted from the tax return. What is the appropriate action for Sam to take?

A. Sam must immediately advise the Internal Revenue Service examiner of the omitted income.

B. Sam must notify the Internal Revenue Service that he is no longer representing Fred by withdrawing his Form 2848.

C. Sam must advise Fred promptly of the omission and the consequences provided by the Internal Revenue Code and regulations for such omission.

D. Sam must advise Fred on how to keep the omission from being discovered by the Internal Revenue Service.

Answer (C) is correct.

REQUIRED: The proper action for the enrolled agent to take upon discovery of an omission from a representative's tax return.

DISCUSSION: Circular 230 addresses the possibility of an omission from a taxpayer's tax return in Section 10.21. It states that, when a practitioner discovers that a client has made an error or omission from any document filed with the IRS, the practitioner must notify the client of the error or omission immediately. In addition, the practitioner must advise the client on the consequences of such an omission as provided by the Internal Revenue Code and regulations.

Answer (A) is incorrect. The practitioner does not necessarily have to notify the Internal Revenue Service when an omission is made. However, (s)he should always advise his or her client on the repercussions of such an omission. **Answer (B) is incorrect.** The practitioner must advise his or her client on the consequences of an omission when this is discovered. **Answer (D) is incorrect.** The practitioner should not encourage the concealment of facts from the IRS. This could result in suspension or disbarment from practice before the IRS.

9. Jack, a return preparer, did not retain copies of all returns that he prepared but did keep a list that reflected the taxpayer's name, identification number, tax year, and type of return for each of his clients. Which of the following statements best describes this situation?

A. Jack is in compliance with the provisions of Sec. 6107 if he retains the list for a period of 1 year after the close of the return period in which the return was signed.

B. Jack is in compliance with the provisions of Sec. 6107 provided he retains the list for a 3-year period after the close of the return period in which the return was signed.

C. Jack is not in compliance with Sec. 6107 since he must retain copies of all returns filed.

D. Jack is not in compliance with Sec. 6107 since he has not kept all the information required by the Code.

Answer (B) is correct.

REQUIRED: The statement that best describes the situation.

DISCUSSION: The person who is an income tax return preparer of any return or claim for refund shall "retain a completed copy of the return or claim for refund; or retain a record by list, card file, or otherwise of the name, taxpayer identification number, and taxable year of the taxpayer for whom the return or claim for refund was prepared and the type of return or claim for refund prepared." The material shall be retained and kept available for inspection for the 3-year period following the close of the return period during which the return or claim for refund was presented for signature to the taxpayer.

Answer (A) is incorrect. The list must be retained for a 3-year period. **Answer (C) is incorrect.** Jack is in compliance with Sec. 6107. **Answer (D) is incorrect.** Jack is in compliance with Sec. 6107.

10. Which of the following is false regarding the filing of information returns concerning employees who prepare tax returns?

A. Annual listings of preparers, identification numbers, and place of work are required for preparers who employ others to prepare returns.

B. The period for which the information return is required is a 12-month period beginning July 1 of each year.

C. No information return is actually required to be submitted; a list is made and kept by the employing preparer.

D. Information returns of income tax return preparers must be maintained by the preparer for 2 years.

Answer (D) is correct.

REQUIRED: The false statement regarding the filing of information returns concerning employees who prepare tax returns.

DISCUSSION: Under Sec. 6060(a), a person who employs one or more tax return preparers to prepare a return or claim for refund must file a return setting forth the name, identifying number, and place of work of each income tax return preparer employed by him or her. Section 6060(b) allows the IRS to approve an alternative method of reporting. Regulation 1.6060-1 states that the requirements of Sec. 6060 are satisfied by retaining a record of the name, identifying number, and principal place of work of each income tax return preparer employed, and making that record available for inspection upon request by the commissioner for the 3-year period following the close of the return period to which that record relates. The return period means the 12-month period beginning July 1 of each year [Reg. 1.6060-1(b)].

11. Identify the item below that does NOT describe information a preparer must maintain about every return prepared.

A. The taxpayer's name and taxpayer identification number.

B. The date the return or claim for refund was prepared.

C. The taxable year of the taxpayer (or nontaxable entity) for whom the return was prepared.

D. The type of return or claim for refund prepared.

Answer (B) is correct.

REQUIRED: The information that must be maintained by a return preparer.

DISCUSSION: Section 6107(b) requires a tax return preparer to retain a completed copy of each return or claim prepared or a list of the names and taxpayer identification numbers of the taxpayers for whom such returns or claims were prepared. Under Reg. 1.6107-1(b)(1)(i)(B), the list must include the taxable year of the taxpayer and the type of return or claim for refund prepared. This copy or list must be retained by the income tax return preparer for 3 years after the close of the return period.

12. A tax return preparer must complete the paid preparer's area of the return if

A. The taxpayer prepares his or her own return.

B. The individual volunteers to complete the return for no cost.

C. The individual was paid to prepare, assist in preparing, or review the tax return.

D. An employee prepares a tax return for his or her employer by whom (s)he is regularly and continuously employed.

Answer (C) is correct.

REQUIRED: The situation in which a tax return preparer must complete the paid preparer's area of the return.

DISCUSSION: Section 7701(a)(36) states that the term "tax return preparer" means any person who prepares for compensation, or who employs one or more persons to prepare for compensation, all or a substantial portion of any return of tax imposed by the IRC or any claim for refund of tax imposed by the IRC.

Answer (A) is incorrect. The taxpayer is not a paid preparer. **Answer (B) is incorrect.** The preparer is not a paid preparer. **Answer (D) is incorrect.** The employee is not hired as a return preparer but simply as an employee in another capacity.

2.2 Disclosure of Taxpayer Information

13. In which of the following situations may the tax return preparer disclose the tax return information requested without first obtaining the consent of the taxpayer/client?

A. The preparer receives a state grand jury subpoena requesting copies of federal and state income tax returns.

B. An IRS agent, in his or her official capacity, visits the preparer and requests copies of state and federal income tax returns, related returns, schedules, and records of the taxpayer used in the preparation of the tax returns.

C. A partner in a partnership, who was not involved with the return preparation or partnership records, requests a copy of the partnership return, including the Schedule K-1s for all partners.

D. All of the answers are correct.

Answer (D) is correct.

REQUIRED: The situation(s) that do not require a preparer to obtain the client's permission to disclose tax information.

DISCUSSION: Generally, a preparer is prohibited from disclosing a taxpayer's information without the client's consent. However, several exceptions exist, including a disclosure made pursuant to a court order, pursuant to an IRS inquiry, or among partners in a partnership.

14. Which of the following situations describes a disclosure of tax information by an income tax preparer that would subject the preparer to a penalty?

A. Ron died after furnishing tax return information to his tax return preparer. Ron's tax return preparer disclosed the information to Jerry, Ron's nephew, who is not the fiduciary of Ron's estate.

B. In the course of preparing a return for Duck Company, Jan obtained information indicating the existence of illegal kickbacks. Jan gave the information to Bill, an auditor in her firm, who was performing a financial audit of the company. Bill confirmed illegal kickbacks were occurring and brought the information to the attention of Duck Company officers.

C. Glade informed the proper federal officials of actions he mistakenly believed to be illegal.

D. Les, a return preparer, obtained information from Tom while selling Tom life insurance. The information was identical to tax return information that had been furnished to him previously. Les discussed this information with Mary, his wife, who was not an employee of any of his businesses.

Answer (A) is correct.

REQUIRED: The situation in which an income tax return preparer is subject to penalty for disclosure of tax information.

DISCUSSION: Section 6713 imposes a $250 penalty (limited to $10,000 per year) on an income tax return preparer who discloses information furnished in connection with preparation of any return or uses the information for any purpose other than to prepare, or assist in preparation of, the return. The preparer is subject to up to $1,000 in fines and up to 1 year in prison if convicted of knowingly or recklessly disclosing the information. This answer choice is such a disclosure described in Sec. 6713 to which no exception applies. Section 7216 imposes criminal penalties for knowingly or recklessly making such disclosure.

Answer (B) is incorrect. A tax return preparer may disclose tax return information to another employee or member of the preparer's law or accounting firm who may use it to render other legal or accounting services to the taxpayer [Reg. 301.7216-2(e)(1)].
Answer (C) is incorrect. Disclosure made in a bona fide but mistaken belief that the activities constituted a violation of criminal law does not subject the preparer to liability under Secs. 6713 or 7216 [Reg. 301.7216-2(n)].
Answer (D) is incorrect. The information disclosed was obtained in a capacity other than as a return preparer [Reg. 301.7216-2(j)].

15. Matt, an enrolled agent, provided tax advice to XYZ corporation on a federal tax matter. The Securities and Exchange Commission (SEC) is reviewing a required filing of the XYZ corporation and asks to see a copy of Matt's tax advice. The tax advice is NOT protected by the federally authorized tax practitioner privilege under IRC Sec. 7525 from disclosure to the SEC because

A. Matt is not a lawyer.

B. Matt is not a CPA.

C. The federally authorized tax practitioner privilege protects advice only against disclosure to the IRS, not other government agencies.

D. The federally authorized tax practitioner privilege protects only advice to individuals.

Answer (C) is correct.

REQUIRED: The statement that correctly identifies why the tax advice given in this question is not protected under IRC Sec. 7525.

DISCUSSION: The confidentiality privilege is extended to certain nonattorneys. In noncriminal tax proceedings before the IRS, a taxpayer is entitled to the same common-law protections of confidentiality, with respect to the tax advice given any "federally authorized tax practitioner," as a taxpayer would have if the advising individual were an attorney [Sec. 7525(a)(1)]. However, tax advice is not protected from disclosure to the SEC because the privilege protects only against disclosure to the IRS, not the SEC.

Answer (A) is incorrect. Matt's status as a lawyer is not covered under IRC Sec. 7525. **Answer (B) is incorrect.** Matt's status as a CPA does not shelter written correspondence between him and his client. **Answer (D) is incorrect.** The tax practitioner privilege act protects advice to entities as well.

2.3 Tax Shelters

16. What are listed transactions?

A. Tax avoidance transactions the IRS has identified by notice, regulation, or other forms of published guidance.

B. Transactions offered under conditions of confidentiality.

C. Transactions when taxpayers claim losses under Sec. 165 exceeding certain thresholds.

D. Transactions when the taxpayer has the right to a full or partial refund of fees paid for tax guidance, if the fees are contigent on realization of tax benefits.

Answer (A) is correct.

REQUIRED: The definition of listed transactions.

DISCUSSION: Listed transactions are tax avoidance transactions the IRS has identified by notice, regulation, or other forms of published guidance that are expected to obtain the same or substantially similar types of tax consequences.

Answer (B) is incorrect. These are confidential transactions. **Answer (C) is incorrect.** These are loss transactions. **Answer (D) is incorrect.** These are transactions with contractual protection.

2.4 Penalties

17. If you are employed as a tax preparer employee by a tax preparation firm, which of the following penalties may be assessed to you as a tax preparer?

A. $50 per return for failure to furnish a copy of the return to the taxpayer.

B. $50 per return for failure to furnish preparer's identifying number to the taxpayer.

C. $50 per return for failure to maintain copies of returns prepared or maintain a listing of clients.

D. None of the answers are correct.

Answer (D) is correct.

REQUIRED: The penalties that may be assessed against a tax preparer employee of a tax preparation firm.

DISCUSSION: According to Reg. 1.6107-1(c), in a situation in which one or more persons are employed as tax return preparers, only the employer is considered to be a tax return preparer. Thus, only the preparer, in this case, the employer, may be assessed the penalties.

18. A penalty may be assessed on any preparer or

A. Any person who prepares and signs a tax return or claim for refund.

B. Any member of a firm who gives advice (written or oral) to a taxpayer or to a preparer not associated with the same firm.

C. Any person who prepares and signs a tax return or claim for refund and the individual with overall supervisory responsibility for the advice given by the firm with respect to the return or claim.

D. The individual with overall supervisory responsibility for the advice given by the firm with respect to the return or claim.

Answer (C) is correct.

REQUIRED: The individual(s), other than a preparer, on which a penalty may be assessed.

DISCUSSION: A penalty may be assessed on any individual who prepares and signs a tax return or claim for a refund. Additionally, an individual with overall supervisory responsibility for advice given by the firm with respect to the return or claim may also be assessed the penalty.

Answer (A) is incorrect. A penalty may also be assessed on any individual with overall supervisory responsibility for the advice given by the firm. **Answer (B) is incorrect.** Any member of a firm who gives advice (written or oral) to a taxpayer is not considered a preparer of the return. Additionally, the individual must be associated with the return in order to be assessed the penalty. **Answer (D) is incorrect.** A penalty may also be assessed on any person who prepares and signs a tax return or claim for refund.

19. To satisfy the due diligence requirements for various credits and head of household filing status, a preparer must do all of the following EXCEPT

A. Complete Form 8867, *Paid Preparer's Due Diligence Checklist*.

B. Retain the records described in the due diligence checklist in Part VI of Form 8867.

C. Provide the taxpayer or the signing preparer with a copy of Form 8867.

D. Retain a copy of the Social Security cards for the taxpayer and each qualifying child.

Answer (D) is correct.

REQUIRED: The requirements of a preparer to satisfy the due diligence requirements.

DISCUSSION: Under the regulations, the preparer must complete Form 8867. A copy of Form 8867 must be attached to the tax return. The preparer must record how and when the information was obtained by the preparer, including the identity of any person furnishing such information. The retention of a copy of the Social Security cards for the taxpayer and each qualifying child is not required.

Answer (A) is incorrect. Form 8867 must be completed. **Answer (B) is incorrect.** The due diligence records must be maintained by the preparer. **Answer (C) is incorrect.** A copy of the tax return must be given to the taxpayer, and Form 8867 is required to be filed with the return.

20. Which of the following persons would be subject to the penalty for improperly negotiating a taxpayer's refund check?

A. A tax return preparer who operates a check cashing agency that cashes, endorses, or negotiates tax refund checks for returns he prepared.

B. A tax return preparer who operates a check cashing business and cashes checks for her clients as part of a second business.

C. The firm that prepared the tax return and is authorized by the taxpayer to receive a tax refund but not to endorse or negotiate the check.

D. A business manager who prepares tax returns for clients who maintain special checking accounts against which the business manager is authorized to sign certain checks on their behalf. The clients' federal tax refunds are mailed to the business manager, who has the clients endorse the checks and then deposits them in the special accounts.

Answer (A) is correct.

REQUIRED: The person subject to the penalty for negotiation of a refund check.

DISCUSSION: Section 6695(f) provides that any tax return preparer who endorses or otherwise negotiates any check issued to a taxpayer with respect to taxes imposed by the IRC will be subject to a penalty of $545 for each such check. A tax return preparer who operates a check cashing agency that cashes, endorses, or negotiates tax refund checks for returns that (s)he prepared is subject to the penalty.

Answer (B) is incorrect. The preparer's second business meets the definition of a bank. **Answer (C) is incorrect.** A preparer may receive checks provided (s)he does not cash it. **Answer (D) is incorrect.** The clients endorsed the checks.

21. Which one of the following would result in a penalty against the tax return preparer for failure to furnish a copy of the 2021 tax return to the taxpayer?

A. The paid preparer's copy machine broke in December 2021, and (s)he was not able to get it fixed until after filing season.

B. The paid preparer prepared one return that affected amounts reported on another return.

C. Failure was due to reasonable cause and not due to willful neglect.

D. The preparer gave advice on a specific issue of law.

Answer (A) is correct.

REQUIRED: The situation that would result in a penalty for failure to furnish a copy of the return.

DISCUSSION: Section 6695(a) provides that a tax return preparer with respect to any return or claim for refund who fails to furnish a copy of the return or claim for refund to the taxpayer when the return is presented for the taxpayer's signature must pay a penalty of $50 unless the failure is due to reasonable cause and not willful neglect. The copy machine breaking on April 13 could qualify for reasonable cause, but in this case, 4 months had elapsed without the preparer addressing the problem.

22. Bernard is a tax return preparer. While preparing a 2021 tax return for a client, Bernard determines the client owes a substantial amount of tax. In order to generate a refund for the client, Bernard substantially overstates itemized deductions and expenses claimed on the Schedule C. Bernard is subject to a penalty of

A. $5,000 or 75% of his fee, whichever is greater.

B. $1,000 or 50% of his fee, whichever is greater.

C. $505 or 50% of his fee, whichever is greater.

D. $250 or 50% of his fee, whichever is greater.

Answer (A) is correct.

REQUIRED: The penalty for willful or reckless conduct by a return preparer.

DISCUSSION: Section 6694(b) provides for a penalty of the greater of $5,000 or 75% of income derived by the preparer as to the return, to be assessed against a return preparer whose willful or reckless conduct in preparing a tax return causes an understatement of liability. The penalty is applied if the understatement is due either to a willful attempt to understate the tax liability or to any reckless or intentional disregard of rules or regulations by the return preparer. The penalty is assessed against each return containing an understatement of liability caused by the return preparer's willful or reckless conduct.

23. When a prepared return claims the Child Tax Credit, which of the following is false?

A. Due diligence requirements apply.

B. No special requirements apply to returns claiming the Child Tax Credit.

C. The preparer may be penalized $545 if no attempt is made to determine eligibility for the credit.

D. The preparer must take additional steps to ensure that a client is eligible for the Child Tax Credit.

Answer (B) is correct.

REQUIRED: The false statement concerning the Child Tax Credit.

DISCUSSION: Section 6695(g) imposes a $545 penalty on a preparer with respect to any return or claim for refund for each failure to comply with the due diligence requirements imposed by regulations with respect to determining a taxpayer's eligibility for the EIC, American Opportunity Tax Credit, or Child Tax Credit or the amount of any allowable credit.

Answer (A) is incorrect. Due diligence requirements for the Child Tax Credit do apply and are enforced by a penalty under Sec. 6695(g). **Answer (C) is incorrect.** Section 6695(g) does impose a $545 penalty for failure to determine a taxpayer's eligibility for the Child Tax Credit. **Answer (D) is incorrect.** The additional steps are the specific Child Tax Credit due diligence requirements in the regulations.

24. Frankie is a truck driver who is also a licensed return preparer and specializes in preparing income tax returns claiming the Earned Income Credit (EIC). Frankie will not be subject to a preparer penalty for an erroneously claimed EIC if he complies with which one of the following?

A. Completion of an eligibility checklist based upon information provided by the client.

B. Completion of the computation worksheet for the EIC based upon information provided by the client.

C. Knowledge or reason to know that the information used to determine eligibility for an amount of the EIC is correct.

D. All of the answers are correct.

Answer (D) is correct.

REQUIRED: The procedure(s) that exempt(s) a preparer who erroneously claims the EIC from a preparer penalty.

DISCUSSION: Frankie will not be subject to a preparer penalty for an erroneously claimed EIC if he meets the four due diligence requirements outlined in Publication 3107, including completion of an eligibility checklist based on information provided by the client, completion of the appropriate computation worksheet for the EIC based on information provided by the client, and no knowledge or reason to know that the information used to determine the client's eligibility and amount of EIC is incorrect.

STUDY UNIT THREE

REPRESENTATION

(8 pages of outline)

This study unit describes the rules concerning the representation of taxpayers before the IRS under the authority of a power of attorney. These rules apply to all offices of the IRS and apply to "practicing before the IRS." In general, a power of attorney is a document signed by the taxpayer, as principal, by which an individual is appointed to perform certain specified acts on behalf of the principal.

3.1 REPRESENTATION

1. Representation is defined as acts performed on behalf of a taxpayer by a representative in practice before the Internal Revenue Service (IRS).
   a. However, any person may appear as a witness for the taxpayer before the Internal Revenue Service, or furnish information at the request of the Internal Revenue Service or any of its officers or employees.

Power of Attorney

2. A power of attorney is a document signed by the taxpayer, as principal, by which an individual is appointed as attorney-in-fact to perform certain specified act(s) or kinds of act(s) on behalf of the principal. Specific types of powers of attorney include the following:
   a. **General power of attorney.** The attorney-in-fact is authorized to perform any or all acts the taxpayer can perform.
   b. **Durable power of attorney.** A power of attorney which specifies that the appointment of the attorney-in-fact will not end due to either the passage of time (i.e., the authority conveyed will continue until the death of the taxpayer) or the incompetency of the principal (e.g., the principal becomes unable or is adjudged incompetent to perform his or her business affairs).
   c. **Limited (or special) power of attorney.** A power of attorney which is limited in any facet (i.e., a power of attorney authorizing the attorney-in-fact to perform only certain specified acts as contrasted to a general power of attorney authorizing the representative to perform any and all acts the taxpayer can perform).

Recognized Representative

3. A recognized representative is an individual who is appointed as an attorney-in-fact under a power of attorney, is a member of one of the following categories, and files a declaration of representative:

   a. **Attorney**, which is any individual who is a member in good standing of the bar of the highest court of any state, possession, territory, commonwealth, or the District of Columbia

   b. **Certified public accountant**, which is any individual who is duly qualified to practice as a certified public accountant in any state, possession, territory, commonwealth, or the District of Columbia

   c. **Enrolled agent**, which is any individual who is enrolled to practice before the Internal Revenue Service and is in active status pursuant to the requirements of Circular 230

      1) Temporary recognition. Any individual who is granted temporary recognition as an enrolled agent by the Director of Practice.

   d. **Enrolled actuary**, which is any individual who is enrolled as an actuary by and is in active status with the Joint Board for the Enrollment of Actuaries

   e. Practice based on a relationship or special status with a taxpayer. Any individual authorized to represent a taxpayer with whom/which a special relationship exists. (For example, an individual may represent another individual who is his or her regular full-time employer or a member of his or her immediate family; an individual who is a bona fide officer or regular full-time employee of a corporation or certain other organizations may represent that entity.)

   f. **Annual Filing Season Program (AFSP) participant.** Any AFSP participant who signs a return as having prepared it for a taxpayer, or who prepared a return with respect to which the instructions or regulations do not require that the return be signed by the preparer. The acts an AFSP participant may perform are limited to representation of a taxpayer before revenue agents and examining officers of the Examination Division in the offices of District Director with respect to the tax liability of the taxpayer for the taxable year or period covered by a return prepared by the AFSP participant.

      1) All unenrolled return preparers must provide a valid PTIN to represent a taxpayer before the IRS. Only unenrolled return preparers who participate in the AFSP program may represent a taxpayer, and only with respect to returns the AFSP participant prepared and signed.

   g. Special appearance. Any individual who, upon written application, is authorized by the IRS to represent a taxpayer in a particular matter.

Signing Tax Returns

4. The filing of a power of attorney does not authorize the recognized representative to sign a tax return on behalf of the taxpayer unless such act is both

   a. Permitted under the Internal Revenue Code and the regulations thereunder and
   b. Specifically authorized in the power of attorney.

Power of Attorney -- Other Items

5. Situations in which a power of attorney is not required.
   a. Disclosure of confidential tax return information. The submission of a tax information authorization to request the disclosure of confidential tax return information does not constitute practice before the Internal Revenue Service. Nevertheless, if a power of attorney is properly filed, the recognized representative also is authorized to receive and/or inspect confidential tax return information concerning the matter(s) specified in the power of attorney (provided the power of attorney places no limitations upon such disclosure).
6. Copy of power of attorney. The Internal Revenue Service will accept either the original or a copy of a power of attorney.
7. If a power of attorney fails to include all required information, the attorney-in-fact can correct the existing power of attorney without obtaining a new power of attorney.
8. Cases where taxpayer may be contacted directly. Where a recognized representative has unreasonably delayed or hindered an examination, collection, or investigation by failing to furnish, after repeated requests, nonprivileged information necessary to the examination, collection, or investigation, the Internal Revenue Service employee conducting the examination, collection, or investigation may request the permission of his or her immediate supervisor to contact the taxpayer directly for such information.
   a. Effect of direct notification. Permission to bypass a recognized representative and contact a taxpayer directly does not automatically disqualify an individual to act as the recognized representative of a taxpayer in a matter. However, such information may be referred to the IRS for possible disciplinary proceedings under Circular 230.
9. A power of attorney does not give an individual the right to represent someone before a court. The practitioner must be admitted to practice before the court.

POA, Form 2848

10. A *Power of Attorney and Declaration of Representative* (POA, Form 2848) or a substitute Form 2848 (i.e., a non-IRS POA form) is generally required when a taxpayer wants to authorize another individual who is recognized to practice before the IRS to perform at least one of the following acts on his or her behalf:
    a. Represent the taxpayer at a conference with the IRS
    b. File a written response to the IRS
    c. Sign a consent or an extension
11. The declaration of representative states the following:
    a. I am not currently suspended or disbarred from practice, or ineligible for practice, before the Internal Revenue Service;
    b. I am subject to regulations contained in Circular 230 (31 CFR, Subtitle A, Part 10), as amended, governing practice before the Internal Revenue Service;
    c. I am authorized to represent the taxpayer identified in Part 1 (POA) for the tax matter(s) specified there; and
    d. I am one of the individuals described in 26 CFR 601.502.

Return Information

12. Return information includes data received or prepared by the IRS regarding a return, deficiency, or penalty.
    a. A change in a return is also considered return information.

Disclosure

13. Tax returns and return information are confidential and are generally not subject to disclosure. Disclosure of return information is permitted to
    a. A person designated by the taxpayer
    b. Congressional committees
    c. State tax officials
    d. Certain other persons

Tax Information Authorization (TIA)

14. A representative must file a *Tax Information Authorization* (TIA, Form 8821) to receive or inspect confidential tax information on behalf of the taxpayer unless the representative has filed a POA to perform those specific acts.
    a. The IRS will accept a POA or TIA other than one on Form 2848 or 8821, respectively, provided that it includes all of the information required by the official form.
        1) However, for purposes of processing into the Centralized Authorization File, a Form 2848 must be attached to the nonstandard form.
            a) The Form 2848 must be completed, but it does not need to be signed by the taxpayer.
    b. With respect to disclosure, a TIA or POA is not required of a representative who
        1) Represents a taxpayer at a conference attended by the taxpayer.
        2) Represents an executor or administrator at a conference on an estate tax case if the representative presents evidence that (s)he
            a) Prepared the estate tax return on behalf of the executor or administrator,
            b) Is recognized to practice before the IRS, and
            c) Is the attorney of record for the executor or administrator before the court where the will is probated or the estate is administered.
        3) Is appointed by a court as a trustee, a receiver, or an attorney for the taxpayer as a debtor.
        4) Practices in cases before the Tax Court if
            a) The taxpayer's petition to the Tax Court was signed by the representative as counsel admitted to practice before the Tax Court.

Multiple Representatives

    c. The IRS will provide copies of written communications to no more than two designated representatives.
        1) The IRS practice is to give copies to the representative named first on the most recent POA unless it lists not more than two representatives to receive them.
        2) The limit to two individuals does not apply to TIA appointees.

Scope of Authority

15. A TIA or POA may relate to several matters, e.g., income taxes for several years.
    a. A power of attorney is a written authorization for an individual to act on behalf of an individual in tax matters. It is required by the IRS when the taxpayer wishes to authorize a recognized representative to act on his or her behalf.
        1) If the authorization is not limited, the individual can generally perform all acts that the taxpayer can perform.

2) In general, a representative can do all of the following:
   a) Represent the taxpayer before any office of the IRS
   b) Sign a waiver agreeing to a tax adjustment
   c) Sign a consent to extend the statutory time period for assessment or collection of a tax
   d) Sign a closing agreement
   e) Receive, but not endorse or cash, a refund check
   f) Record the interview
3) An unenrolled return preparer is limited in scope to appearing before revenue agents and examining officers.

b. Technical language is not necessary, but
   1) The instrument must clearly specify which acts the representative is authorized to perform.
   2) "In all tax matters" does not sufficiently describe the representative's scope of authority.

c. The scope of authority should be specific as to the
   1) Tax matters, e.g., type of tax
   2) Years or periods

d. A power of attorney may concern only a tax period listed on the form that ends no later than 3 years after the date a power of attorney is received by the IRS.

e. The instrument need not list the divisions of the IRS involved in the matter.

POA Requirements

16. A POA must contain the following information:
   a. Name and address of the taxpayer
   b. Identification number of the taxpayer
   c. Employee plan number (if applicable)
   d. Name, address, and title (if employed full-time) of the recognized representative
   e. The state in which the representative is admitted to practice, if the representative is an attorney or a CPA
   f. Description of the matter(s) for which representation is authorized, which, if applicable, must include the
      1) Type of tax involved
      2) Federal tax form number
      3) Specific years involved
      4) Decedent's date of death (for estate matters)
   g. A clear expression of the taxpayer's intention concerning the scope of authority granted to the recognized representative
   h. Signature of the appointed representative

TIA Limitations

17. A TIA does not authorize an appointee to
   a. Advocate the taxpayer's position with respect to federal tax laws;
   b. Execute waivers, consents, or closing agreements; or
   c. Otherwise represent the taxpayer before the IRS.

Change of Authority

18. The authority granted a representative by a POA may be changed by filing a new POA.
    a. A new POA is deemed to revoke a prior POA unless the new one contains a clause specifically stating that it does not revoke a prior POA.
    b. A new POA revokes a prior POA if the taxpayer signs a statement listing the names and addresses of the individuals listed under the prior POA whose authority is revoked. "REVOKE" should be written across the power of attorney.

Execution of a POA or TIA

19. Form 2848 is used to appoint a representative to act on behalf of a taxpayer before the IRS.
    a. A representative recognized to practice before the IRS need only execute a declaration on the POA that (s)he is so recognized.
    b. A TIA or POA for a specific type of taxpayer is properly executed when it is signed by the appropriate individual(s), as indicated below.
        1) Joint return, for representation by one party -- by both spouses unless one spouse is duly authorized in writing to sign for the other
        2) Partnership -- by all partners or a duly authorized partner
            a) If a dissolved partnership is involved, each of the former living partners must execute a power of attorney.
        3) Corporation -- by an officer with authority to bind the corporation
        4) Person with a court-appointed guardian -- by the one appointed
        5) Decedent -- by the executor or administrator
    c. Form 2848 should be mailed or faxed directly to the IRS.

Substitution

20. A properly executed POA and Declaration of Representative does permit the representative to make substitution of representatives by the taxpayer in the original POA.
    a. The POA must, however, state the intention to grant authority of substitution.
    b. A substitution is made by filing the following items with the IRS:
        1) Notice of substitution
        2) A new declaration of representative
        3) A power of attorney that authorizes a substitution
    c. Only the newly recognized representative will be considered the taxpayer's representative.
21. A POA is required for executing a waiver of notice to disallow a claim for credit or refund.

Partnership Audits

22. In an administrative or judicial proceeding concerning partnership items, the determination of the tax treatment of partnership items is made at the partnership level in a single administrative partnership proceeding, rather than in individualized proceedings.
    a. Special rules govern proceedings that must be conducted at the partnership level for the assessment and collection of tax deficiencies or for tax refunds arising out of the partners' distributive shares of income, deductions, credits, etc.

b. Notice of the beginning of administrative proceedings and the resulting final partnership administrative adjustment must be given to all partners except those with less than a 1% interest in partnerships with more than 100 partners.

   1) However, a group of partners having an aggregate profits interest of 5% or more may request notice to be mailed to a designated partner.

c. Each partnership is supposed to name a partnership representative who is to receive notice on behalf of small partners not entitled to notice and to keep all partners informed of all administrative and judicial proceedings at the partnership level.

d. Settlement agreements may be entered into between the partnership representative and the IRS that bind the parties to the agreement and may extend to other partners who request to enter into consistent settlement agreements.

Representing a Decedent

23. A **personal representative** of an estate is an executor, administrator, or anyone who is in charge of the decedent's property.

    a. Generally, an **executor** is named in a decedent's will to administer the estate and distribute properties as the decedent has directed.

    b. An **administrator** is usually appointed by the court if no will exists, if no executor was named in the will, or if the named executor cannot or will not serve.

       1) Generally, an administrator performs the same duties and has the same responsibilities as an executor.

24. For estate tax purposes, if there is no executor or administrator appointed, qualified, and acting within the United States, the term "executor" includes anyone in actual or constructive possession of any property of the decedent.

25. The **primary duties** of a personal representative are to collect all the decedent's assets, pay his or her creditors, and distribute the remaining assets to the heirs or other beneficiaries. The personal representative must also perform the following duties:

    a. Apply for an employer identification number (EIN) for the estate.
    b. File all tax returns, including income, estate, and gift tax returns, when due.
    c. Pay the tax determined up to the date of discharge from duties.

26. It is the personal representative's duty to file the returns for the decedent and the estate when due.

    a. Reliance on an agent (attorney, accountant, etc.) is not reasonable cause for late filing.

27. All personal representatives must include fees paid to them from an estate in their gross income.

Notice of Fiduciary Relationship

28. The term **fiduciary** means any person acting for another person. It generally includes a guardian, trustee, executor, administrator, receiver, or conservator.

    a. A personal representative appointed to act in a fiduciary capacity for another must file a written notice with the IRS stating this. Form 56, *Notice Concerning Fiduciary Relationship*, is used for this purpose.

    b. Form 56 should also be filed to notify the IRS if the fiduciary relationship is terminated or when a successor fiduciary is appointed if the estate has not been terminated.

STOP AND REVIEW! **You have completed the outline for this subunit. Study multiple-choice questions 1 through 17 beginning on page 77.**

3.2 CENTRALIZED AUTHORIZATION FILE (CAF)

1. A Centralized Authorization File (CAF) system is a computer file containing information regarding the authority of individuals appointed under powers of attorney or designated under the tax information authorization system. This system gives IRS personnel quicker access to authorization information.
2. A CAF number generally will be issued to
   a. A recognized representative who files a POA and a written Declaration of Representative
   b. An appointee authorized under a TIA
3. The issuance of a CAF number does not indicate that a person is either recognized or authorized to practice before the Internal Revenue Service. This determination is made under the provisions of Circular 230, 31 CFR Part 10.
4. A recognized representative or an appointee should include the same CAF number on every POA or TIA filed. However, because the CAF number is not a substantive requirement, a TIA or POA will not be rejected based on the absence of a CAF number.
5. Information from both POAs and TIAs is recorded on the CAF system.
   a. This information enables IRS personnel who do not have access to the actual POAs or TIAs to send copies or computer-generated notices and communications to appointees or recognized representatives authorized by taxpayers.
6. Only documents that concern a tax period that ends no later than 3 years after the date a POA is received by the IRS will be recorded on the CAF system.
   a. Documents that concern any tax period that ended prior to the date on which a POA is received by the IRS will be recorded on the CAF system provided that matters concerning such years are under consideration by the IRS.

STOP AND REVIEW! **You have completed the outline for this subunit. Study multiple-choice questions 18 through 20 on page 84.**

QUESTIONS

3.1 Representation

1. A power of attorney is required in all of the following situations EXCEPT to

A. Represent an individual at a conference with the IRS.

B. File a written response to the IRS on behalf of another individual.

C. Sign a consent to extend the statute of limitations on behalf of another individual.

D. Furnish copies of pre-existing documents at the request of the IRS.

Answer (D) is correct.

REQUIRED: The situation that does not require a power of attorney.

DISCUSSION: A power of attorney is required when an individual wants to authorize another individual to perform at least one of the following acts on his or her behalf:

1. Represent the individual at a conference with the IRS
2. File a written response to the IRS
3. Sign a consent or an extension

Answer (A) is incorrect. Representing an individual at a conference with the IRS is a situation that requires a power of attorney. **Answer (B) is incorrect.** Filing a written response to the IRS on behalf of another individual is a situation that requires a power of attorney. **Answer (C) is incorrect.** Signing a consent to extend the statute of limitations on behalf of another individual is a situation that requires a power of attorney.

2. A declaration of representative, which accompanies a power of attorney, includes all of the following statements EXCEPT

A. I am authorized to represent the taxpayer(s) identified in the power of attorney.

B. I am aware of the regulations in Circular 230.

C. I am an individual described in 26 CFR 601.502(a) (such as an attorney, a CPA, an enrolled agent, etc.).

D. I have never been sanctioned (e.g., reprimand, suspension, or disbarment) by the IRS.

Answer (D) is correct.

REQUIRED: The statement not required for a declaration of representative.

DISCUSSION: A recognized representative must attach to the power of attorney a written declaration stating the following:

1. I am not currently suspended or disbarred from practice, or ineligible for practice, before the Internal Revenue Service;
2. I am subject to regulations contained in Circular 230 (31 CFR, Subtitle A, Part 10), as amended, governing practice before the Internal Revenue Service;
3. I am authorized to represent the taxpayer identified in Part 1 (POA) for the tax matter(s) specified there; and
4. I am one of the individuals described in 26 CFR 601.502.

A declaration of representative does not require an individual to state that they have never been sanctioned.

3. A taxpayer must use a power of attorney to do which of the following?

A. Authorize an individual to prepare the taxpayer's return.

B. Authorize an individual to represent a taxpayer at a conference with the IRS.

C. Authorize the IRS to disclose tax information to an individual.

D. Authorize an individual to provide information to the IRS.

Answer (B) is correct.

REQUIRED: The action that requires a taxpayer to use a power of attorney.

DISCUSSION: A power of attorney is required when a taxpayer wants to authorize another individual to appear on his or her behalf at a conference with the IRS.

Answer (A) is incorrect. A power of attorney is not necessary for engaging a tax return preparer. **Answer (C) is incorrect.** A *Tax Information Authorization* (TIA) may also be used to authorize the IRS to disclose confidential information. **Answer (D) is incorrect.** A power of attorney is not required to authorize an individual to provide information to the IRS.

4. If a representative chooses to use a non-IRS power of attorney form, which of the following "Declaration of Representative" statements is NOT required in order for the power of attorney to be valid?

A. A declaration that the representative is not currently under suspension or disbarment from practice before the IRS or other practice of his or her profession by any other authority.

B. A declaration that the representative is aware of the regulations contained in Treasury Department Circular 230 concerning the practice of enrolled agents, attorneys, CPAs, etc.

C. A declaration that the representative is not currently under investigation by the IRS.

D. A declaration that the representative is authorized to practice before the IRS in his or her capacity as an attorney, a certified public accountant, an enrolled agent, etc.

Answer (C) is correct.

REQUIRED: The statement not required in a Declaration of Representative.

DISCUSSION: The Declaration of Representative is a statement made by a representative under the penalty of perjury that (s)he is (1) authorized to practice before the IRS in his or her capacity as an attorney, a CPA, an enrolled agent, etc.; (2) not currently suspended or disbarred from practice before the IRS; (3) authorized to represent the taxpayer for the matter specified in the power of attorney; and (4) aware of the regulations governing practice before the IRS. It is filed with a power of attorney, and its failure to indicate current investigation by the IRS will not invalidate the power of attorney.

5. Which of the following is true regarding a refund check?

A. Form 2848, *Power of Attorney and Declaration of Representative*, may be used to authorize cashing of a refund check.

B. Form 2848, *Power of Attorney and Declaration of Representative*, may be used to authorize receipt of a refund check.

C. Form 8821, *Tax Information Authorization*, must be signed before a refund check may be applied to a fee for electronic filing.

D. Both Form 2848 and Form 8821 must be used to authorize cashing a refund check.

Answer (B) is correct.

REQUIRED: The true statement regarding a refund check.

DISCUSSION: A power of attorney (POA, Form 2848) is generally required when a taxpayer wants to authorize another individual to perform at least one of the following acts on his or her behalf:

1. Represent the taxpayer before any office of the IRS
2. Sign a waiver agreeing to a tax adjustment
3. Sign a consent to extend the statutory time period for assessment or collection of a tax
4. Sign a closing agreement
5. Receive, but not endorse or cash, a refund check
6. Record the interview

Answer (A) is incorrect. A POA does not grant the authority to cash a refund check. **Answer (C) is incorrect.** The statement is false with regard to the scope of the *Tax Information Authorization* form. **Answer (D) is incorrect.** Form 2848 and Form 8821 do not authorize the cashing of a refund check.

6. Phil, an enrolled agent, prepares William's income tax return. William gives Phil power of attorney, including the authorization to receive his federal income tax refund check. Accordingly, the IRS sends William's $100 refund check to Phil's office. William is very slow in paying his bills and owes Phil $500 for tax services. Phil should

A. Use William's check as collateral for a $100 loan to tide him over until William pays him.

B. Refuse to give William the check until William pays him the $500.

C. Get William's written authorization to endorse the check, cash the check, and reduce the amount William owes him to $400.

D. Turn the check directly over to William.

Answer (D) is correct.

REQUIRED: The action that should be taken by an unpaid enrolled agent who receives a taxpayer's refund.

DISCUSSION: When Phil was granted a power of attorney to receive William's federal income tax refund check, Phil must act in William's best interest. It is in William's best interest if he receives the $100 refund check as soon as possible. Even though William is slow to pay his tax bill, it does not negate Phil's responsibility to act in William's best interest. Therefore, Phil's obligation requires him to turn the check over directly to William.

Answer (A) is incorrect. Phil is not allowed to keep the refund check as collateral because that is not acting in William's best interest. **Answer (B) is incorrect.** Phil is not allowed to withhold the refund check as a means of extracting payment from William. **Answer (C) is incorrect.** Phil is not permitted to endorse the refund check.

7. A power of attorney is required when a taxpayer wishes to authorize a recognized representative to perform one or more of the following services on behalf of the taxpayer, EXCEPT to

A. Execute a closing agreement.

B. Request confidential tax return information.

C. Represent the taxpayer before an appeals officer.

D. Execute a consent to extend the statutory period of assessment.

Answer (B) is correct.

REQUIRED: The service that does not require a power of attorney.

DISCUSSION: In general, a representative can do all of the following:

1. Represent the taxpayer before any office of the IRS
2. Sign a waiver agreeing to a tax adjustment
3. Sign a consent to extend the statutory time period for assessment or collection of a tax
4. Sign a closing agreement
5. Receive, but not endorse or cash, a refund check
6. Record the interview

Form 8821 is used to request confidential tax information.

8. A power of attorney is required when you want to authorize any individual to do the following:

A. To represent you at a conference with the IRS.

B. To prepare and file a written response to the IRS.

C. To sign the offer or a waiver of restriction on assessment or collection of tax deficiency.

D. All of the answers are correct.

Answer (D) is correct.

REQUIRED: The situations in which a power of attorney is required.

DISCUSSION: A power of attorney is required when an individual wishes to authorize someone to provide representation at a conference with the IRS, to prepare and file a written response with the IRS, as well as to sign an offer or waiver of restriction on an assessment or collection of any tax deficiency (Publication 947).

9. A representative who signs a Form 2848, *Power of Attorney and Declaration of Representative*, declares under penalty of perjury that (s)he is aware of which of the following?

A. The federal income tax regulations.

B. The regulations in Treasury Department Circular No. 230.

C. Recent tax law developments that relate to the tax matter(s) listed on line 3 of the Form 2848.

D. All of the answers are correct.

Answer (B) is correct.

REQUIRED: The information a representative who signs a Form 2848 declares under penalty that (s)he is aware of.

DISCUSSION: The declaration of representative states that the representative is subject to regulations contained in Circular 230 (31 CFR, Subtitle A, Part 10), as amended, governing practice before the IRS.

Answer (A) is incorrect. By signing Form 2848, the representative does not declare (s)he is aware of federal income tax regulations. **Answer (C) is incorrect.** Form 2848 does not require the representative to declare that (s)he is aware of recent tax law developments relating to the listed tax matters. **Answer (D) is incorrect.** It is not declared by the representative when signing Form 2848 that (s)he is aware of the federal income tax regulations or recent law developments that relate to the tax matter(s) listed on line 3 of the Form 2848.

10. The filing of a power of attorney does not authorize the recognized representative to sign a tax return on behalf of the taxpayer unless such act is

A. Permitted under the Internal Revenue Code and the regulations thereunder.

B. Specifically authorized in the power of attorney.

C. Neither permitted under the Internal Revenue Code and the pertinent regulations nor specifically authorized in the power of attorney.

D. Both permitted under the Internal Revenue Code and the regulations thereunder and specifically authorized in the power of attorney.

Answer (D) is correct.

REQUIRED: The requirements for a representative to sign a tax return on behalf of the taxpayer.

DISCUSSION: The filing of a power of attorney does not authorize the recognized representative to sign a tax return on behalf of the taxpayer unless such act is both

1. Permitted by the Code and regulations and
2. Specifically authorized in the power of attorney.

Answer (A) is incorrect. It must also be specifically authorized in the power of attorney. **Answer (B) is incorrect.** It must also be permitted under the Code and regulations. **Answer (C) is incorrect.** It must be permitted by the Code and specifically authorized in the power of attorney.

11. Which of the following statements with respect to executing a power of attorney is false?

A. The Internal Revenue Service will accept a power of attorney other than Form 2848, provided such document satisfies the requirements of Reg. 601.504(a).

B. In the case of any matter concerning a joint return in which both husband and wife are not to be represented by the same recognized representative(s), the power of attorney must be executed by the spouse who is to be represented.

C. In the case of a corporation, a power of attorney may be executed only by the officer or employee who signs the return.

D. In the case of a partnership, a power of attorney must be executed by all partners, or if executed in the name of the partnership, by the partner or partners duly authorized to act for the partnership. The partner or partners must certify that they have such authority.

Answer (C) is correct.

REQUIRED: The false statement regarding the execution of a power of attorney.

DISCUSSION: Except when Form 2848 (or its equivalent) is executed by an attorney-in-fact under the provisions of Sec. 601.503(b)(3), the individual who must execute a Form 2848 depends on the type of taxpayer involved. In the case of a corporation, a power of attorney must be executed by an officer of the corporation with authority to legally bind the corporation. The officer must certify that (s)he has such authority.

12. Judith wants to revoke a power of attorney that she previously executed and does not want to name a new representative. In order to do this, what is Judith's most appropriate action?

A. Judith must call the Internal Revenue Service toll free number, verify that she is Judith, and inform them she wants to revoke the current power of attorney that is on file.

B. Judith must send a letter to her nearest Internal Revenue Service Center informing them that she wants to revoke the current power of attorney that is on file.

C. Judith must send a copy of the previously executed power of attorney to the Internal Revenue Service (with an original signature) and write "REVOKE" across the top of the power of attorney.

D. Judith must send a new power of attorney to the Internal Revenue Service office(s) where the prior power was originally filed and name herself as the representative.

Answer (C) is correct.

REQUIRED: The proper action for revoking a power of attorney.

DISCUSSION: The authority granted a representative by a POA may be changed by filing a new POA [26 CFR 601.505(c)(1)]. A new POA is deemed to revoke a prior POA unless the new one contains a clause specifically stating that it does not revoke a prior POA. A new tax information authorization notice revokes a prior POA if the taxpayer signs a statement listing the names and addresses of the individuals under the prior POA whose authority is revoked. "REVOKE" should be written across the top of the POA.

13. Regarding a *Tax Information Authorization*, Form 8821, which of the following statements is true?

A. The appointee can advocate the taxpayer's position.

B. The appointee can execute waivers.

C. The appointee can represent the taxpayer by correspondence.

D. None of the answers are correct.

Answer (D) is correct.

REQUIRED: The true statement regarding a *Tax Information Authorization*, Form 8821.

DISCUSSION: Form 8821 states that it does not authorize an appointee to advocate the taxpayer's position with respect to the federal tax laws; to execute waivers, consents, or closing agreements; or to otherwise represent the taxpayer before the IRS.

14. With regard to the declaration of the representative on a power of attorney, all of the following statements are true EXCEPT

A. A fiduciary is required to show his or her relationship.

B. An attorney must indicate the state in which (s)he is admitted to practice.

C. A CPA must include the state in which (s)he is licensed to practice.

D. A full-time employee must show his or her title.

Answer (A) is correct.

REQUIRED: The false statement regarding the declaration of the representative on a power of attorney.

DISCUSSION: A fiduciary stands in the position of a taxpayer and acts as the taxpayer. Therefore, a fiduciary does not act as a representative and should not file a power of attorney (Instructions for Form 2848).

Answer (B) is incorrect. An attorney must enter the two-letter abbreviation for the state in which (s)he is admitted to practice in the jurisdiction column (Instructions for Form 2848). **Answer (C) is incorrect.** A certified public accountant must enter the two-letter abbreviation of the state in which (s)he is licensed to practice in the jurisdiction column (Instructions for Form 2848). **Answer (D) is incorrect.** A full-time employee must enter his or her title or position in the jurisdiction column (Instructions for Form 2848).

15. All of the following statements regarding changes to powers of attorney are true EXCEPT

A. A recognized representative may withdraw from representation in a matter in which a power of attorney has been filed.

B. A taxpayer may revoke a power of attorney without authorizing a new representative.

C. If specifically authorized on the power of attorney, a recognized representative may delegate authority to another recognized representative.

D. After a substitution of a representative is made, both the old representative and the newly recognized representatives will be considered the taxpayer's representative.

Answer (D) is correct.

REQUIRED: The false statement regarding changes to powers of attorney.

DISCUSSION: A properly executed POA and Declaration of Representative does permit the representative to make substitution of representatives by the taxpayer in the original POA. The POA must, however, state the intention to grant authority of substitution. Only the most recent representative is considered the taxpayer's representative.

16. A properly executed power of attorney must contain all of the following EXCEPT

A. Identification number of the taxpayer (i.e., Social Security number or employer identification number).
B. The specific year(s) and period(s) involved.
C. Name of the preparer of the return for the year(s) and period(s) involved.
D. Signature of the appointed representative.

Answer (C) is correct.
REQUIRED: The information not contained in a properly executed power of attorney.
DISCUSSION: Form 2848 constitutes the power of attorney and declaration of representative. The identification number of the taxpayer, the specific year(s) and period(s) involved, and the signature of the appointed representatives must appear on a properly executed power of attorney. The name of the preparer of the return for the year(s) and period(s) involved is not included on the POA.

17. Nancy, who is enrolled to practice before the Internal Revenue Service, has been granted power of attorney to represent Lee in a matter before the IRS. Nancy wants to delegate that authority to another representative. Regarding this substitution of authority, which of the following statements is false?

A. The power of attorney, whether it is IRS Form 2848, *Power of Attorney and Declaration of Representative*, or a non-IRS power of attorney, must specifically provide that Nancy can substitute her authority.
B. The new representative must be an individual who is recognized to practice before the IRS.
C. The new representative must file a written declaration in accordance with the regulations with the appropriate IRS offices.
D. Nancy need only file a signed statement (notice of substitution or delegation) with the appropriate IRS offices.

Answer (D) is correct.
REQUIRED: The false statement regarding the substitution of authority.
DISCUSSION: A substitution is made by filing the following items with the IRS: (1) a notice of substitution or delegation signed by the practitioner who was appointed under the power of attorney, (2) a declaration of representative made by the new representative, and (3) a power of attorney that authorizes the substitution or delegation.

3.2 Centralized Authorization File (CAF)

18. A Centralized Authorization File (CAF) number may be issued to which of the following?

A. An attorney licensed by the state of Texas who represents taxpayers before the IRS solely at IRS offices in Texas.

B. An attorney licensed by the state of Texas who files powers of attorney at the Austin Service Center.

C. A financial advisor named as a designee in a tax information authorization.

D. All of the answers are correct.

Answer (D) is correct.

REQUIRED: The individual(s) who may be issued CAF numbers.

DISCUSSION: A CAF number is the Centralized Authorization File number assigned by the IRS to each representative whose power of attorney, or to each designee whose tax information authorization, has been recorded on the CAF. All of the individuals may be issued CAF numbers.

19. What is the purpose of the Centralized Authorization File (CAF) number?

A. This is the number a preparer would use to sign an electronically filed return.

B. The CAF number is another means of tracing enrolled agents.

C. Use of the CAF number allows the IRS to verify an individual's authority to practice before the IRS.

D. None of the answers are correct.

Answer (D) is correct.

REQUIRED: The purpose of the CAF number.

DISCUSSION: The CAF system is a computer file containing information regarding individuals appointed under powers of attorney or designated under the tax information authorization system. The CAF system gives IRS personnel quicker access to authorization information. The CAF does not indicate that a person is either recognized or authorized to practice before the IRS.

Answer (A) is incorrect. CAF numbers are used on powers of attorney, not on returns. **Answer (B) is incorrect.** A CAF number may be assigned to any individual appointed to represent another before the IRS by a power of attorney, not just enrolled agents. **Answer (C) is incorrect.** The CAF does not indicate that a person is either recognized or authorized to practice before the IRS.

20. With regard to the Centralized Authorization File (CAF) number on powers of attorney, which of the following is true?

A. Powers of attorney that relate to specific tax periods, or to any other federal tax matter such as application for an employee identification number, will be entered on the CAF system.

B. A CAF number is an indication of authority to practice before the Internal Revenue Service.

C. The fact that a power of attorney cannot be entered on the CAF system affects its validity.

D. A power of attorney that does not include a CAF number will not be rejected.

Answer (D) is correct.

REQUIRED: The true statement regarding the CAF number on powers of attorney.

DISCUSSION: A recognized representative or an appointee should include the same CAF number on every power of attorney (POA) or *Tax Information Authorization* (TIA) filed. However, because the CAF number is not a substantive requirement [i.e., as listed in Sec. 601.503(a)], a TIA or POA will not be rejected based on the absence of a CAF number.

Answer (A) is incorrect. Only documents that concern a matter(s) relating to a specific tax period will be recorded on the CAF system. Applications for an employer identification number cannot be recorded on the CAF system [Reg. 601.506(d)(3)(i)]. **Answer (B) is incorrect.** The issuance of a CAF number does not indicate that a person is either recognized or authorized to practice before the IRS [Reg. 601.506(d)(2)(ii)]. **Answer (C) is incorrect.** Specific-use powers of attorney are not processed into the CAF.

STUDY UNIT FOUR

EXAMINATION OF RETURNS AND THE APPEALS PROCESS

(13 pages of outline)

Although the U.S. tax system is founded on self-assessment and payment, the IRS examines and adjusts a percentage of returns filed to verify the tax reported is correct. This study unit addresses the examination and appeals process the IRS uses to monitor taxpayer behavior and resolve disputes as they arise.

4.1 EXAMINATION OF RETURNS

1. A tax return may be examined for a variety of reasons, and the examination may take place in any one of several ways.

Computer Scoring

   a. A tax return may be selected for examination on the basis of computer scoring. A computer program called the **Discriminant Function System (DIF)** assigns a numeric score to each individual and some corporate tax returns after they have been processed.

      1) The scoring formula determines which tax returns are most likely to be in error.

         a) Returns selected from DIF have high scores.

Third-Party Information

   b. A return may be selected for examination on the basis of matching information on the return with information received from third parties such as Forms 1099 and W-2.

      1) For example, wages reported on the Form 1040 return should match wages per Form W-2 on the employer's return.

   c. Returns may be selected to address both the questionable treatment of an item and to study the behavior of similar taxpayers (a market segment) in handling a tax issue.

   d. Tax returns may be selected as a result of information received from other sources on potential noncompliance with the tax laws or inaccurate filing.

Other Contacts

2. The IRS must give the taxpayer **reasonable notice** before contacting other persons in examining or collecting a tax liability. The IRS also must provide the taxpayer with a record of persons contacted. The contact record is provided on both a periodic basis and upon taxpayer request.

   a. The notice does not apply

      1) To any pending criminal investigation,
      2) When providing notice would jeopardize collection of any tax liability,
      3) When providing notice may result in reprisal against any person, or
      4) When the taxpayer authorized the contact.

Rights/Process Explained

3. Prior to the initial in-person interview, an officer or employee of the IRS must provide to the taxpayer an explanation of the audit or collection process and Publication 1, *Your Rights as a Taxpayer*.

Representation

4. A taxpayer may act on his or her own behalf or have someone represent or accompany him or her.
   a. If a joint return was filed, either spouse or both can meet with the IRS.
   b. The taxpayer can be represented by a federally authorized practitioner or the person who prepared and signed the return.

Examination Location

5. If the IRS notifies the taxpayer that the IRS will conduct an examination of the taxpayer's return through a personal interview, or the taxpayer requests such an interview, the taxpayer has the right to ask that the examination take place at a reasonable time and place that is convenient for both the taxpayer and the IRS.

Jurisdiction

6. The examination may be transferred to another IRS district office if
   a. The taxpayer's books and records are kept in another district,
   b. The taxpayer has changed domiciles, or
   c. An executor or administrator has moved to another district.

Proposed Changes

7. If the IRS examiner proposes any changes to the taxpayer's return, the IRS examiner will explain the reasons for the changes. If the taxpayer does not agree with these changes, the taxpayer can meet with the examiner's supervisor.
   a. The detailed document describing an IRS examiner's audit findings and stating the amount of deficiency or refund the agent found the taxpayer to owe or be owed is called the Revenue Agent's Report (RAR). This is the same as the 30-day letter discussed later in Subunit 4.2.

Statute of Limitations

8. The IRS has a general statute of limitations of 3 years from the due date of the tax return to assess any deficiency in tax payments.
   a. If the taxpayer grossly misstates the income (for more than 25% of the gross income of the return) by not reporting income or understating the basis of an asset, the statute of limitations is 6 years.
   b. If the taxpayer files a fraudulent return, there is no statute of limitations on that return.
   c. If the taxpayer does not file a return, there is no statute of limitations on that return.

Agreement

9. If the taxpayer agrees with any proposed changes, (s)he can sign an agreement form and pay any additional tax due. The taxpayer must pay interest on any additional tax.
    a. If payment is made when the agreement is signed, the interest is generally figured from the due date of the return to the date of payment.
    b. If payment is not made when the agreement is signed, the taxpayer will receive a bill that includes interest.
        1) If payment is made within 10 business days of the billing date, no additional interest or penalties will be due.
        2) This period is extended to 21 calendar days if the amount due is less than $100,000.

Interest and Penalties

10. Taxpayers must pay interest on penalties and on additional tax for
    a. Failing to file returns,
    b. Overstating valuations,
    c. Understating valuations on estate and gift tax returns, and
    d. Substantially understating tax liability.
11. Interest is generally figured from the date (including extensions) the tax return is due to the date the taxpayer pays the penalty and/or additional tax.

Abatement

12. The IRS may **abate** (reduce) the amount of interest owed if the interest is due to an unreasonable error or delay by an IRS officer or employee performing a ministerial or managerial act.
    a. Only the amount of interest on income, estate, gift, generation-skipping, and certain excise taxes can be reduced.
13. If, for the same period of time that a taxpayer owes interest to the IRS on an underpayment, the IRS owes the taxpayer interest on an overpayment, on equivalent underpayments and overpayments, the net rate of interest on such amounts will be zero for such period.
    a. Therefore, during an audit, the IRS nets underpayments and additional taxes owed plus interest against overpayments of tax plus interest paid.
14. If a practitioner or taxpayer believes overpayment of tax has occurred, Form 843, *Claim for Refund and Request for Abatement*, must be filed at the same service center in which the disputed return was filed.
    a. If the taxpayer does not remember where (s)he filed this tax return, (s)he may file the form at the last service center (s)he filed a return.
    b. When the taxpayer has already paid the tax, Form 843 must be filed within 3 years from the due date (plus the filing extension time) or 2 years from the time (s)he paid the interest, whichever is later.

Notices Sent by the IRS

15. IRS notices are often form letters referred to by the IRS as computer paragraphs. Accordingly, the following five notices are all designated CP (computer paragraph).
16. CP 12, Changes to Tax Return, Overpayment
    a. When the IRS makes a correction to a tax return, it sends a math error notice to explain the changes to the taxpayer who filed the return.
        1) This notice explains the nature of the changes and includes an account statement showing how the changes affected the tax return.
        2) The notice also includes a short description of the changes.
            a) If the taxpayer agrees with the correction made, (s)he does not need to reply to the notice.
        3) The IRS will issue a refund in 6 to 8 weeks unless the taxpayer owes other amounts the IRS is required to collect.
            a) Examples include unpaid tax, penalty, or interest on another tax account.
17. CP 14, Balance Due, No Math Error
    a. Notice CP 14 is not a math error notice.
        1) It shows the taxpayer the amount of underpaid tax according to IRS records.
            a) The middle section of the notice shows the tax reported on the return, the credits applied, and the underpayment.
18. CP 49, Overpaid Tax Applied to Other Taxes You Owe
    a. Reports an overpayment on one account and an underpayment on another.
        1) The first part of the notice deals with the overpaid account.
        2) The second part of the notice also deals with the overpaid account.
        3) The third part of the notice deals with the balance due account.
19. CP 90, Final Notice - Notice of Intent to Levy and Notice of Your Right to a Hearing
    a. This notice tells the taxpayer that the IRS intends to issue a levy against any federal payments due the taxpayer, such as contractor/vendor payments, OPM retirement benefits, SSA benefits, salary, or employee travel advances or reimbursements because (s)he still has a balance due on his or her tax account.
        1) Property, or rights to property, such as real estate, automobiles, business assets, bank accounts, wages, commissions, and other income are also subject to levy.
        2) CP 90 also tells the taxpayer that the IRS may file a Federal Tax Lien if it has not already done so.
20. CP 2000, We Are Proposing Changes to Your Tax Return
    a. This notice is to inform the taxpayer of changes the IRS proposes to the tax return because information reported by the taxpayer on it does not match what was reported to the IRS by the taxpayer's employers, banks, and other payers.
        1) The IRS sends a CP 2000 to provide detailed information about the differences, the changes proposed, and what to do if the taxpayer agrees or disagrees with the proposal.

IRS Authority to Investigate

21. Any investigator, agent, or other internal revenue officer by whatever term designated, whom the Secretary charges with duty of enforcing any of the criminal, seizure, or forfeiture provisions of any law of the United States pertaining to the commodities subject to tax may
    a. Carry firearms;
    b. Execute and serve search warrants and arrest warrants, and serve subpoenas and summonses issued under authority of the United States;
    c. In respect to the performance of such duty, make arrests without warrant for any offense against the United States committed in an officer's presence, or for any known felony under the laws of the United States if the officer has reasonable grounds to believe that the person to be arrested has committed, or is committing, such felony; and
    d. In respect to the performance of such duty, make seizures of property subject to forfeiture to the United States.

Audit Reconsideration

22. This is a process used by the IRS to help the taxpayer when the taxpayer disagrees with the results of an IRS audit or a return created for the taxpayer by the IRS because the taxpayer did not file a tax return as authorized by Internal Revenue Code 6020(b).
    a. The taxpayer is permitted to request an audit reconsideration if the taxpayer
        1) Did not appear for the audit
        2) Moved and did not receive correspondence from the IRS
        3) Has additional information to present that the taxpayer did not provide during the original audit
        4) Disagrees with the audit assessment
    b. Audit reconsideration requests will be **accepted** if
        1) Information is submitted that the IRS has not considered previously
        2) The taxpayer files a return after the IRS completed a return for the taxpayer
        3) The taxpayer believes the IRS made a computational or processing error in assessing the tax
        4) The liability is unpaid or credits are denied
    c. Audit reconsideration requests are **not accepted** if the
        1) Taxpayer previously agreed to pay the amount of tax owed by signing an agreement such as a Form 906, *Closing Agreement On Final Determination Covering Specific Matters*; a compromise agreement; or an agreement on Form 870-AD with the Appeals office.
        2) Amount of tax owed is the result of final partnership item adjustments under the Bipartisan Budget Act of 2015 (BBA).
        3) United States Tax Court, or another court, has issued a final determination on the taxpayer's tax liability.

STOP AND REVIEW! **You have completed the outline for this subunit.** **Study multiple-choice questions 1 through 3 beginning on page 97.**

4.2 APPEALS WITHIN THE IRS

Scope of Tax Law

1. Because people sometimes disagree on tax matters, the IRS has established an **appeals system**.
   a. The IRS has concluded that most disagreements can be settled within this system without expensive and time-consuming court trials.
      1) The disagreements must arise within the scope of the tax laws.
         a) For example, a case cannot be appealed based only on moral, religious, political, constitutional, conscientious, or similar grounds.
      2) Appeals officers have no prior involvement with the case.
   b. If a taxpayer wishes to bypass the IRS appeals system, (s)he may take his or her case directly to court.
      1) The IRS also offers fast-track mediation services to help taxpayers resolve many disputes resulting from examinations, offers in compromise, trust fund recovery penalties, and certain other collection actions.
   c. Taxpayers may be represented by attorneys, certified public accountants, or enrolled agents before appeals officers, revenue officers, counsel, or similar officers or employees of the Internal Revenue Service or the Treasury Department.

Appeals Location

2. An appeal can be made to a local appeals office, which is separate from and independent of the IRS office taking the action the taxpayer disagrees with.
3. In order to request an appeals conference, the taxpayer must follow the instructions in the 30-day letter received from the IRS.
   a. The IRS letter will contain a time limit during which the taxpayer may file a protest.
   b. The letter notifies the taxpayer of his or her right to appeal the proposed changes within 30 days and includes
      1) A copy of the examination report explaining the examiner's proposed changes,
      2) An agreement or waiver form, and
      3) A copy of Publication 5, *Your Appeal Rights and How To Prepare a Protest If You Don't Agree*.
   c. The taxpayer generally has 30 days from the date of the 30-day letter to tell the IRS whether (s)he will accept or appeal the proposed changes.
   d. The letter will explain what steps the taxpayer should take, depending on which action is chosen.
   e. If a taxpayer does not respond to a 30-day letter and does not reach an agreement with an Appeals Officer, the IRS will send the taxpayer a 90-day letter (covered on the next page).

90-Day Letter

f. A **Notice of Deficiency** is a 90-day letter (150-day letter if it is addressed to a taxpayer outside the U.S.) that requires a taxpayer who wants to dispute the adjustments to the tax owed to file a petition within 90 days (150 days for a taxpayer outside the U.S.) from the date the notice is mailed to the taxpayer.

1) The 90-day notice notifies the taxpayer of the proposed additional liability.
2) The taxpayer has 90 days to petition the Tax Court to hear the case.
   a) If the taxpayer does not respond within 90 days of the notice, additional tax is assessed.

g. If the petition to have the Tax Court hear the case is not filed on time, the tax will be due within 10 days, and the case cannot be taken to Tax Court.

Appeals Procedure

4. The proposed increase or decrease in tax determines the appeals procedure.

a. If the total amount for any tax period is not more than $25,000, a **small case** request may be filed.

b. If the total amount for any tax period is more than $25,000, a formal written protest must be submitted. The protest should contain

1) The name, address, identification number (i.e., EIN, SSN, etc.), and a daytime phone number of the taxpayer
2) A statement that the taxpayer wants to appeal the IRS findings to the appeals office
3) The date and office symbols from the letter showing the proposed changes and findings in disagreement (or a copy of the 30-day letter)
4) The tax periods or years involved
5) An itemized schedule of the changes with which there are disagreements
6) A statement of facts supporting the taxpayer's position on any issue with which there is a disagreement
7) A statement stating the law or other authority on which the argument is based
8) A declaration that the statement of facts is true under penalties of perjury
   a) To satisfy this submission requirement, the taxpayer must add the following signed declaration:

      "Under the penalties of perjury, I declare that I have examined the statement of facts presented in this protest and in any accompanying schedules and, to the best of my knowledge and belief, it is true, correct, and complete."

   b) Alternatively, if a representative submits the protest for the taxpayer, (s)he can substitute a declaration stating
      i) That (s)he prepared the protest and accompanying documents and
      ii) Whether (s)he knows personally that the statement of facts in the protest and the accompanying documents is true and correct.

c. An interview with the IRS must be suspended immediately if the taxpayer indicates a desire to consult with a representative.

d. In all partnership and S corporation cases, a written protest must be filed without regard to the dollar amount at issue.

Repetitive Review

5. If the same items were examined in either of the previous 2 years and the examination resulted in no change to the tax liability, the taxpayer should notify the person whose name and phone number appear in the appointment letter.
   a. The IRS will suspend (not cancel) an audit while reviewing its files to determine whether to proceed.
   b. This avoids repetitive examinations of the same items.

Statutory Period

6. A claim for refund must be filed within 3 years from the due date (plus the filing extension time) or 2 years from the time the tax was paid, whichever is later.
   a. In order to toll (suspend) the statute of limitations, the IRS must mail a Statutory Notice of Deficiency to the taxpayer before the end of the statutory period.
   b. The Statutory Notice of Deficiency tolls the assessment statute of limitations but not the refund statute of limitations.
   c. A refund claim for a prior year is made by filing an amended return such as Form 1040X for individuals or Form 1120X for corporations. Form 843 is used to claim a refund of any other tax.
7. If a tax is properly assessed, the statute of limitations for collecting the assessed amount is extended by 10 years from the assessment date.

Contesting Determination

8. If, after a Collection Due Process hearing with the Office of Appeals to discuss an IRS levy or lien, the taxpayer does not agree with the appeals determination, the taxpayer has 30 days from the date of the determination to bring suit in court to contest the determination.

STOP AND REVIEW! **You have completed the outline for this subunit. Study multiple-choice questions 4 through 13 beginning on page 98.**

4.3 APPEALS TO THE COURTS

1. If a taxpayer and the IRS still disagree after an appeals conference or the election was made to bypass the IRS appeals system, the case may be taken to the U.S. Tax Court, the U.S. Court of Federal Claims, or a U.S. District Court.

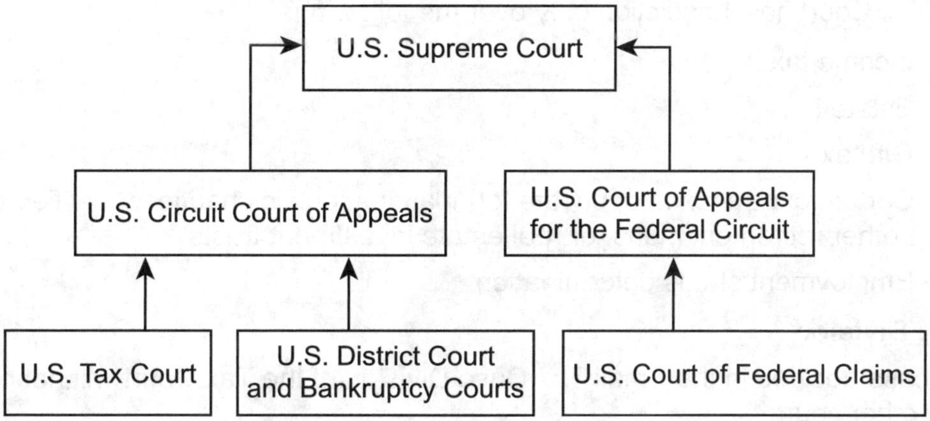

Figure 4-1

a. In any court proceeding, the burden of proof shifts to the IRS for any factual issue if the taxpayer has introduced credible evidence for the issue, provided that the taxpayer has done all of the following:
   1) Complied with substantiation requirements in the Code
   2) Maintained all records required by the Code
   3) Cooperated with all reasonable requests for information from the IRS
   4) Had a net worth of $7 million or less if the tax return is for a corporation, partnership, or trust
b. After the filing of a petition in the Tax Court, the Appeals office will have exclusive settlement jurisdiction, for a period of 4 months, over cases docketed in the Tax Court. There is also vested in the Appeals offices authority to represent the regional commissioner in the commissioner's exclusive authority to settle
   1) All cases docketed in the Tax Court and designated for trial at any place within the territory comprising the region, and
   2) All docketed cases originating in the office of any district director situated within the region, or in which jurisdiction has been transferred to the region, which are designated for trial at Washington, D.C., unless the petitioner resides in, and the petitioner's books and records are located or can be made available in, the region that includes Washington, D.C.

2. **Tax Court**

   a. Generally, the Tax Court hears cases before any tax has been assessed or paid.
   b. In order to petition, the taxpayer must first receive a Notice of Deficiency.

Jurisdiction

   c. The Tax Court has jurisdiction only over the following:
      1) Income tax
      2) Estate tax
      3) Gift tax
      4) Certain excise taxes of private foundations, public charities, qualified pension and other retirement plans, or real estate investment trusts
      5) Employment status determination

Small Tax Case Division

   d. Any case decided in the Small Tax Case Division of the Tax Court will not be reviewed by any other court.
      1) The limit to be heard in the Small Tax Case Division is $50,000.
      2) The Tax Court must approve the request that the case be handled under the small tax case procedure.

Practice before the Tax Court

   e. With respect to docketed Tax Court cases, status solely as an enrolled agent or a CPA will not allow that person to practice before the Tax Court.
      1) An individual other than an attorney must demonstrate his or her qualifications satisfactorily to the Tax Court by means of a written examination given by the Tax Court.

(Non)Acquiescence

   f. The IRS may announce an acquiescence or a nonacquiescence to any court decision except a decision of the Supreme Court.
      1) Acquiescence means that the IRS accepts the holding of the court in a case and that the IRS will follow it in disposing of cases with the same controlling facts. It does not indicate approval or disapproval of the reasons assigned by the court for its conclusions.
      2) Nonacquiescence signifies that, although the decision was not appealed or was not reviewed by the Supreme Court, the IRS does not agree with the holding of the court and will not follow it nationwide in disposing of other cases. With respect to opinions of an appellate court, the IRS will generally follow the holding of the circuit court in cases appealable to that circuit due to the binding nature of that opinion in lower courts, even when the office concludes that the opinion is erroneous.

Decision Types

g. The Tax Court issues two types of decisions: regular decisions and memorandum decisions.

1) Regular decisions usually involve questions of law.
2) Memorandum decisions usually involve questions of fact.

3. **District Court and Court of Federal Claims**

a. Generally, District Courts and the Court of Federal Claims hear tax cases only after the tax has been paid and a claim for a refund has been filed.

b. Claims for refund may be filed when a tax is deemed incorrect or excessive.

c. The claim can be taken to court only if it is rejected or not acted on within 6 months from the date it is filed.

1) A taxpayer may request, in writing, immediate rejection from the IRS to facilitate his or her court claim.

d. The taxpayer must file suit no later than 2 years after the time of mailing of the rejected claim.

e. A trial by jury is available in a District Court but not in the Tax Court.

Appeal

4. If either the taxpayer or the IRS Commissioner disagrees with the decision of the District Court, the decision may be appealed to the appropriate Circuit Court of Appeals.

***STOP AND REVIEW!* You have completed the outline for this subunit. Study multiple-choice questions 14 through 23 beginning on page 102.**

4.4 PENALTIES

NOTE: The penalties in this subunit are assessed against the taxpayer.

Negligence

1. A 20% penalty will be imposed on the taxpayer for an understatement of tax due to negligence.
    a. Negligence is defined as a failure to make a reasonable attempt to comply with the regulations issued by the IRS.
        1) Included in a failure to make a reasonable attempt are any attempts that show a "careless, reckless, or intentional disregard" for the rules.

Fraud

2. The IRS will impose a penalty of 75% of the tax owed when the taxpayer is party to tax fraud.
3. If the taxpayer files a frivolous income tax return, a $5,000 frivolous return penalty, in addition to any other applicable penalty, is assessed against the taxpayer.

Abatement

a. Taxpayers have the right to challenge the assessment of a penalty and may request the following:
    1) A review of the penalty prior to assessment (e.g., deficiency procedures)
    2) A penalty abatement after it is assessed and either before or after it is paid (post-assessment review)
    3) An abatement and refund after payment (claim for refund)

b. A reduction or elimination of tax, penalties, or interest. Taxes may be abated when the IRS determines that there was an overassessment.
    1) General rule. The Secretary of the Treasury is authorized to abate the unpaid portion of the assessment of any tax or any liability in respect thereof, which is
        a) Excessive in amount,
        b) Assessed after the expiration of the period of limitation properly applicable thereto, or
        c) Erroneously or illegally assessed.

Reasonable Cause

c. The amount of interest owed may be abated by the IRS if the interest is due to unreasonable errors and delays by the IRS. In general,
    1) This applies in the case of any assessment of interest on any deficiency attributable in whole or in part to any unreasonable error or delay by an officer or employee of the IRS (acting in his or her official capacity) in performing a ministerial or managerial act; or
    2) If late payment of any tax was caused by office or employee error, the taxpayer can request the abatement of all or any part of such interest for any period.
        a) This only applies if the taxpayer was not significantly responsible for the delay or error.
        b) The taxpayer must contact the IRS in writing to request abatement.

Interest Abatement

d. An abatement of interest is requested by writing “Request of abatement of interest under Sec. 6404(e)” at the top of Form 843.

Passport Revocation

4. The IRC authorizes the IRS to certify seriously delinquent tax debt to the State Department for action.
   a. Seriously delinquent tax debt is an individual’s unpaid, legally enforceable federal tax debt totaling more than $54,000 (including interest and penalties) for which
      1) A Notice of Federal Tax Lien has been filed and all administrative remedies under the IRC have lapsed or been exhausted or
      2) A levy has been issued.
   b. Upon receiving certification, the State Department shall deny the taxpayer’s passport application and/or may revoke his or her current passport. If the taxpayer is overseas, the State Department may issue a limited validity passport good only for direct return to the United States.

STOP AND REVIEW! **You have completed the outline for this subunit. Study multiple-choice questions 24 and 25 on page 106.**

QUESTIONS

4.1 Examination of Returns

1. Caroline received an audit notification letter scheduling an appointment for July 1, 2020, for the examination of her tax year 2018 Form 1040 return. The week before the scheduled appointment, she received a telephone call from the Internal Revenue Service office canceling the appointment. She was told that she would be contacted at a later date to reschedule the appointment. She was not contacted until July 1, 2021, when she was advised of a new appointment date. Errors identified in the examination resulted in her owing additional tax of $4,000 plus accrued interest of $600. Caroline does not believe that she should have to pay interest for the period that she was waiting for her appointment to be rescheduled. How should she proceed?

A. Pay the tax and interest and deduct the interest on her 2021 return, the year paid.

B. Immediately request an appeals conference to contest the interest.

C. Request an abatement of the interest by filing a Form 843 with the Internal Revenue Service service center where she filed her 2018 return.

D. Immediately petition the Tax Court to contest the interest.

Answer (C) is correct.

REQUIRED: The appropriate procedures to take to reduce the interest owed due to an unreasonable delay on the part of the IRS.

DISCUSSION: Caroline must file Form 843 at the same service center in which she filed her return. If she does not remember where she filed her 2018 tax return, she can file this form at the last service center she filed a tax return. If Caroline had already paid the tax due and interest, she must file Form 843 within 3 years from the due date (plus the filing extension time) or 2 years from the time she paid the interest, whichever is later.

2. All of the following reasons are acceptable for transferring an examination from one IRS district to another EXCEPT

A. The place of examination is solely for the convenience of the taxpayer's representative (books and records are located at his or her client's office, which is located within the current IRS district).

B. Books and records are located in another district.

C. An executor or administrator has moved to another district.

D. The taxpayer's residence has changed since the return was filed.

Answer (A) is correct.

REQUIRED: The reason that is not acceptable for transferring an examination from one IRS district office to another.

DISCUSSION: When a request is received to transfer a return to another district for examination, the district director having jurisdiction may transfer the case to the district director of the other district. The IRS will determine the time and place of the examination. In determining whether a transfer should be made, circumstances considered include the change of the taxpayer's domicile, discovery that the taxpayer's books and records are kept in another district, change of domicile of an executor or administrator to another district, and the effective administration of the tax laws [26 CFR 601.105(k)]. The convenience of the taxpayer's representative is not an acceptable reason to transfer an examination.

3. Under what circumstances may the examination of a tax return be transferred to another district?

A. The taxpayer moved and now resides in another district.

B. The books and records are located in another district.

C. The taxpayer requests a transfer to another district.

D. All of the answers are correct.

Answer (D) is correct.

REQUIRED: The circumstances in which the examination of a tax return may be transferred to another district.

DISCUSSION: In most cases, an income tax examination is conducted in the Internal Revenue Service district office nearest the taxpayer's place of residence. The examination may be transferred to another IRS district office if the taxpayer's books and records are kept in another district, the taxpayer has changed domiciles, or an executor or administrator has moved to another district [26 CFR 601.105(k)]. The IRS has authority to determine the time and place of the examination.

4.2 Appeals within the IRS

4. Sam is the sole shareholder in an S corporation. The S corporation was examined and the IRS proposed a $20,000 deficiency. What must Sam do to request an appeals conference?

A. File a formal written protest.

B. Pay the deficiency.

C. Hire a federally authorized tax practitioner to represent the S corporation.

D. Nothing because he is eligible for the small case procedure.

Answer (A) is correct.

REQUIRED: The requirements to request an appeals conference.

DISCUSSION: In order to request an appeals conference, the taxpayer must follow the instructions in the letter received from the IRS. The taxpayer needs to file a formal written protest in all partnership and S corporation cases without regard to the dollar amount.

Answer (B) is incorrect. The deficiency must generally be paid before a case can be brought before a District Court or Court of Federal Claims. **Answer (C) is incorrect.** The taxpayer does not need to hire a federally authorized tax practitioner unless (s)he feels it is necessary. **Answer (D) is incorrect.** The taxpayer needs to file a formal written protest in all partnership and S corporation cases without regard to the dollar amount.

5. Peter's return was examined, and the result was additional tax of $36,000 due to unreported lottery winnings. Peter has received a letter notifying him of his right to appeal the proposed changes within 30 days. Which of the following should Peter do in preparing his appeal?

A. Call the examiner and request a conference.

B. Provide a brief written statement of the disputed issues.

C. Submit a written protest within the time limit specified.

D. Submit a written protest explaining additional expenses not previously claimed.

Answer (C) is correct.

REQUIRED: The action required to prepare for an appeal.

DISCUSSION: If a taxpayer wants an appeals conference, (s)he must follow the instructions in the IRS letter sent to him or her. A taxpayer whose proposed increase or decrease in tax, including penalties or claimed refund, is more than $25,000 must submit a written protest of disputed issues.

Answer (A) is incorrect. A formal written protest is required when the proposed tax increase exceeds $25,000. **Answer (B) is incorrect.** A formal written protest is required when the proposed tax increase exceeds $25,000. **Answer (D) is incorrect.** A written protest should contain only information supporting the taxpayer's position and should not introduce new information.

6. At the conclusion of an audit, the taxpayer can appeal the tax decision to a local appeals office. Which statement regarding appeal procedures is false?

A. If the total amount for any tax period is not more than $25,000, a formal written protest is not required.

B. A taxpayer may represent himself at an appeals conference.

C. Written protests do not require a signature.

D. All partnership and S corporation cases require formal written protests.

Answer (C) is correct.

REQUIRED: The false statement regarding appeal procedures.

DISCUSSION: Publication 5 states that a taxpayer must sign a written protest stating that it is true, under the penalties of perjury.

Answer (A) is incorrect. Publication 5 states that the taxpayer may make a small case request instead of filing a formal written protest if the total amount for any tax period is not more than $25,000. **Answer (B) is incorrect.** It is a true statement according to Publication 5. **Answer (D) is incorrect.** It is a true statement according to Publication 5.

7. The examination of Greta's tax return for 2019 resulted in adjustments creating a tax liability in the amount of $30,000. Greta does not believe she owes anything. A Notice of Proposed Income Tax Deficiency is issued to Greta, who wants to appeal the Revenue Agent's adjustments to the IRS Office of Appeals. Greta must file a written protest letter no later than which of the following periods?

A. 10 days.

B. 30 days.

C. 90 days.

D. None of the answers are correct.

Answer (B) is correct.

REQUIRED: The time period for filing a written protest letter upon receipt of a Notice of Deficiency.

DISCUSSION: In order to request an appeals conference with the IRS, both Publication 5 and Publication 556 state that the taxpayer must follow the instructions in the letter received from the IRS. This letter should specify a time limit during which the taxpayer may file a protest. Publication 556 also states that, within a few weeks after the closing conference with the examiner and/or supervisor, the taxpayer will receive a package with a letter (known as a "30-day letter") notifying him or her of his or her right to appeal the proposed changes within 30 days. The taxpayer generally has 30 days from the date of the 30-day letter to tell the IRS whether (s)he will accept or appeal the proposed changes.

8. Wesley timely filed his tax year 2018 Form 1040 tax return on April 15, 2019, and paid the $2,000 tax as shown on the return at the time of filing. The return was subsequently examined, and Wesley signed an agreement form for the proposed changes on January 31, 2020. He paid the additional tax due of $10,000 on March 31, 2020. In 2021, Wesley located missing records that he believes would make $5,000 of the additional assessment erroneous. Which of the following statements accurately states the date by which Wesley must file a claim for refund?

A. January 31, 2022, 2 years from signing the agreement form.

B. April 15, 2022, 3 years from the due date of the original return.

C. March 31, 2022, 2 years from when the additional tax was paid.

D. No claim for refund can be filed since an examination agreement form was signed.

Answer (B) is correct.

REQUIRED: The deadline to file a claim for refund.

DISCUSSION: Sections 6511(a) and (b) state that a claim for refund must be filed within 3 years from the time the return was due or 2 years from the time the tax was paid, whichever is later. Thus, the deadline would either be April 15, 2022 (3 years from the time the return was due), or March 31, 2022 (2 years from the time the tax was paid). Because April 15, 2022, is later, this is the date by which the claim for refund must be filed.

9. Which of the following statements relating to the statutory Notice of Deficiency is false?

A. If a taxpayer receives a Notice of Deficiency and sends money to the IRS without written instructions, the IRS will treat it as a payment, and the taxpayer will not be able to petition the Tax Court.

B. A Notice of Deficiency is not an assessment.

C. If the taxpayer consents, the IRS can withdraw any Notice of Deficiency. However, after the notice is withdrawn, the taxpayer cannot file a petition with the Tax Court based on the withdrawn notice, and the IRS may later issue a Notice of Deficiency greater or less than the amount in the withdrawn deficiency.

D. The Notice of Deficiency provides the taxpayer 90 days (150 days if the taxpayer lives outside the United States) to either agree to the deficiency or file a petition with the Tax Court for a redetermination of the deficiency.

Answer (A) is correct.

REQUIRED: The false statement about the Notice of Deficiency.

DISCUSSION: Normally, once a taxpayer pays the tax, the Tax Court does not have jurisdiction, and the taxpayer must file a claim for a refund in U.S. District Court or the U.S. Court of Federal Claims. However, Sec. 6213(b)(4) provides that payment of additional tax due after the mailing of a Notice of Deficiency does not deprive the Tax Court of jurisdiction over the deficiency. Section 6213(a) provides that a taxpayer may file a petition with the Tax Court for a redetermination of the deficiency within 90 days (or 150 if the taxpayer lives outside the U.S.) after the Notice of Deficiency is mailed. If 90 (or 150) days pass and a petition is not filed, taxes may be assessed, and the taxpayer must pay the tax and file a claim for refund.

10. Marty timely filed his federal income tax return for 2017. It was selected for examination. During the course of the examination, the Revenue Agent first assigned to the case retired. A second Revenue Agent proposed adjustments to the tax return that Marty believed were erroneous. The second Revenue Agent was assigned to an extended training assignment. Before going on training, Marty and the second Revenue Agent orally agreed that the statute of limitations could be extended to December 31, 2021. Which of the following statements is applicable in order for the IRS to protect its rights?

A. An assessment of income taxes must be made before December 31, 2021.

B. A Statutory Notice of Deficiency must be mailed on or before December 31, 2021.

C. A Statutory Notice of Deficiency must be mailed on or before April 15, 2021.

D. The assessment of tax can be made at any time.

Answer (C) is correct.

REQUIRED: The requirement for extending the statute of limitations.

DISCUSSION: Because an agreement to extend the statute of limitations is not valid if it is not in writing, the IRS must mail the Statutory Notice of Deficiency within the statute of limitations period. Marty's tax return for 2017 would have been due on April 15, 2018. Therefore, the IRS must mail the notice by April 15, 2021.

Answer (A) is incorrect. The assessment is not sufficient; the IRS must mail a Notice of Deficiency to the taxpayer. **Answer (B) is incorrect.** The oral agreement to extend the statute of limitations is not valid. **Answer (D) is incorrect.** The IRS must make any assessment of tax within the statute of limitations period, which ends on or before April 15, 2021.

11. Which of the following statements concerning the procedure for a formal written protest submitted by a representative to obtain an appeals office conference is false?

A. A formal written protest is required when the tax due, including penalties, is more than $25,000.

B. A formal written protest must contain the tax years involved and a statement that the taxpayer wants to appeal to the appeals office.

C. A formal written protest must contain a statement of facts for each disputed issue and a statement of law or other authority relied upon for each issue.

D. A formal written protest must contain a declaration under penalties of perjury, signed by the taxpayer, that the statement of facts is true and correct.

Answer (D) is correct.

REQUIRED: The false statement regarding the procedure for a written protest.

DISCUSSION: Generally, a formal written protest must contain a sworn statement made by the taxpayer under penalty of perjury declaring that the statement of facts presented in the protest is true, correct, and complete. However, a substitute declaration may be submitted by the taxpayer's representative stating that the representative prepared the protest and accompanying documents, and whether the representative knows personally that the statement of facts in the protest and the accompanying documents is true and correct.

12. A claim for refund must be filed

A. No later than 3 years after the due date.

B. No later than 2 years from the date you paid the tax.

C. No later than 3 years after the return due date (plus extension) or no later than 2 years from the date you paid the tax, whichever is later.

D. 4 years after making estimated payments.

Answer (C) is correct.

REQUIRED: The deadline for filing a claim for a refund.

DISCUSSION: A claim for refund must be filed within 3 years from the due date (plus the filing extension time) or 2 years from the time the tax was paid, whichever is later. Section 6511(a) states that if no return was filed, the claim for refund is due within 2 years from the time the tax was paid.

Answer (A) is incorrect. The deadline is within 3 years from the due date (plus the filing extension time) or 2 years from the time the tax was paid, whichever is later, not either independently. **Answer (B) is incorrect.** The deadline is within 3 years from the due date (plus the filing extension time) or 2 years from the time the tax was paid, whichever is later, not either independently. **Answer (D) is incorrect.** The deadline for a refund claim is determined under Secs. 6511(a) and (b) to be 3 years or 2 years, not 4 years.

13. D's tax return for 2019 was examined by the IRS for contributions and medical expenses. The examination resulted in "no change" to his tax liability. He received notification of an examination for the same items for his 2021 tax return. What action should he take?

A. Notify the IRS of the prior year's examination as soon as possible.

B. Do not respond to the audit notification.

C. Set up an appointment for the current examination and do not discuss the prior examination.

D. Call the IRS Problem Resolution Office.

Answer (A) is correct.

REQUIRED: The proper action when an examination is based on a previously resolved issue.

DISCUSSION: If the same items were examined in either of the previous 2 years and the examination resulted in no change to the tax liability, the taxpayer should notify the person whose name and phone number appear in the appointment letter. The IRS will suspend but not cancel an audit (while reviewing its files to determine whether to proceed) so as to avoid repetitive examinations of the same items (Publication 556).

Answer (B) is incorrect. Taxpayers are required to respond to audit notification. **Answer (C) is incorrect.** Discussing the previous audit may cancel or suspend the current audit. **Answer (D) is incorrect.** The taxpayer should attempt to work out any differences with the IRS employees before contacting the Problem Resolution Office.

4.3 Appeals to the Courts

14. If a taxpayer and the IRS still disagree after an appeals conference, the taxpayer can take his or her case to

A. United States Tax Court.

B. United States Court of Federal Claims.

C. United States District Court.

D. All of the answers are correct.

Answer (D) is correct.

REQUIRED: The court a taxpayer may take his or her case to when still disagreeing with the IRS after an appeals conference.

DISCUSSION: If a taxpayer and the IRS still disagree after an appeals conference, or the election was made to bypass the IRS appeals system, the case may be taken to the U.S. Tax Court, the U.S. Court of Federal Claims, or a U.S. District Court.

15. The small tax case procedures in the Tax Court allow resolution of cases under a set of rules that are simpler than the normal Tax Court procedures. A case may be designated a small tax case in the Tax Court if the amount of tax at issue for each tax year or period is not more than

A. $50,000

B. $100,000

C. $125,000

D. $150,000

Answer (A) is correct.

REQUIRED: The maximum deficiency that may be handled by the Small Tax Case Division of the U.S. Tax Court.

DISCUSSION: Any case decided in the Small Tax Case Division of the Tax Court will not be reviewed by any other court. The limit to be heard in the Small Tax Case Division is $50,000 [Sec. 7463(a)]. The Tax Court must approve the request that the case be handled under the small tax case procedure.

16. To which court may a taxpayer petition, without first paying the disputed tax, regarding a disagreement with the Internal Revenue Service?

A. District Court.

B. Court of Federal Claims.

C. Tax Court.

D. All of the answers are correct.

Answer (C) is correct.

REQUIRED: The court a taxpayer may petition regarding a disagreement with the IRS without first paying the tax.

DISCUSSION: Federal District Courts and the U.S. Court of Federal Claims have refund jurisdiction, meaning a disputed tax must be paid before an action can be brought for a refund. A disputed tax does not have to be paid before a petition to the Tax Court is made.

Answer (A) is incorrect. A disputed tax must be paid before an action can be brought for a refund in District Court. **Answer (B) is incorrect.** A disputed tax must be paid before an action can be brought for a refund in the Court of Federal Claims. **Answer (D) is incorrect.** Federal District Courts and the U.S. Court of Federal Claims have refund jurisdiction.

17. Disputes involving which areas of taxation may not be resolved in a deficiency determination proceeding in United States Tax Court?

A. Income tax.

B. Gift tax.

C. Employment tax.

D. Estate tax.

Answer (C) is correct.

REQUIRED: The tax law disputes that cannot be resolved by the United States Tax Court.

DISCUSSION: The Tax Court has jurisdiction only over the following:

1. Income tax
2. Estate tax
3. Gift tax
4. Certain excise taxes of private foundations, public charities, qualified pension and other retirement plans, or real estate investment trusts
5. Employment status determination

Thus, employment tax is not a tax over which the United States Tax Court has jurisdiction.

18. Harry claimed gambling losses on his income tax return. The return was examined by the IRS, and the losses were disallowed. Harry pursued an appeal before the IRS Appeals Office, which sustained the Revenue Agent's adjustment. Harry now wants to take his case to a judge. In which of the following courts can Harry file a tax action?

A. United States Court of Federal Claims.

B. United States District Court.

C. United States Tax Court.

D. All of the answers are correct.

Answer (D) is correct.

REQUIRED: The court(s) that can be selected for an appeal.

DISCUSSION: If a taxpayer still disagrees with the IRS after an appeals conference, the taxpayer may bring his or her case to the United States Tax Court, the United States Court of Federal Claims, or a United States District Court. Harry must file his claim within 90 days of receiving a Notice of Deficiency if he wants to take his case to Tax Court. To file in either District Court or the Court of Federal Claims, Harry must pay the deficiency and file a claim for refund. Harry should request that the IRS immediately reject his claim so he may file his court case quickly.

19. Julie, who lives in Washington, D.C., operated a business without books and records. Her business income and expenses were reported on Schedule C. Julie's tax return for 2021 was examined, and substantial adjustments were proposed. Julie disagreed with the adjustments and wants to take her case directly to Tax Court. A Statutory Notice of Deficiency was issued to Julie by the IRS Area Director. Julie can file a petition for a small tax case before the U.S. Tax Court during which of the following periods beginning from the date of the issuance of the notice?

A. 30 days.

B. 90 days.

C. 150 days.

D. None of the answers are correct.

Answer (B) is correct.

REQUIRED: The time limit for petitioning the Tax Court.

DISCUSSION: After receiving a Statutory Notice of Deficiency, a taxpayer has 90 days to file a petition in Tax Court. Provided that the amount in dispute in Julie's case is under $50,000, she may petition the Small Tax Case Division of the Tax Court; however, the period to file a petition is 90 days for both the Small Tax Case Division and the main Tax Court.

20. Nicholas wants his income tax case to be handled under the Tax Court's small tax case procedure. All of the following statements regarding the small tax case procedure are true EXCEPT

A. The amount in the case must be $50,000 or less.

B. The amount must be paid before going to Tax Court.

C. The Tax Court must approve the request that the case be handled under the small tax case procedure.

D. The decision is final and cannot be appealed.

Answer (B) is correct.

REQUIRED: The false statement regarding the small tax case procedure.

DISCUSSION: The IRS Restructuring and Reform Act of 1998 increased the deficiency or overpayment limit for cases that may be heard by the Small Tax Case Division of the Tax Court. The limit is $50,000 [Sec. 7463(a)]. It is the taxpayer's option (subject to agreement by the Tax Court) for the case to be heard by the Small Tax Case Division. Generally, the Tax Court hears cases before any tax has been assessed or paid. In order to petition, the taxpayer must first receive a Notice of Deficiency. Any case decided in the Small Tax Case Division of the Tax Court will not be reviewed by any other court.

21. Gina disagreed with the results of an IRS examination of her tax return. She pursued the appeals procedures and disagreed with the appeals officer. If she wishes to appeal further, Gina may

A. Request a conference with a new appeals officer in a different district.

B. Wait for a Notice of Deficiency, fail to pay the tax, and petition the District Court.

C. Wait for a Notice of Deficiency, fail to pay the tax, and petition the Tax Court.

D. Submit a revised written protest that outlines the issues and authority for the position taken.

Answer (C) is correct.

REQUIRED: The true statement regarding an appeal of an IRS examination.

DISCUSSION: If there is no resolution of the tax dispute in the appeals conference, the IRS will issue a 90-day letter (Notice of Deficiency) to the taxpayer. Within 90 days of receipt of the notice, the taxpayer may file a petition with the Tax Court.

Answer (A) is incorrect. There is no authority that allows a taxpayer to attempt to move his or her case into a different district solely on the grounds of a previous denial. **Answer (B) is incorrect.** The District Court deals with cases in which the taxes have been paid. **Answer (D) is incorrect.** A written protest is used only for the initial contact with the IRS appeals officer.

22. If you don't agree with the Internal Revenue Service examination conclusion, you may take your case to the United States Tax Court for the following:

A. State income tax examination.

B. Federal income tax examination.

C. Federal estate tax examination.

D. Both federal income tax and federal estate tax examination.

Answer (D) is correct.

REQUIRED: The tax examination case that can be taken to the U.S. Tax Court.

DISCUSSION: If a taxpayer and the IRS still disagree after an appeals conference or the election was made to bypass the IRS appeals system, the case may be taken to the U.S. Tax Court, the U.S. Court of Federal Claims, or a U.S. District Court. State income tax matters, however, are not handled by the U.S. Tax Court.

Answer (A) is incorrect. State income tax matters are not handled by the U.S. Tax Court. **Answer (B) is incorrect.** Both federal income tax and federal estate tax issues may be handled by the U.S. Tax Court. **Answer (C) is incorrect.** Both federal income tax and federal estate tax issues may be handled by the U.S. Tax Court.

23. Anna's 2021 individual tax return was examined, and the IRS proposed changes resulting in additional tax. Anna wishes to bypass the IRS's appeal system and file a refund suit in the U.S. Court of Federal Claims on contested income tax issues. Your advice to Anna should be that she

A. Request that her return be reexamined.

B. Pay all of the additional tax and file another 1040 tax return.

C. Pay all of the additional tax and then file a claim for refund and request in writing that the claim be immediately rejected.

D. File a claim for refund and do nothing else.

Answer (C) is correct.

REQUIRED: The best action to take in order to file a refund suit directly to the claims court.

DISCUSSION: A taxpayer may file a refund suit in the appropriate District Court or the U.S. Court of Federal Claims only after the IRS rejects a refund claim. Thus, if the taxpayer does not want to appeal within the IRS, (s)he should request in writing that the claim be immediately rejected to enable jurisdictional requirements for court proceedings to be satisfied earlier.

Answer (A) is incorrect. Only the IRS appeals office will reexamine a return. **Answer (B) is incorrect.** The filing of another 1040 tax return is not required. **Answer (D) is incorrect.** Requesting immediate rejection allows the refund suit to bypass the IRS appeals system.

4.4 Penalties

24. Ron's tax returns were examined for 2016, 2017, and 2018, all of which resulted in adjustments increasing income reported on Schedule C of the returns. The Revenue Agent determined that the failure to report the income was intentional. The Revenue Agent proposed a fraud penalty. The adjustment for each year was in the amount of $100,000. The fraud penalty for each year should be in which of the following amounts?

A. $50,000

B. $75,000

C. $18,800

D. $28,200

Answer (B) is correct.

REQUIRED: The amount of the fraud penalty.

DISCUSSION: Publication 17 states, "If there is any underpayment of tax on your return due to fraud, a penalty of 75% of the underpayment due to fraud will be added to your tax." Ron, therefore, owes $75,000 ($100,000 × 75%) for each year.

25. A frivolous income tax return is one that does not include enough information to figure the correct tax or that certain information clearly showing that the tax that was reported is substantially incorrect. If a taxpayer files a frivolous return, which penalty applies specifically to the taxpayer for the frivolous return?

A. $50 for failure to supply your Social Security number.

B. 20% of the underpayment, reduced for those items for which there was adequate disclosure made.

C. $5,000 frivolous return penalty, applied in addition to any other applicable penalty or penalties.

D. $100 for the failure to furnish the tax shelter registration number.

Answer (C) is correct.

REQUIRED: The frivolous return penalty.

DISCUSSION: If the taxpayer files a frivolous income tax return, a $5,000 frivolous return penalty, in addition to any other applicable penalty, is assessed.

Answer (A) is incorrect. This question mentions nothing about a missing Social Security number.
Answer (B) is incorrect. Section 6662(c) does not offer disclosure as a tactic for circumventing the rule.
Answer (D) is incorrect. This question does not specifically address tax shelters.

STUDY UNIT FIVE

THE COLLECTION PROCESS

(14 pages of outline)

The purpose of the IRS is to collect the proper amount of tax revenue while minimizing cost; serve the public by continually improving the quality of its products and services; and perform in a manner warranting the highest degree of public confidence in its integrity, efficiency, and fairness. This study unit explains the taxpayer's rights and responsibilities regarding payment and collection of federal tax.

5.1 COLLECTIONS

Notice

1. When a taxpayer does not pay the full amount of tax owed, (s)he will receive an **assessment**.
   a. This assessment notifies the taxpayer of the balance due, demands payment, and begins the collection process.
      1) The notice requests payment within 10 days.
      2) Notices requesting payment are generated at the IRS service center.

Statutory Period

2. The IRS has 10 years from the date of assessment to collect the amount of tax assessed. This limit of time for collection of a debt is generally referred to as the **statute of limitations**. During this period, the tax may be collected by levy or by a proceeding in court.
   a. However, the taxpayer and the IRS may agree upon an extension of the period of time in which to collect.
   b. The 10-year collection period may be extended after it has expired if
      1) There has been a levy on any part of the taxpayer's property prior to the expiration and
      2) The extension is agreed to in writing before the levy is released.
   c. The statute of limitations on collection can be suspended by various acts. The IRS must notify the taxpayer that (s)he may refuse to extend the statute of limitations.
      1) Filing a petition in bankruptcy under Title 11 of the U.S. Code automatically stays assessment and collection of tax.
         a) The stay remains in effect until the bankruptcy court discharges liabilities or lifts the stay.
         b) Although the bankruptcy court has the authority to state the amount or legality of the tax liability charged against the taxpayer filing for bankruptcy, it may not determine the amount or legality of a tax liability that has already been decided by the appropriate jurisdiction before the filing of the bankruptcy petition.
   d. Form 872-A, *Special Consent to Extend the Time to Assess Tax*, indefinitely extends the period within which a tax may be assessed.

3. If a taxpayer is unable to pay the bill in full, (s)he is expected to pay as much as possible and contact the IRS for assistance.
   a. The IRS will attempt to determine the best method of payment based on the taxpayer's current financial condition as reported on Forms 433 A, B, and F.
      1) In determining the taxpayer's general financial health, these forms require the reporting of, among many other items, the taxpayer's history of bankruptcy filings, financial obligations (e.g., settlement of lawsuits), and court ordered payments (e.g., garnishments). This information assists in determining whether the taxpayer is solvent or insolvent, i.e., the taxpayer's ability to pay an assessed tax liability.

Installment Agreements

   b. The IRS is authorized to, and in certain cases must, enter into a written agreement for payments to be made in installments. The payment plan is based on an individual's current financial condition. The plan is subject to the following stipulations:
      1) Interest and penalties continue to accrue.
      2) The payments must be made on time, and the taxpayer must provide a financial update if requested by the IRS.
         a) Otherwise, the agreement may be subject to termination.
         b) The agreement also may be terminated if the IRS determines that the taxpayer's financial condition has significantly changed.
      3) The IRS must notify a taxpayer 30 days in advance before any changes in the agreement may be made.
         a) The IRS must provide the opportunity for an independent administrative review of any termination of an installment agreement.
      4) In order to obtain an installment agreement, the taxpayer must file all of his or her tax returns and make the current estimated tax payment, if required. The IRS will assess a one-time fee to set up the agreement.
         a) The IRS also may require that the taxpayer fill out Form 433-F, *Collection Information Statement*, explaining his or her situation.
            i) For amounts between $25,001 and $50,000, installment agreements do not require the taxpayer to complete Form 433-F, *Collection Information Statement*. However, direct debit information (e.g., routing number and account number of the taxpayer's bank account) or a completed Form 2159, *Payroll Deduction Agreement*, must be provided.
         b) The IRS may still file a Notice of Federal Tax Lien to secure the government's interest until the final payment is made.
         c) The IRS cannot take any collection actions
            i) While it considers a request for an installment agreement,
            ii) While the agreement is in effect,
            iii) For 30 days after an agreement is rejected, or
            iv) For any period while an agreement rejection is being appealed.

Guaranteed Installment Agreements

c. Under the following conditions, the IRS must enter into an installment agreement with any taxpayer requesting such an arrangement. These requirements also apply to the taxpayer's spouse if the liability proposed to be paid in installments relates to a joint return.

1) The taxpayer must not owe more than $10,000;
2) During the past 5 years, the taxpayer must not have
   a) Failed to file any income tax return,
   b) Failed to pay any income tax, or
   c) Entered into any installment agreement for payment of any income tax;
3) The taxpayer is financially unable to pay the liability in full when due;
4) The taxpayer must agree to pay in full within 3 years; and
5) The taxpayer must agree to file and pay all tax returns while the agreement is in effect.

Extension of Time to Pay

4. Taxpayers can receive an extension of time for payment due to undue hardship. They must file a Form 1127, *Application for Extension of Time for Payment of Tax Due to Undue Hardship*. For estate tax and GSTT, the taxpayer uses Form 4768, *Application for Extension of Time to File a Return and/or Pay U.S. Estate (and Generation-Skipping Transfer) Taxes*.

a. **Undue hardship** means more than an inconvenience. The taxpayer must show a substantial financial loss (e.g., selling property at a sacrifice price) if the tax is paid on the date it is due.

b. Generally, the full amount of the income tax owed, plus interest and any other penalties, must be paid on or before the 6-month extension due date (e.g., October 15). With a few exceptions, an extension of more than 6 months may be granted if the taxpayer is out of the country.

1) If the request for an extension of time to pay is granted, it will only affect the failure-to-pay penalty. The taxpayer will still owe interest and any other penalties on the unpaid amount from the original due date (e.g., April 15) until the tax is paid in full.
2) If full payment of the amount of the tax for which the taxpayer requested the extension, plus interest and other penalties, is not paid on or before the payment extension date, a failure-to-pay penalty will be imposed and calculated from the original due date.

Collection Appeals Program

5. In addition to contesting IRS assessments, a taxpayer may appeal collection activities.
   a. A taxpayer, or third party whose property is subject to a collection action, may appeal the following actions under the Collection Appeals Program (CAP):
      1) Levy or seizure action that has been or will be taken
      2) A Notice of Federal Tax Lien (NFTL) that has been or will be filed
      3) The filing of a notice of lien against an alter-ego or nominee's property
      4) Denials of requests to issue lien certificates, such as subordination, withdrawal, discharge, or non-attachment
      5) Rejected, proposed for modification or modified, or proposed for termination or terminated installment agreements
      6) Disallowance of taxpayer's request to return levied property
      7) Disallowance of property owner's claim for return of property
      8) Denial of a lien withdrawal
   b. If a taxpayer disagrees with the decision of the IRS employee and wishes to appeal, the taxpayer must first request a conference with the employee's manager.
   c. If the taxpayer does not resolve the disagreement with the collection manager, (s)he may submit Form 9423, *Collection Appeal Request*, to request consideration by Appeals. The taxpayer must let the collection office know within 2 business days after the conference with the collection manager that the taxpayer plans to submit Form 9423. The Form 9423 must be received or postmarked within 3 business days of the conference with the collection manager, or collection action may resume.
      1) If the taxpayer requests an appeal after the IRS makes a seizure, the taxpayer must appeal to the collection manager within 10 business days after the Notice of Seizure is provided to the taxpayer or left at the taxpayer's home or business.
   d. If the taxpayer requests a conference and is not contacted by a manager or designee within 2 business days of the request, the taxpayer can contact the collection manager again or submit Form 9423. If submitting Form 9423, the taxpayer should note the date of the request for a conference in Block 15 and indicate that the taxpayer was not contacted by a manager. The Form 9423 should be received or postmarked within 4 business days of the taxpayer's request for a conference, as collection action may resume.
   e. On the Form 9423, the taxpayer checks the collection action(s) disagreed with and explains why the disagreement exists. The taxpayer must also explain the solution to resolve the tax problem. Form 9423 is to be submitted to the collection office involved in the lien, levy, or seizure action.
   f. In situations where the IRS action(s) create economic harm or the taxpayer wants help because the tax problem has not been resolved through normal channels, the taxpayer can contact the Taxpayer Advocate Service.
   g. A taxpayer may appeal an installment agreement that has been rejected, proposed for modification or modified, or proposed for termination or terminated.
      1) If the taxpayer disagrees with the decision regarding the installment agreement, the taxpayer should appeal by completing a Form 9423.
      2) The taxpayer should provide it to the office or revenue officer who took the action regarding the installment agreement within 30 calendar days.

h. What will happen when the taxpayer appeals the case? Normally, the IRS will stop the collection action(s) the taxpayer disagrees with until the appeal is settled, unless the IRS has reason to believe that collection or the amount owed is at risk.

i. A taxpayer may represent himself or herself at an Appeals conference, or (s)he may be represented by an attorney, certified public accountant, or a person enrolled to practice before the IRS.

   1) If the taxpayer wants his or her representative to appear without him or her, the taxpayer must provide a properly completed Form 2848, *Power of Attorney and Declaration of Representative*.

j. Once Appeals makes a decision regarding the taxpayer's case, that decision is binding on both the taxpayer and the IRS. The taxpayer cannot obtain a judicial review of Appeals' decision following a CAP. However, there may be other opportunities to obtain administrative or judicial review of the issue raised in the CAP hearing. For example, a third party may contest a wrongful levy by filing an action in district court.

   1) Providing false information, failing to provide all pertinent information, or fraud will void Appeals' decision.

Administrative Summons

6. The administrative summons is among the IRS's most powerful tools for tax determination and collection. Unlike levies and federal tax liens, which directly seize or encumber assets, the summons is an administrative discovery device that is similar in intent and reach to a grand jury subpoena, and the IRS uses it to locate assets.

   a. The IRS normally issues a summons during the investigative stage of an examination to compel production of records not voluntarily produced. If such summons is issued to a third party, the taxpayer identified in such summons is generally entitled to notice of the summons and is given an opportunity to begin a proceeding to quash the summons.

   b. After the taxpayer's liability has been determined, the IRS may issue a summons to locate assets. The collection summons may request the same types of records as an investigative summons, that is, any books, records, papers, or other data that may be relevant to the collection of taxes. Typically, a collection summons requests bank records, financial statements and records, property records and records of property transfers, and transactions.

   c. The IRS must provide advance notice to the taxpayer that third-party contacts will be made in connection with the collection of the taxpayer's liability. This notice requirement does not apply to John Doe summonses or to certain emergency summonses. In addition, the IRS is required to periodically provide the taxpayer with a list of specific contacts and also to provide the list upon the taxpayer's request. These rules do not apply, however, if the collection is in jeopardy or the taxpayer authorizes the contact.

   d. Unlike an investigative summons issued during the examination of the taxpayer, if a collection summons is issued to any third party, the IRS is not required to notify the taxpayer of the summons and the taxpayer may not file a petition to quash the summons.

Refund Offset

7. Taxpayers owing past-due federal tax, state income tax, state unemployment compensation debts, child support, spousal support, or certain federal nontax debts, e.g., student loans, may have all or part of their refund used (offset) to pay the past-due amount. Offsets for federal taxes are made by the IRS. All other offsets are made by the Treasury Department's Bureau of Fiscal Services (BFS). For federal tax offsets, the taxpayer will receive a notice from the IRS. For all other offsets, the taxpayer will receive a notice from BFS.

IRS Collection Financial Standards

8. Collection Financial Standards are used to help determine a taxpayer's ability to pay a delinquent tax liability. Allowable living expenses include those expenses that meet the necessary expense test.
   a. The necessary expense test is defined as expenses that are necessary to provide for a taxpayer's (and his or her family's) health and welfare and/or production of income.
9. **National Standards** apply nationwide and include
   a. A standard monthly amount for food, clothing, and other items based on family size.
   b. Minimum allowances for out-of-pocket healthcare expenses for which taxpayers and their dependents are allowed the standard amount monthly on a per-person basis.
10. Maximum allowances for monthly housing and utilities and transportation, known as the **Local Standards**, vary by location.
11. Generally, the total number of persons allowed for necessary living expenses should be the same as those allowed as dependents on the taxpayer's most recent year income tax return.
12. If the IRS determines that the facts and circumstances of a taxpayer's situation indicate that using the standards is inadequate to provide for basic living expenses, the IRS may allow for actual expenses.
    a. The taxpayer must provide documentation that supports a determination that using national and local expense standards leaves them an inadequate means of providing for basic living expenses.

STOP AND REVIEW! **You have completed the outline for this subunit. Study multiple-choice questions 1 through 7 beginning on page 121.**

5.2 OFFER IN COMPROMISE

1. The IRS may accept an offer in compromise to settle unpaid tax accounts for less than the full amount of the balance due.
   a. The amount offered must reflect the taxpayer's maximum ability to pay.
      1) Present and future earning capacity are considered.
   b. The Commissioner of the IRS has the authority to compromise all taxes, interest, and penalties other than those relating to alcohol, tobacco, and firearms.
2. A compromise may be made on one, two, or all of three grounds:
   a. Doubt as to the liability for the amount owed
      1) Doubt as to the liability for the amount owed must be supported by the evidence.
   b. Doubt as to the taxpayer's ability to make full payment
      1) The total amount owed must be greater than the sum of the taxpayer's assets and future income.
   c. Promotion of effective tax administration
      1) Existence of economic hardship or other special circumstance
3. There are two types of offer in compromise payment terms:
   a. Lump sum cash payments must be paid within 5 or fewer installments within 5 or fewer months after the offer is accepted.
   b. Periodic payments must be paid monthly until paid in accordance with the provisions of the offer. They must be payable in 6 or more monthly installments and within 24 months after the offer is accepted.
4. The submission for payment terms must include the $205 application fee. In addition to the application fee, the following are required with the submission:
   a. A nonrefundable 20% of the offered amount for lump sum cash offers. The remaining balance is paid by the five or fewer installments.
   b. An initial proposed payment for periodic offers. The remaining proposed periodic payments must continue to be made while the offer is being evaluated.

   NOTE: There is an exemption of these submission requirements for taxpayers at or below income levels based on poverty guidelines.
5. If the taxpayer is basing the **offer in compromise on doubt as to collectibility or promotion of effective tax administration**, the taxpayer must also submit Form 433-A, *Collection Information Statement for Wage Earners and Self-Employed Individuals*, or Form 433-B, *Collection Information Statement for Businesses*, with supporting documentation. Submission of both forms may be required.
   a. If the taxpayer is basing the **offer in compromise on doubt as to liability**, the taxpayer must file a Form 656-L, *Offer in Compromise (Doubt as to Liability)*, instead of Form 656 and Form 433-A (OIC) and/or Form 433-B (OIC).

6. After acceptance of an offer, the taxpayer must remain current with filing and paying requirements for 5 years or until the amount of the offer is paid in full, whichever is longer.
   a. The taxpayer may ask the IRS Office of Appeals to review a rejection of the offer in compromise.

Taxpayer Assistance Orders

7. The National Taxpayer Advocate Office performs the following functions:
   a. Assists taxpayers in resolving problems with the IRS
      1) The National Taxpayer Advocate is responsible for issuing Taxpayer Assistance Orders (TAOs) through the Problem Resolution Office.
         a) TAOs are issued in assisting taxpayers suffering significant hardship as a result of how the revenue laws are being enforced.
         b) The order may require the IRS to release levied property or stop any action, or refrain from taking further action, under any section of the IRS Code.
         c) A TAO is requested by submitting Form 911.
   b. Identifies areas in which taxpayers have problems in dealing with the IRS
   c. Proposes changes to IRS administrative practices that would mitigate the problems that exist between the IRS and taxpayers
   d. Identifies possible law changes that might mitigate the problems identified between the IRS and taxpayers

Interest

8. Interest is generally figured from the due date of the return to either (a) the date payment is made, if paid when agreement of assessment is signed, or (b) the billing date, if paid within 21 days (10 days if the balance exceeds $100,000).

Injured Spouse

9. Form 8379, *Injured Spouse Allocation*, is filed by one spouse on a MFJ tax return when the joint overpayment was applied to a past-due obligation of the other spouse. The injured spouse may be able to get back his or her share of the joint refund.

Collection Statute Expiration Date

10. The last date the IRS can collect unpaid tax from the taxpayer consists of the year, month, and day.
    a. The IRS generally has 10 years from the date of assessment to collect tax.
       1) Certain actions by taxpayers either suspend or extend the collection statute of limitations.
       2) Examples include filing a Collection Due Process hearing request and submitting offers in compromise or installment agreements.

Stop and Review! **You have completed the outline for this subunit. Study multiple-choice questions 8 through 12 beginning on page 123.**

5.3 LIENS AND LEVIES

Lien

1. If a person neglects or refuses to pay a deficiency after demand, a lien attaches to all the person's property.
   a. A lien is a claim against the assets of a taxpayer who has failed to pay a debt.
   b. When the IRS files a Notice of Federal Tax Lien, all creditors of the taxpayer are notified of the lien. This results in an attachment of the lien to all of the taxpayer's property, including property that is acquired after the notice is filed.

Attachment Requirements

   c. Before the IRS files a Notice of Federal Tax Lien, three requirements must be met for the statutory lien to attach:
      1) The IRS must assess the liability.
      2) The IRS must send notice of tax due and demand for payment, unless waived by the taxpayer.
      3) The taxpayer must neglect or refuse to pay the tax within 10 days after notification.

Notice

   d. The IRS must notify the taxpayer in writing within 5 business days after filing a lien.
   e. Recording the notice provides constructive notice to potential purchasers and creditors that the government has a claim against the property.
      1) Recording restricts the ability to transfer or encumber the property.

Prepayment Removal

   f. There are several circumstances in which the lien is removed prior to the payment of the tax. The Secretary is the authority with the ability to withdraw a notice of a lien filed.

Release

   g. The IRS will issue a Release of the Notice of Federal Tax Lien within 30 days after the tax due is satisfied.
      1) The tax due also includes all fees charged by the state or other jurisdiction for both filing and releasing the lien.
         a) The fees are added to the balance owed.
      2) Failure by the IRS to release a lien allows the taxpayer to bring a civil suit for damages.
   h. The IRS will discharge a lien on taxpayer property if the property has declined in value and a sale of the property will not generate any proceeds for the IRS.

Appeal

i. A taxpayer may appeal the filing of a Notice of Federal Tax Lien if the taxpayer believes the IRS filed in error.

1) Form 12153, *Request for a Collection Due Process or Equivalent Hearing*, is completed and sent to the address from which the lien (or levy, discussed below) came. The request must be received within 30 days.

2) Upon the conclusion of the CDP hearing, the IRS will issue a determination stating whether the lien will be removed or will continue its existence.

   a) If the taxpayer disagrees with the outcome of the hearing, (s)he has 30 days from the receipt of the letter to bring a suit to contest the determination.

3) A lien is considered incorrect if it is filed while a taxpayer is in bankruptcy and subject to the automatic stay during bankruptcy.

Levy

2. The IRS is authorized to levy on a person's property to collect unpaid assessed taxes.

   a. Levy is defined as the power of distraint and seizure by any means.

Assessment

   b. Before levy action can begin, the IRS must make a determination of tax liability and assess it.

      1) Interest is assessed from the date the taxes are required to be paid, usually the due date of the return.

Notice and Demand

   c. Within 60 days after making the assessment, the IRS is required to provide a notice and demand for payment to the person.

      1) It must be left at the person's home or usual place of business or sent by mail to the person's last known address.

      2) The notice is accompanied by a publication outlining the person's rights.

      3) The right to discuss the matter with the collection employee's manager is provided at any step of the collection process.

      4) The Taxpayer Advocate Service (TAS) is an independent organization within the IRS and is the taxpayer's "*voice at the IRS*."

         a) TAS helps taxpayers whose problems are causing financial difficulty.

         b) The taxpayer may be eligible for help if the taxpayer tried to resolve the tax problem through normal IRS channels or the taxpayer believes an IRS procedure is not working as designed.

      5) If the taxpayer agrees to the assessment of the deficiency and pays the amount within 21 calendar days (10 business days if ≥ $100,000) after the date of the notice and demand, interest will not be imposed after the date of the notice and demand.

         a) This suspension of interest does not apply to interest on penalties and additions to tax for failure to file, for failure to pay the stamp or asset transfer tax, and for the accuracy-related and fraud penalties.

      6) A deposit of cash by the taxpayer, if (s)he believes additional tax is owed, may stop the further accrual of interest on the amount sent, but interest will continue to accrue on accrued interest.

Final Notice

d. If the taxpayer does not pay the tax within 10 days after notice and demand, a Notice of Intent to Levy must be provided at least 30 days in advance of levy.

1) This notice may be given in person, left at the taxpayer's home or usual place of business, or sent by certified mail.

Jeopardy Levy

e. If the IRS makes a finding that assessment or collection of a tax deficiency is in jeopardy, the IRS may waive the 10-day notice and demand period and/or the 30-day Final Notice of Intent to Levy period.

1) A jeopardy levy is based on the collection of tax, interest, penalties, etc., being endangered by delay.

2) In most cases, the following are insufficient bases for a jeopardy levy:

a) A bankruptcy petition filed by the person
b) Seized property that is perishable
c) Drug Enforcement Administration participation

Exercise of Levy

f. The IRS is authorized to seize (take) and sell property of persons with unpaid assessed liability after proper notice.

1) Certain property is exempt from levy. The exempt property includes the following:

a) Wearing apparel necessary for the taxpayer or for family members
b) School books and tools of a trade
c) Undelivered mail
d) Unemployment benefits
e) Workers' compensation
f) Certain annuity and pension benefits
g) Minimum exemption for wages, salary, and other income
h) Principal residence, unless the levy is approved in writing by a judge or magistrate of a U.S. District Court
i) Tangible personal or nonrental real property used in a trade or business, unless the levy is approved in writing by an area director or assistant area director of the IRS, or unless the collection is in jeopardy

2) In most states that have state income taxes, the IRS can levy a state refund check and apply the state refund to a federal tax debt.

Sale

g. After seizing property, the IRS gives notice of its pending sale to the person from whom it was seized and to the public.

   1) Sale must occur between 10 and 40 days after public notice is given.

      a) The property may be sold by public auction or sealed bids.

   2) Perishable goods. If the taxpayer posts a bond or pays the appraised value, seized perishable goods must be returned.

      a) Otherwise, they must be sold immediately.

   3) If real estate was sold, the taxpayer or anyone with an interest in the property may redeem it at any time within 180 days after the sale by paying the purchaser the amount paid for the property plus a certain percentage of interest.

   4) Before the date of sale, the IRS computes a "minimum bid price," which is the lowest amount the IRS will accept for the sale of that property to protect the taxpayer's interest in that property.

   5) The sale proceeds are applied first against the expenses of the proceedings, next against any federal excise tax imposed directly on the property, and then against the tax liability for which the levy was made.

   6) Any real property used as a residence by the taxpayer may not be seized to satisfy a levy of $5,000 or less.

Wages

h. A levy on wages begins from the date the levy is enacted until

   1) The tax liability assessed is satisfied,
   2) The levy is released, or
   3) The levy becomes unenforceable due to lapse of time.

i. An exemption exists for an amount of weekly income equal to the standard deduction divided by 52.

   1) For example, a single taxpayer's weekly levy exemption is $241.35 ($12,550 ÷ 52).

j. The IRS will release a levy if the IRS determines the levy is creating an economic hardship for the taxpayer.

Discharging Taxes through Bankruptcy

3. Income tax debts may be eligible for discharge under Chapter 7 or Chapter 13 of the Bankruptcy Code. Chapter 7 provides for full discharge of allowable debts. However, tax liens will not be removed with a Chapter 7 bankruptcy. Chapter 13 provides a payment plan to repay some debts, with the remainder of debts discharged. In order to remove the tax debts completely, the taxpayer must liquidate non-exempt assets (determined by each state) and meet certain qualifications or conditions.
   a. The IRS will not discharge taxes through bankruptcy unless certain conditions are met. These conditions are applicable to tax returns and tax assessments independently. If any one of the following qualifications are not met, or are off by a day or two, the taxes will still be due at the end of the bankruptcy proceedings:
      1) Solely income taxes -- Only income taxes can be discharged in bankruptcy as opposed to payroll taxes and other types of taxes.
      2) Taxes must be at least 3 years old -- The tax debts and their respective returns must be filed at least 3 years before filing for bankruptcy. This is often called the 3-year rule. Understand that this includes filing extensions as well. So if the taxpayer received a 6-month extension, it would be 3 years from the extension date (typically October 15).
      3) Tax returns filed 2 years before bankruptcy filing -- Any IRS taxes to be discharged must have been filed 2 years before filing for bankruptcy. Therefore, a taxpayer cannot file unfiled tax returns today from 3 years ago and then file for Chapter 7. Substitute tax returns do not count.
      4) Taxes were assessed at least 240 days ago -- The IRS must have assessed applicable taxes at least 240 days before a petition is filed. Taxes can be assessed more than once in a year. An assessment is when the IRS reviews unpaid taxes and makes any changes (e.g., adding to the balance) to the tax return and taxes owed. Therefore, any taxes that do not meet this 240-day rule will not be discharged.
      5) No fraudulent tax activities or evasion -- A taxpayer convicted of tax evasion or fraudulent tax activities will not qualify to have his or her taxes discharged.
      6) A taxpayer must prove to the court that the last 4 years of tax returns have been filed and must have a copy of the most recent return.

STOP AND REVIEW! **You have completed the outline for this subunit. Study multiple-choice questions 13 through 22 beginning on page 126.**

5.4 TRUST FUND RECOVERY PENALTY

1. The trust fund recovery penalty was enacted to encourage the prompt payment of withheld income and employment taxes, including Social Security and collected excise taxes.
   a. Excise taxes are taxes paid when purchases are made on a specific good, such as gasoline.
   b. Excise taxes are often included in the price of the product.
2. Trust fund taxes are composed of
   a. Income taxes withheld, plus
   b. The employee's portion of FICA taxes withheld.
3. The penalty is imposed against any person who is responsible for collecting or paying withheld income and employment taxes and who willfully fails to collect or pay them.
   a. A person is responsible if (s)he has the duty to perform and the power to direct the collecting, accounting, and paying of trust fund taxes. This person may be a(n)
      1) Officer or employee of a corporation
      2) Member or employee of a partnership
      3) Corporate director or shareholder
      4) Member of a board of trustees

      NOTE: Non-officer and/or non-equity employees have a low likelihood of receiving the penalty.
   b. A person's failure to pay or collect taxes is willful if (s)he has free will or choice yet either intentionally disregards the law or is plainly indifferent to legal requirements.
   c. An employee is not responsible if his or her function was solely to pay the bills as directed by a supervisor, rather than to determine which creditors would or would not be paid.
4. The penalty amount is 100% of the amount of trust fund taxes that were not paid.
5. The additional Medicare tax under Sec. 1411 is not designated as a trust fund tax.
6. Trust fund recovery penalties are excepted from discharge whether or not they were provided for in the plan or included on a timely filed proof of claim.
7. Trust fund recovery penalty assessments are based on liabilities recorded on the following tax forms:

Form Number	Form Title
Form CT-1	*Employer's Annual Railroad Retirement Tax Return*
Form 720	*Quarterly Federal Excise Tax Return*
Form 941	*Employer's Quarterly Federal Tax Return*
Form 943	*Employer's Annual Federal Tax Return for Agricultural Employees*
Form 944	*Employer's Annual Federal Tax Return*
Form 945	*Annual Return of Withheld Federal Income Tax*
Form 1042	*Annual Withholding Tax Return for U.S. Source Income of Foreign Persons*
Form 8288	*U.S. Withholding Tax Return for Dispositions by Foreign Persons of U.S. Real Property Interests*
Form 8804	*Annual Return for Partnership Withholding Tax (Section 1446)*

***STOP AND REVIEW!* You have completed the outline for this subunit. Study multiple-choice questions 23 through 25 on page 130.**

QUESTIONS

5.1 Collections

1. The collection process begins

A. At the IRS service center where notices are generated requesting payment.

B. In an IRS automated collection branch when telephone contact is made with the taxpayer.

C. Only after the problem resolution officer has acted upon the taxpayer's claim.

D. With the filing of a Notice of Federal Tax Lien.

Answer (A) is correct.

REQUIRED: The true statement concerning the IRS collection process.

DISCUSSION: Section 6301 authorizes the Internal Revenue Service, on behalf of the Secretary of the Treasury, to collect taxes imposed by the Internal Revenue laws. The collection process begins at the IRS service center where notices are generated requesting payment. Regulation 301.6303-1 states that the district director or the director of the regional service center shall, after making a tax assessment, give notice to the person liable for the unpaid tax, stating the amount of the tax and demanding payment.

2. When dealing with IRS employees, taxpayers have certain rights. Which of the following most accurately reflects those rights?

A. A right of appeal is available for most collection actions.

B. A right of representation is only available in audit matters; it is not available for collection matters.

C. A case may not be transferred to a different IRS office, even if your authorized representative is located in an area different from your residence.

D. If you disagree with the IRS employee who handles your case, you must first have the employee's permission before requesting a meeting with the manager.

Answer (A) is correct.

REQUIRED: The rights of the taxpayer in dealing with IRS employees.

DISCUSSION: Among the rights of the taxpayer is the right to appeal for most collection actions (Pub. 17).

Answer (B) is incorrect. Representation is permitted for collection as well as audit matters. **Answer (C) is incorrect.** A case may be transferred to a different IRS office regardless of the location of the authorized representative. **Answer (D) is incorrect.** A taxpayer does not need the permission of the IRS employee to request a meeting with the manager.

3. The initial action required in the collection process is

A. The filing of a Notice of Levy.

B. An assessment.

C. The receipt of the fourth notice by certified mail.

D. A notification of a pending examination audit.

Answer (B) is correct.

REQUIRED: The initial action required in the collection process.

DISCUSSION: Section 6201(a) authorizes the Internal Revenue Service to make a determination of all taxes. If the IRS makes a determination that a tax liability exists, the IRS has the authority under Sec. 6201(a) to assess the tax. The assessment of the taxes is the initial action required in the collection process.

Answer (A) is incorrect. It is a step in the collection process that occurs subsequent to the assessment. **Answer (C) is incorrect.** It is a step in the collection process that occurs subsequent to the assessment. **Answer (D) is incorrect.** A notification of a pending examination is part of the examination process, not the collection process.

4. With regard to an installment agreement with the IRS to pay a federal tax debt, which of the following statements is false?

A. Once an installment payment plan has been approved, the IRS will not continue to charge the taxpayer's account with interest on the taxpayer's unpaid balance of penalties and interest.

B. Installment payments may be paid by electronic transfers from the taxpayer's bank account.

C. While the taxpayer is making installment payments, the IRS may require the taxpayer to provide financial information on his or her financial condition to determine any change in his or her ability to pay.

D. The IRS may file a Notice of Federal Tax Lien to secure the government's interest until the taxpayer makes the final payment.

Answer (A) is correct.

REQUIRED: The false statement concerning an installment agreement.

DISCUSSION: Under Sec. 6159, the IRS is authorized to enter into a written agreement with a taxpayer for the payment of a tax liability in installments. Once an installment agreement is made, the taxpayer must make each payment on time. Interest and penalties will continue to accrue. Failure to pay an installment can result in the termination of the agreement.

5. Late payments by a taxpayer on an installment agreement to pay a tax liability will

A. Necessitate payment by certified check.

B. Extend the statute of limitations.

C. Generate a Notice of Intent to Levy.

D. Generate a 30-day notice as to the cessation of the agreement.

Answer (D) is correct.

REQUIRED: The action taken by the IRS as a result of late installment payments.

DISCUSSION: The IRS must notify a taxpayer 30 days in advance before it may change a payment agreement. The IRS may not take any enforcement action until after it has tried to contact the taxpayer and given him or her a chance to voluntarily pay any tax due.

6. After assessment, as a general rule, the Internal Revenue Service has the authority to collect outstanding federal taxes for which of the following?

A. Three years.

B. Five years.

C. Ten years.

D. Twenty years.

Answer (C) is correct.

REQUIRED: The collection period for taxes owed to the IRS.

DISCUSSION: Under Sec. 6502(a)(1), the IRS has 10 years from the date of assessment to collect the amount of tax assessed.

7. A guaranteed installment agreement is one of the acceptable methods of paying off a tax debt to the United States Treasury. The IRS must enter into an installment agreement provided all of the following requirements are met, EXCEPT the taxpayer

A. Must not owe more than $10,000.

B. Filed income tax returns without fail.

C. Did not fail to pay any income tax.

D. Previously entered into a nonguaranteed installment agreement.

Answer (D) is correct.

REQUIRED: The false statement regarding requirements for guaranteed installment agreements.

DISCUSSION: If the taxpayer owes the IRS less than $10,000, an installment agreement must be entered into by the IRS if the taxpayer had not failed to file any income tax return, failed to pay any income tax, or entered into any installment agreement for payment of any income tax. The taxpayer need not have previously entered into a nonguaranteed installment agreement.

Answer (A) is incorrect. The taxpayer must not owe more than $10,000. Previously entering into a nonguaranteed installment agreement is not a requirement. **Answer (B) is incorrect.** The taxpayer must not have failed to file any income tax return. Previously entering into a nonguaranteed installment agreement is not a requirement. **Answer (C) is incorrect.** The taxpayer must not have failed to pay any income tax. Previously entering into a nonguaranteed installment agreement is not a requirement.

5.2 Offer in Compromise

8. The Internal Revenue Service may accept an Offer in Compromise to settle unpaid tax accounts for less than the full amount due. A *Collection Information Statement* (financial statement) is NOT required with the offer when the reason for the offer is

A. Doubt as to liability.

B. Doubt as to collectibility.

C. To promote effective tax administration.

D. Economic hardship.

Answer (A) is correct.

REQUIRED: The instance in which a *Collection Information Statement* would not be required.

DISCUSSION: The IRS will permit less than full payment of amounts owed in certain instances. These include doubt as to a taxpayer's liability, collectibility, a resulting economic hardship if full payment was required, or full payment by the taxpayer would harm voluntary compliance by the taxpayer or others. Additionally, a *Collection Information Statement* is not required if the compromise is based on doubt of the liability (Pub. 594).

9. Which of the following statements is false with respect to taxpayers' offers in compromise on unpaid tax liabilities?

A. A compromise may be made only when doubt exists as to the liability for the amount owed.

B. The Commissioner of Internal Revenue has the authority to compromise all taxes (including any interest, penalty, or addition to the tax) arising under the revenue laws of the United States, except those relating to alcohol, tobacco, and firearms.

C. Submission of an offer in compromise will usually extend the statute of limitations on collection of an account.

D. Taxpayers have a right by law to submit an offer in compromise on their unpaid tax liability.

Answer (A) is correct.

REQUIRED: The false statement regarding an offer in compromise.

DISCUSSION: Under Sec. 7122, the Commissioner of the Internal Revenue Service has the authority to compromise all taxes, interest, and penalties arising under the internal revenue laws, except those relating to alcohol, tobacco, and firearms. A compromise may be made on one, two, or all three grounds: (1) doubt as to the liability for the amount owed, (2) doubt as to the taxpayer's ability to make full payment, or (3) promotion of effective administration [Reg. 301.7122-1(a)(b)]. The doubt as to the liability for the amount owed must be supported by the evidence. In the case of inability to pay, the amount offered must exceed the total value of the taxpayer's equity in all his or her assets and must give sufficient consideration to present and future earning capacity. The IRS may enter into a compromise with a taxpayer at any time before, during, or after collection proceedings.

10. If the taxpayer cannot resolve a collection problem through discussions with the revenue officer or his or her manager, the taxpayer should contact

A. An IRS taxpayer service representative.

B. The IRS district problem resolution officer.

C. The IRS area director.

D. The IRS regional appeals office.

Answer (B) is correct.

REQUIRED: The person or office contacted when a problem with the IRS exists.

DISCUSSION: The IRS has a Problem Resolution Program for people who have been unable to solve their problems with an IRS employee. A taxpayer should try to resolve the problem with a supervisor before contacting the Problem Resolution Program. The Problem Resolution Office is under the authority of the National Taxpayer Advocate.

11. Which of the following statements with respect to taxpayers' offers in compromise on unpaid tax liabilities is true?

A. A taxpayer does not have the right to submit an offer in compromise on his or her tax bill but is given the opportunity in order to increase voluntary compliance with the tax laws.

B. Doubt as to the liability for the amount owed must be supported by evidence, and the amount acceptable under the offer in compromise will depend on the degree of doubt found in the particular case.

C. Submission of an offer in compromise automatically suspends the collection of an account.

D. If the offer in compromise is made on the grounds that doubt exists as to the taxpayer's ability to make full payment on the amount owed, the amount offered must give sufficient consideration only to the taxpayer's present earning capacity.

Answer (B) is correct.

REQUIRED: The statement that is true regarding an offer in compromise.

DISCUSSION: Under Sec. 7122, the Commissioner of the Internal Revenue Service has the authority to compromise all taxes, interest, and penalties arising under the internal revenue laws, except those relating to alcohol, tobacco, and firearms. A compromise may be made on one, two, or all three grounds: (1) doubt as to the liability for the amount owed, (2) doubt as to the taxpayer's ability to make full payment, or (3) promotion of effective tax administration [Reg. 301.7122-1(a)]. The doubt as to the liability for the amount owed must be supported by the evidence. In the case of inability to pay, the amount offered must exceed the total value of the taxpayer's equity in all his or her assets and must give sufficient consideration to present and future earning capacity. A compromise may be entered into by the IRS, whether a suit has been instituted or not, and may be entered into after a judgment has been rendered.

Answer (A) is incorrect. A taxpayer has the right to submit an offer in compromise. **Answer (C) is incorrect.** Regulation 301.7122-1(d)(2) states that submission of an offer in compromise does not automatically suspend collection of an account. **Answer (D) is incorrect.** An offer in compromise gives consideration to present and future earning capacity.

12. Which of the following is true with respect to an offer in compromise?

A. The taxpayer may be allowed to pay less than the full amount owed.

B. Collection actions, such as levy, may be delayed.

C. A rejected offer may be appealed.

D. All of the answers are correct.

Answer (D) is correct.

REQUIRED: The true statement with respect to an offer in compromise.

DISCUSSION: The IRS may accept an offer in compromise to settle unpaid tax accounts for less than the full amount of the balance due when the facts support the likelihood that the IRS will be unable to collect the debt in full. The amount offered must reflect the taxpayer's maximum ability to pay. The IRS is also permitted to delay collection actions, and a taxpayer may appeal a rejected offer.

Answer (A) is incorrect. Collection actions may be delayed and rejected offers may be appealed. **Answer (B) is incorrect.** A taxpayer may be able to pay less than the full tax owed and appeal a rejected offer. **Answer (C) is incorrect.** A taxpayer may be allowed to pay less than the full amount owed, and the IRS may delay collections if deemed necessary.

5.3 Liens and Levies

13. With regard to the IRS filing a Notice of Federal Tax Lien, which of the following statements is NOT a requirement?

A. The IRS must assess the tax.

B. The IRS must send the taxpayer a notice and demand for payment.

C. The IRS must give individual notices to all of the taxpayer's creditors.

D. The taxpayer must neglect or refuse to pay the tax or otherwise neglect or refuse to resolve his or her tax liability problems.

Answer (C) is correct.

REQUIRED: The item that is not a requirement for the filing of a Notice of Federal Tax Lien.

DISCUSSION: Before the IRS files a Notice of Federal Tax Lien, three requirements must be met for the statutory lien to attach:

1. The IRS must assess the liability.
2. The IRS must send notice of tax due and demand for payment unless waived by the taxpayer.
3. The taxpayer must neglect or refuse to pay the tax within 10 days.

By filing a Notice of Federal Tax Lien, the government is providing a public notice to all creditors.

14. Once a notice of federal tax lien has been filed, all of the following are true EXCEPT

A. The lien applies to all of the taxpayer's real and personal property and to all of his or her rights to property until the tax is paid or the lien is removed.

B. The IRS will issue a release of the notice of federal tax lien within 15 business days after the taxpayer satisfies the tax due (including interest and other additions) by paying the debt, by having it adjusted, or if the IRS accepts a bond that the taxpayer submits, by guaranteeing a payment of the debt.

C. By law, a filed notice of tax lien can be withdrawn if withdrawal will speed collecting the tax.

D. The law requires the IRS to notify the taxpayer in writing within 5 business days after the filing of a lien.

Answer (B) is correct.

REQUIRED: The situation that is not true once a notice of federal tax lien has been filed.

DISCUSSION: The IRS will issue a Release of the Notice of Federal Tax Lien within 30 days after the tax due is satisfied. The tax due also includes all fees charged by the state or other jurisdiction for both filing and releasing the lien. The fees are added to the balance owed.

Answer (A) is incorrect. A federal tax lien attaches to all property and rights to property, whether real or personal, belonging to the taxpayer at the time the lien arises, as well as to property subsequently acquired during the period of the lien. The lien can be removed before the payment of the tax. Section 6323(j) lists several items where the lien is removed before the payment of the tax. **Answer (C) is incorrect.** A filed notice of tax lien can be withdrawn if withdrawal will speed collection. **Answer (D) is incorrect.** The IRS must notify the taxpayer in writing within 5 business days after the filing of a lien.

15. Which of the following taxes may be discharged in bankruptcy?

A. Gift.

B. Estate.

C. Income.

D. Employment.

Answer (C) is correct.

REQUIRED: The tax(es) that may be discharged in bankruptcy.

DISCUSSION: The IRS will not discharge taxes through bankruptcy unless certain conditions are met. These conditions are applicable to tax returns and tax assessments independently. One of the conditions is that the tax to be discharged must be an income tax. Therefore, gift tax, estate tax, and employment taxes do not qualify for bankruptcy.

Answer (A) is incorrect. Gift tax is a tax distinct from income tax. Only income tax may be discharged in bankruptcy. **Answer (B) is incorrect.** Estate tax, not to be confused with estate income tax, is a tax distinct from income tax. Only income tax may be discharged in bankruptcy. **Answer (D) is incorrect.** Employment taxes are distinct from income tax. Only income tax may be discharged in bankruptcy.

16. With regard to the levy method used by the IRS to collect tax that has not been paid voluntarily, which of the following statements is false?

A. The IRS cannot levy any state income tax refund checks and apply the state refund to a federal tax debt.

B. If the IRS levies a taxpayer's bank account, the bank is required to hold the funds the taxpayer has on deposit, up to the amount the taxpayer owes, for 21 days.

C. Levies can be made on property that is the taxpayer's but is held by third parties.

D. The IRS will release a levy if the IRS determines the levy is creating an economic hardship for the taxpayer.

Answer (A) is correct.

REQUIRED: The false statement regarding a levy.

DISCUSSION: A levy allows the IRS, by legal authority, to take a taxpayer's property in order to satisfy a tax debt. The IRS may levy on property that is held by the taxpayer or on property belonging to the taxpayer but held by a third party. In most states that have state income taxes, the IRS can levy a state refund check and apply the state refund to a federal tax debt.

17. Mr. Alomar's income tax return was examined by the IRS, and he agreed with the proposed changes. He has several ways by which he may settle his account and pay any additional tax that is due. Which of the following statements with respect to this situation is false?

A. If he pays when he signs the agreement, the interest is generally figured from the due date of the return to the date of his payment.

B. If he does not pay the additional tax when he signs the agreement, he will receive a bill. The interest on the additional tax is generally figured from the due date of the return to the billing date.

C. If the bill is delayed, he will not be billed for additional interest for more than 60 days from the date he signed the agreement.

D. If he pays the amount due within 21 days of the billing date, he will not have to pay more interest or penalties.

Answer (C) is correct.

REQUIRED: The false statement regarding the collection of taxes.

DISCUSSION: Although the IRS may lower the interest on tax owed when the interest is due to an error or delay by an IRS official performing a procedural or mechanical act, it will not suspend the billing of interest until the payment is made.

18. Which of the following statements in respect to IRS seizure and sale of a taxpayer's property to satisfy his or her federal tax bill is false?

A. A taxpayer does not have the right to redeem any property seized once the IRS has sold it.

B. Unless the property is perishable and must be sold immediately, the IRS will wait at least 10 days after seizure before conducting the sale.

C. Before the date of sale, the IRS may release the property to the taxpayer if (s)he pays the amount equal to the amount of the government's interest in the property.

D. The taxpayer may request a recomputation if (s)he is in disagreement with the minimum price the IRS has determined it will accept for the property.

Answer (A) is correct.

REQUIRED: The false statement with respect to IRS seizure and sale of a taxpayer's property.

DISCUSSION: Section 6331(b) authorizes the seizure and sale of any property upon which the IRS may levy. Section 6337(a) provides a right of redemption by paying the amount due, together with expenses, at any time prior to sale of the property. For real property, the right of redemption continues until 180 days after the sale [Sec. 6337(b)].

19. Jeopardy levies may occur when the IRS waives the 10-day notice and demand period and/or the 30-day Final Notice (Notice of Intent to Levy) period because

A. The taxpayer has filed for bankruptcy protection.

B. The seized property is perishable in nature.

C. The IRS is working in conjunction with the Drug Enforcement Administration.

D. A delay would endanger the collection of tax.

Answer (D) is correct.

REQUIRED: The reason jeopardy levies may occur.

DISCUSSION: Under Sec. 6331(a), a taxpayer has 10 days to pay the tax after receiving a Notice and Demand for Tax. If the taxpayer neglects or refuses to pay the tax within that time, the IRS may issue a Final Notice (Notice of Intent to Levy) giving the taxpayer 30 days to pay the tax. If the tax is not paid within that period, the IRS may proceed to collect the tax by levy upon the taxpayer's property. If the IRS makes a finding that the assessment or collection of the tax deficiency is in jeopardy, the IRS may waive the 10-day notice and demand period and/or the 30-day Final Notice (Notice of Intent to Levy) period. Jeopardy levies may occur when delay would endanger collection of the tax, interest, penalties, etc. (Sec. 6861).

20. Which of the following statements with respect to IRS seizure and sale of a taxpayer's property to satisfy the taxpayer's tax bill is false?

A. A seizure may not be made on any property if the estimated cost of the seizure and sale exceeds the fair market value of the property to be seized.

B. A taxpayer has the right to an administrative review of a seizure action when the IRS has taken personal property that is necessary to the maintenance of the taxpayer's business.

C. The IRS must wait 30 days after seizure before conducting a sale.

D. After the sale, proceeds are applied first to the expenses of the levy and sale.

Answer (C) is correct.

REQUIRED: The false statement regarding IRS seizures and sales.

DISCUSSION: After seizure of property, the IRS gives notice of sale to the public and to the taxpayer from whom the property was seized. Under Sec. 6335(d), the time of sale must be not less than 10 days nor more than 40 days from the time of giving public notice. Section 6336 provides an exception to this rule in the case of perishable goods, which must be returned to the taxpayer if (s)he pays the appraised value of the goods or posts a bond. If the taxpayer does not pay such amount or post a bond, the goods must be sold immediately.

21. When levies are attached, the IRS has the authority to take property to satisfy a tax debt. The IRS may levy all of the following EXCEPT

A. Accounts receivable.

B. Workers' compensation.

C. Rental income.

D. Commissions.

Answer (B) is correct.

REQUIRED: The property exempt from a levy.

DISCUSSION: A levy is the seizure of a taxpayer's property in order to satisfy a tax debt. A levy can be made on property that is held by the taxpayer or property that is held for a taxpayer by third parties. However, a taxpayer has the legal right to keep workers' compensation.

22. With respect to the IRS's seizures and sales of personal property to satisfy a federal tax debt, which of the following statements is false?

A. After the notice of sale has been given to the taxpayer, the IRS must wait 10 days before conducting the sale unless the property is perishable and must be sold immediately.

B. After the sale, the IRS uses the proceeds first to satisfy the tax debt.

C. If real estate was sold, the taxpayer, or anyone with an interest in the property, may redeem it at any time within 180 days after the sale by paying the purchaser the amount paid for the property plus a certain percentage of interest.

D. Before the date of sale, the IRS computes a "minimum bid price," which is the lowest amount the IRS will accept for the sale of that property to protect the taxpayer's interest in that property.

Answer (B) is correct.

REQUIRED: The false statement regarding IRS seizures and sales.

DISCUSSION: The sale proceeds are applied first against the expenses of the proceedings, next against any federal excise tax imposed directly on the property, and then against the tax liability for which the levy was made, including a separate supporting statement containing the basis for the taxpayer's explanation.

5.4 Trust Fund Recovery Penalty

23. With regard to the trust fund recovery penalty assessments for employers, which of the following statements is false?

A. The penalty can be applied regardless of whether a taxpayer is out of business or without assets.

B. The penalty is computed on unpaid income taxes withheld plus the employee's and the employer's portion of the FICA taxes.

C. The two key elements that support an assessment of the penalty against an individual are responsibility and willfulness.

D. The amount of the penalty is equal to the unpaid trust fund tax.

Answer (B) is correct.

REQUIRED: The false statement regarding the trust fund recovery penalty.

DISCUSSION: When a person is responsible for collection and payment of trust fund taxes, (s)he is assessed a penalty equal to the amount of the delinquent trust fund taxes. Trust fund taxes are the taxes an employer is required to withhold from employees. The employer is required to pay FICA taxes equivalent to the amount withheld from the employee, but these are non-trust fund taxes and are not included when determining the amount of the penalty.

24. All of the following persons may be responsible for the trust fund tax EXCEPT

A. An officer of a corporation.

B. An employee in the payroll department.

C. A member of the board of trustees.

D. A corporate director or shareholder.

Answer (B) is correct.

REQUIRED: The person who does not meet the definition of a responsible person for the trust fund tax.

DISCUSSION: A person who has a responsibility to collect withholding taxes imposed on another person may be liable for a penalty equal to the amount of such taxes that (s)he willfully fails to remit to the IRS. The primary factor considered in determining responsibility is the control of funds and the authority to sign or co-sign checks. Included among responsible persons are the officers, employees, directors, and shareholders of a corporation and members of the board of trustees. An employee in the payroll department generally does not have control over funds.

25. With regard to the trust fund recovery penalty assessments for employers, which of the following statements is false?

A. A federal tax lien may be filed against a responsible person.

B. A person is considered willful if (s)he has free will or choice, yet either intentionally disregards the law or is plainly indifferent to legal requirements.

C. The penalty also applies to excise taxes.

D. The amount of the penalty is equal to the unpaid income taxes withheld.

Answer (D) is correct.

REQUIRED: The false statement regarding the trust fund recovery penalty.

DISCUSSION: When a person is responsible for collection and payment of trust fund taxes, (s)he is assessed a penalty equal to the amount of the delinquent trust fund taxes. Trust fund taxes are the taxes an employer is required to withhold from employees, including income taxes withheld and the employee's share of FICA taxes.

STUDY UNIT SIX

TAX AUTHORITY

(11 pages of outline)

Tax law is comprised of three basic sources of authority: statutory law, administrative pronouncements, and judicial decisions. In combination, these sources provide the authority by which both taxpayers and governments must abide. Statutory law is contained in the Internal Revenue Code (IRC), which consists of sections that contain operational, definitional, or procedural rules relating to federal taxes. The Department of the Treasury has the responsibility of issuing administrative pronouncements, including Treasury regulations, that interpret and illustrate the rules contained in the IRC. Finally, if a disagreement arises regarding the interpretation of a tax law, a taxpayer may take his or her case to federal court to settle the dispute. Court decisions may serve as guidance for future tax decisions.

6.1 STATUTORY LAW (LEGISLATIVE LAW)

IRC 1986

1. **The Internal Revenue Code** (IRC) of 1986 is the primary source of federal tax law. It imposes income, estate, gift, employment, and miscellaneous excise taxes as well as provisions controlling the administration of federal taxation. The IRC is found at Title 26 of the titles of the United States Code (U.S.C.).
   a. The courts give great importance to the literal language of the IRC, but not every tax controversy can be resolved by the language in the Code.
      1) In cases where the literal language of the Code is ambiguous, the courts will consider the history of a particular Code section, including committee reports and other legislative history, Treasury regulations and other IRS published guidance interpreting the Code section, and the relationship of the particular Code section to other Code sections.
   b. The Code is continually changing, requiring practitioners to carefully determine the law applicable to the year under examination.
      1) To do so, practitioners determine whether the applicable law has been modified and, if so, the date on which the changes became effective.
      2) Many publishers provide this information in small print immediately following the current Code section.

Committee Reports

2. **Committee reports** are useful tools in determining Congressional intent behind certain tax laws and helping examiners apply the law properly.

Treaties

3. In the U.S., a tax treaty is treated as equivalent to statutory law and overrides the IRC. The United States has income tax treaties with a number of foreign countries. Under these treaties, residents (not necessarily citizens) of foreign countries are taxed at a reduced rate or are exempt from U.S. income taxes on certain items of income they receive from sources within the United States. These reduced rates and exemptions vary among countries and specific items of income. Treaty provisions generally are reciprocal (i.e., apply to both treaty countries and their residents).

STOP AND REVIEW! **You have completed the outline for this subunit. Study multiple-choice questions 1 through 4 beginning on page 142.**

6.2 REGULATIONS, RULES, AND PROCEDURES (ADMINISTRATIVE LAW)

Regulations

1. IRC Sec. 7805(a) grants general authority to the Secretary of the Treasury to "prescribe all needful rules and regulations for the enforcement" of the Code. All regulations are written by the Office of the Chief Counsel, IRS, and approved by the Secretary of the Treasury.
   a. Regulations are issued as interpretations of specific Code sections and are organized in a sequential system consistent with the Code. The prefixed number designates the area of taxation referred to by the regulation.
   b. Treasury Regulations (also referred to as Income Tax Regulations) are authorized by law. Nevertheless, courts are not bound to follow such administrative interpretations to the extent they conflict with the Code.
      1) The IRS is generally bound by regulations; the courts are not.
   c. The Supreme Court has stated that "Treasury Regulations must be sustained unless unreasonable and plainly inconsistent with the revenue statutes."
      1) However, if the regulation is promulgated under the "general authority to prescribe all needful rules and regulations, 26 U.S.C. Sec. 7805 . . . 'we owe the interpretation less deference than a regulation issued under a specific grant of authority to define a statutory term or prescribe a method of executing a statutory provision.'"
      2) The effect of a regulation on the courts depends on whether the regulation is considered legislative, interpretative, or procedural.
2. A regulation can be characterized as one of three types: legislative, interpretative, or procedural.

Legislative

   a. Legislative regulations are issued pursuant to specific authorization from, or direction by, Congress in particular Code sections.
      1) Legislative regulations are not issued pursuant to the authority of Sec. 7805 but under specific authority of a particular statute.
      2) Some Code sections that authorize legislative regulations are very brief.
         a) For example, the consolidated tax return regulations are less than 2 pages, but related legislative regulations are more than 200 pages.
      3) When the Treasury promulgates a legislative regulation, the regulation has the force and effect of law.
         a) A legislative regulation is as binding as a statute if it is
            i) Within the grant of delegated power,
            ii) Issued pursuant to proper procedure, and
            iii) Reasonable.

            NOTE: The delegating statute and the regulation also must be within constitutional bounds.
         b) A reviewing court has no authority to substitute its judgment concerning the regulation's content because Congress granted that discretion to the Treasury and not to the court.
         c) A legislative regulation, however, may be overturned if it exceeds the scope of the power delegated to the Treasury, is contrary to the statute, or is unreasonable.

Interpretative

b. An interpretative regulation explains the meaning of a statutory provision. Unlike a legislative regulation, there is no section-specific grant of authority for the promulgation of an interpretative regulation.

1) Authority to issue an interpretative regulation is derived from the general grant of authority to prescribe all needful rules and regulations for enforcement of the tax laws.

2) Interpretative regulations do not have the force and effect of law.

a) However, the courts customarily accord them substantial weight.

b) A regulation issued at the same time as the enactment of a Code provision is given more weight because it is more likely to represent the legislative intent.

c) Interpretative regulations that have been in existence for a long time are given greater weight than more recent ones.

Procedural

c. Procedural regulations are promulgated under the procedural and administrative provisions of the Code by the Commissioner of the IRS, not the Secretary of the Treasury.

1) Procedural regulations are binding on the IRS insofar as they affect a vital or personal interest of the taxpayer.

2) Procedural regulations describing obligations to file forms and information appear to be given the force and effect of law.

3. Regulations can be further classified as proposed, temporary, or final.

Proposed

a. Proposed regulations are issued to elicit comments from the public. Public hearings are held if written requests are made.

1) Proposed regulations might be used as somewhat of an authority for taking a tax position.

a) The regulations themselves do not state this and must be considered as a weak authority at best.

2) Notices of proposed rulemaking are required for proposed regulations and are published in the Federal Register so that interested parties have an opportunity to participate in the rule-making process.

Temporary

b. Temporary regulations provide guidance to the IRS, tax practitioners, and the public until final regulations are issued.

1) Temporary regulations have the same force and effect of law as final regulations until the final regulations are issued.

a) Public hearings are not held on temporary regulations unless written requests are made.

2) Temporary regulations

a) Can be used as somewhat of an authority
b) May remain effective for a maximum of 3 years
c) Must be issued concurrently as proposed regulations

Final

c. Final regulations are adopted after public comment on the proposed versions has been evaluated by the Treasury.

1) When a proposed regulation becomes final or an existing regulation is amended, the document that describes the finalization or amendment is referred to as a Treasury Decision (TD).

2) Some Code sections do not have final Treasury Regulations.

Authority of the Regulations

4. The IRS is bound by the regulations. The courts are not.

a. If both temporary and proposed regulations have been issued on the same Code section and the text of both are similar, taxpayers' positions should be based on the temporary regulations because they can be cited as an authority for proposing an adjustment.

b. When no temporary or final regulations have been issued, taxpayers may use a proposed regulation to support a position.

1) The taxpayer should indicate that the proposed regulation is the best interpretation of the Code section available.

Revenue Rulings

5. A revenue ruling is an official interpretation of Internal Revenue law as applied to a given set of facts and is issued by the IRS.

a. Revenue rulings are published in Internal Revenue Bulletins (and later the Cumulative Bulletin) to inform and advise taxpayers, the IRS, and others on substantive tax issues.

b. Publication of revenue rulings is intended to promote uniform application of tax laws by IRS employees and to reduce the number of letter ruling requests.

c. Revenue rulings may be cited as precedent and relied upon when resolving disputes, but they do not have the force and effect of regulations.

1) A revenue ruling is not binding on a court.

Revenue Procedures

6. A revenue procedure is an official IRS statement that prescribes procedures that affect the rights or duties of either a particular group of taxpayers or all taxpayers.

a. Revenue procedures primarily address administrative and procedural matters, e.g., in what format and to whom should a letter ruling request be submitted.

b. Revenue procedures do not have the force and effect of law, but they may be cited as precedent.

c. Revenue procedures are directive and not mandatory.

IRB

7. The Internal Revenue Bulletin (IRB) is the authoritative instrument of the Commissioner of Internal Revenue for announcing official IRS rulings and procedures and for publishing Treasury Decisions, Executive Orders, Tax Conventions, legislation, court decisions, and other items of general interest. It is published on a weekly basis by the Government Printing Office.
   a. It is the policy of the IRS to publish in the IRB all substantive rulings necessary to promote a uniform application of the tax laws, including rulings that supersede, revoke, modify, or amend any of those previously published in the IRB.
      1) All published rulings apply retroactively unless otherwise indicated.
8. In addition to revenue rulings and revenue procedures, a number of miscellaneous documents that apply to tax law interpretation and administration are published in the IRB.

Announcements

   a. Announcements are public pronouncements on matters of general interest, such as effective dates of temporary regulations, clarification of rulings, and form instructions.
      1) They are issued when guidance of a substantive or procedural nature is needed quickly.
      2) Announcements can be relied on to the same extent as revenue rulings and revenue procedures.
      3) Announcements are identified by a number representing the year and a sequence number.

Notices

   b. Notices are public announcements issued by the IRS that
      1) Appear in the IRB and are included in the bound Cumulative Bulletin
      2) Are identified by a number representing the year and a sequence number
      3) Can be relied on to the same extent as revenue rulings and revenue procedures

Delegation Orders

   c. Commissioner Delegation Orders formally delegate authority to perform certain tasks or make certain decisions to specified IRS employees.
      1) Delegation orders are identified by a number and are located in the Internal Revenue Manual (IRM).

Authority of Rulings and Procedures

9. Rulings do not have the force and effect of Treasury Department Regulations, but they may be used as precedents.
   a. In applying published rulings, the effects of subsequent legislation, regulations, court decisions, rulings, and procedures must be considered.
   b. Caution is urged against reaching the same conclusion in other cases, unless the facts and circumstances are substantially the same.

Publications

10. IRS Publications explain the law in plain language for taxpayers and their advisors. They typically highlight changes in the law, provide examples illustrating IRS positions, and include worksheets.
    a. Publications are nonbinding on the IRS and do not necessarily cover all positions for a given issue.
    b. While a good source of general information, **publications should not be cited to sustain a position**.

Private Letter Ruling

11. A **Private Letter Ruling** (PLR) represents the conclusion of the IRS for an individual taxpayer.
    a. The application of a PLR is confined to the specific case for which it was issued, unless the issue involved was specifically covered by statute, regulations, ruling, opinion, or decision published in the IRB.

Technical Advice Memos

12. **Technical Advice Memoranda** (TAMs) are requested by IRS area offices after a return has been filed, often in conjunction with an ongoing examination.
    a. TAMs are binding on the IRS in relation to the taxpayer who is the subject of the ruling.
13. A PLR to a taxpayer or a TAM to an area director, which relates to a particular case, should not be applied or relied upon as a precedent in the disposition of other cases.
    a. However, they provide insight with regard to the IRS's position on the law and serve as a guide.

Other Private Letter Rulings and Memos

14. Existing PLRs and memoranda [including Confidential Unpublished Rulings (CURs), Advisory Memoranda (AMs), and General Counsel Memoranda (GCMs)] may not be used as precedents in the disposition of other cases but may be used as a guide with other research material in formulating an area office position on an issue.
15. Whenever an area office finds that a CUR, AM, or GCM represents the sole precedent or guide for determining the disposition of an issue and cannot to its own satisfaction find justification in the Code, regulations, or published rulings to support the indicated position, technical advice should be requested from the Headquarters Office.
    a. Technical advice should be requested when taxpayers or their representatives take the position that the basis for the proposed action is not supported by statute, regulations, or published positions of the IRS.
        1) If it is believed that the position of the IRS should be published, the request for technical advice will contain a statement to that effect.
            a) Instructions for requesting technical advice from the Headquarters Office are contained in the second revenue procedure issued each year.
                i) Questions regarding the procedures should be addressed to the contacts listed in the revenue procedure.

General Counsel Memos

16. General Counsel Memoranda (GCMs) are legal memoranda from the Office of Chief Counsel prepared in connection with the review of certain proposed rulings (Rev. Ruls., PLRs, TAMs).
    a. They contain legal analyses of substantive issues and can be helpful in understanding the reasoning behind a particular ruling and the IRS's response to similar issues in the future.

Technical Memos

17. Technical Memoranda (TMs) function as transmittal documents for Treasury Decisions or Notices of Proposed Rule Making (NPRMs).
    a. They generally summarize or explain proposed or adopted regulations, provide background information, state the issues involved, and identify any controversial legal or policy questions.
    b. TMs are helpful in tracing the history and rationale behind a regulation or regulation proposal.

Internal Revenue Manual

18. The Internal Revenue Manual (IRM) sets forth instructions, policies, and guidelines for the IRS's operations and organizations. The day-to-day conduct of IRS agents and other personnel and the procedures to be followed in various IRS activities are addressed in the Manual.
    a. Because an agency such as the IRS is bound by the procedural rules it adopts, IRS personnel must comply with Manual procedures. However, the policies and guidelines contained in the Manual are not legally binding because they are directory, not mandatory. Strict compliance is not required if the procedure does not affect a significant interest of the taxpayer or if the IRS's failure to comply with Manual procedures occurred in good faith and requiring strict compliance would affect the outcome of the government action at issue.

STOP AND REVIEW! **You have completed the outline for this subunit. Study multiple-choice questions 5 through 12 beginning on page 143.**

6.3 THE COURT SYSTEM (JUDICIAL LAW)

1. The court system is comprised of
   a. U.S. Tax Court
   b. U.S. District Courts and Bankruptcy Courts
   c. U.S. Court of Federal Claims
   d. Appellate courts
   e. U.S. Supreme Court

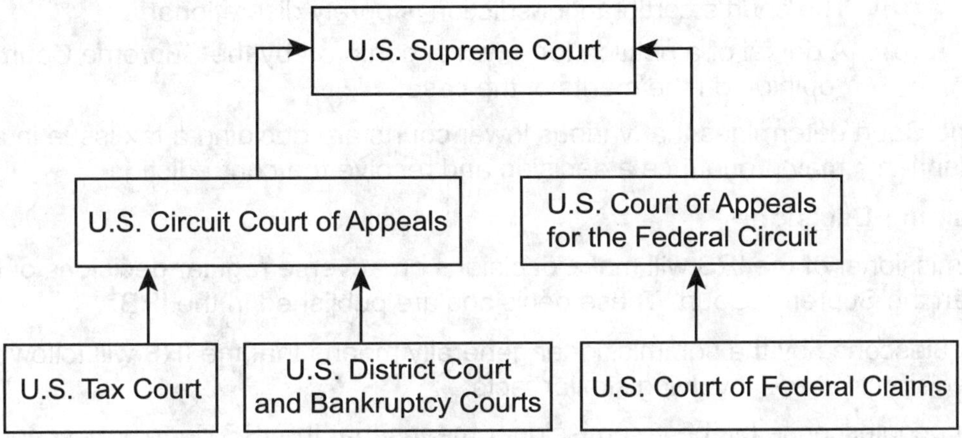

Figure 6-1

2. **Tax Court**
   a. Decisions of the Tax Court are issued as either regular reports or memorandum decisions.
      1) Regular reports are published in bound volumes by the government.
      2) Memorandum decisions are usually published only commercially. A Tax Court memorandum decision is a report of a Tax Court decision thought to be of little value as a precedent because the issue has been decided one or more times before.
3. Cases from the U.S. Tax Court and the U.S. District Courts are appealed to the appropriate U.S. Circuit Court of Appeals. Cases from the U.S. Court of Federal Claims are appealed to the U.S. Court of Appeals for the Federal Circuit.
   a. Bankruptcy courts are separate units of the district court.
      1) They resolve tax matters concerning taxpayers who are involved in an ongoing bankruptcy case.

4. **U.S. Supreme Court**
   a. The U.S. Supreme Court generally reviews decisions of the courts of appeals and other federal courts.
   b. An appellant in an appropriate case may petition the Supreme Court to hear an appeal from the lower court's decision.
      1) A **writ of certiorari** is an order by the Supreme Court to send the case up for its consideration.
         a) The court's certiorari jurisdiction is purely discretionary.
         b) A denial of a petition for a writ of certiorari by the Supreme Court expresses no opinion on the merits of the case.
   c. If the Court determines that various lower courts are deciding a tax issue in an inconsistent manner, it may pronounce a decision and resolve the contradiction.

IRS Commissioner Decisions

5. The Commissioner of the IRS will make decisions on adverse regular decisions of the courts other than the Supreme Court. These decisions are published in the IRB.
   a. Acquiescence by the commissioner generally means that the IRS will follow the court decision in cases involving similar facts.
   b. Nonacquiescence by the commissioner means that the IRS does not accept an adverse decision and will not follow it in cases on the same issue.
   c. An acquiescence or a nonacquiescence may be subsequently revised by the commissioner.
   d. The acquiescence program is not intended as a substitute for a ruling or regulation program.
6. The **citator** contains case histories and recent case developments, such as appeals, writs of certiorari, and related cases. Citators are published commercially.
7. **Dictum** is a court statement of opinion on a legal point that is not necessary for the decision of the case.
   a. It is not controlling but may be persuasive to another court deciding the issue dealt with by the dictum.
8. Decisions of the courts, other than the Supreme Court, are binding on the Commissioner only for the particular taxpayer and for the year litigated; thus, decisions of the lower courts do not require the IRS to alter its position for all taxpayers.
9. The IRC is federal law. All courts are bound by the Code sections.
10. In general, the IRS may exercise executive, judicial, and legislative power.

***STOP AND REVIEW!* You have completed the outline for this subunit. Study multiple-choice questions 13 through 21 beginning on page 146.**

6.4 TAX RESEARCH

1. There are two classes of tax source materials: primary and secondary. Primary authorities consist of the law enacted by the legislature plus its official interpretation and indications of its meaning. Primary reference materials emanate from a branch of the government. Primary reference materials consist of the statutory law, administrative law, and judicial law. All other statements or explanations of what the law is or means are secondary authorities. The supporting authority for a rule of law should always be a primary authority.
2. Primary authorities include the following:

    Constitution
    Internal Revenue Code
    House Ways and Means Committee Report
    House debate
    Senate Finance Committee Report
    Senate debate
    Conference Committee Report
    Post-Conference House and Senate Debate
    Treaties
    Temporary and Final Regulations
    Proposed Regulations
    Revenue Rulings
    Revenue Procedures
    Private Letter Rulings
    Technical Advice Memoranda
    Determination Letters
    IRS Press Releases
    Notices
    Any other similar documents published by the IRS in the Internal Revenue Bulletin
    Court cases

3. Secondary authorities should be used as supporting authority only to supplement supporting primary authorities or when primary authorities in point are nonexistent. Secondary authorities serve chiefly as research tools that help locate primary authorities in point. Examples of secondary reference materials include tax services, citators, textbooks, journals, and newsletters.

***STOP AND REVIEW!* You have completed the outline for this subunit. Study multiple-choice questions 22 and 23 on page 149.**

QUESTIONS

6.1 Statutory Law (Legislative Law)

1. Which of the following is the primary source of federal tax law?

A. The Internal Revenue Code of 1913.

B. Treasury Regulations.

C. The Internal Revenue Code of 1986.

D. The Internal Revenue Bulletin.

Answer (C) is correct.

REQUIRED: The primary source of federal tax law.

DISCUSSION: The Internal Revenue Code of 1986 is the primary source of federal tax law. It imposes income, estate, gift, employment, and miscellaneous excise taxes and provisions controlling the administration of federal taxation. The Code is found at Title 26 of the United States Code.

Answer (A) is incorrect. The Internal Revenue Code (IRC) of 1913 was the first IRC to implement a federal income tax and is superseded by the 1986 Code. **Answer (B) is incorrect.** Treasury Regulations are administrative pronouncements that interpret and illustrate the rules contained in the Internal Revenue Code. They are a secondary source of federal tax law. **Answer (D) is incorrect.** The Internal Revenue Bulletin is an instrument used to publish treasury decisions, executive orders, tax conventions, legislation, court decisions, and other items of general interest.

2. Which of the following are useful tools in determining Congressional intent behind certain tax laws and helping examiners apply the law properly?

A. Committee reports.

B. Treasury regulations.

C. Revenue rulings.

D. Revenue procedures.

Answer (A) is correct.

REQUIRED: The useful tools in determining Congressional intent.

DISCUSSION: Congressional Committee Reports reflect Congress's intent behind certain tax laws and help examiners apply the law properly.

Answer (B) is incorrect. Treasury regulations are prescribed by the Secretary of the Treasury. All regulations are written by the Office of the Chief Counsel, IRS, and approved by the Secretary of the Treasury. They are not the product of Congress. **Answer (C) is incorrect.** Revenue rulings are official interpretations of Internal Revenue law as applied to a given set of facts, and issued by the IRS. They are not the product of Congress. **Answer (D) is incorrect.** Revenue procedures are official IRS statements that prescribe procedures that affect the rights or duties of either a particular group of taxpayers or all taxpayers. They are not the product of Congress.

3. The current Internal Revenue Code is the

A. Internal Revenue Code of 2008.

B. Internal Revenue Code of 1986.

C. Internal Revenue Code of 1954.

D. Internal Revenue Code of 1939.

Answer (B) is correct.

REQUIRED: The current edition of the IRC.

DISCUSSION: The Tax Reform Act of 1986 represented the most extensive overhaul of the tax code in over 30 years, which led Congress to rename the code to the Internal Revenue Code of 1986.

Answer (A) is incorrect. There is no Internal Revenue Code of 2008. **Answer (C) is incorrect.** The Internal Revenue Code of 1954 was later superseded. **Answer (D) is incorrect.** The Internal Revenue Code of 1939 was later superseded.

4. In order to show that a tax preparer's application of tax law was in line with the intent of the tax law, the preparer should cite which of the following types of authoritative sources to make the most convincing case?

A. IRS publication.

B. Technical Advice Memorandum of another, similar case.

C. Committee report.

D. Delegation order.

Answer (C) is correct.

REQUIRED: The authoritative source for determining the intent behind certain tax law.

DISCUSSION: Congressional committee reports are useful tools in determining Congressional intent behind certain tax laws and helping examiners apply the law properly. The committee reports are a very high authority to which the courts are bound.

Answer (A) is incorrect. Publications do an excellent job of plainly explaining the law; however, they are not binding on the IRS or courts. **Answer (B) is incorrect.** TAMs are binding on the IRS only in relation to the taxpayer who is the subject of the ruling. **Answer (D) is incorrect.** Delegation orders are not authoritative sources for tax research. They simply delegate authority to perform tasks/make decisions to specified IRS employees.

6.2 Regulations, Rules, and Procedures (Administrative Law)

5. Which of the following is false with respect to classes of regulations?

A. Temporary regulations are issued to provide guidance for the public and IRS employees until final regulations are issued.

B. Public hearings are not held on temporary regulations unless written requests are made.

C. Proposed regulations have the same force and effect of law as temporary regulations.

D. Public hearings are held on proposed regulations if written requests are made.

Answer (C) is correct.

REQUIRED: The false statement regarding classes of regulations.

DISCUSSION: Although proposed regulations provide guidance for tax planning, taxpayers may not ordinarily rely on them to support a tax position. Courts have generally determined that proposed regulations are not entitled to judicial deference. Temporary regulations have the same force and effect of law as final regulations until they are superseded.

6. Which of the following statements with respect to regulations is false?

A. All regulations are written by the Office of the Chief Counsel, IRS, and approved by the Secretary of Treasury.

B. Public hearings are not held on temporary regulations without a written request.

C. Although IRS employees are bound by the regulations, the courts are not.

D. Public hearings are not held on proposed regulations.

Answer (D) is correct.

REQUIRED: The false statement regarding classes of regulations.

DISCUSSION: The purpose of proposed regulations is to give the public an opportunity to be heard before the regulations are promulgated in their final form. Public hearings are held if written requests for a hearing are made.

7. Which of the following statements with respect to revenue rulings and revenue procedures is false?

A. Revenue procedures are official statements of procedures that either affect the rights or duties of taxpayers or other members of the public or should be a matter of public knowledge.

B. The purpose of revenue rulings is to promote uniform application of the tax laws.

C. Taxpayers cannot appeal adverse return examination decisions based on revenue rulings and revenue procedures to the courts.

D. IRS employees must follow revenue rulings.

Answer (C) is correct.

REQUIRED: The false statement regarding revenue rulings and revenue procedures.

DISCUSSION: Revenue rulings and revenue procedures do not have the force and effect of regulations but are published to provide precedents to be used in the disposition of other cases. While taxpayers may rely on the rulings and procedures, they can also appeal adverse return examination decisions based on those rulings to the Tax Court or other federal courts.

8. Which of the following is NOT one of the three classes of Treasury Regulations?

A. Temporary.

B. Judicial.

C. Final.

D. Proposed.

Answer (B) is correct.

REQUIRED: The answer that is not a class of Treasury Regulations.

DISCUSSION: The three classes of Treasury Regulations are temporary, final, and proposed regulations. Judicial is not a class of Treasury Regulations.

9. Which of the following is NOT a type of administrative regulation?

A. Procedural.

B. Interpretive.

C. Legislative.

D. Executive.

Answer (D) is correct.

REQUIRED: The types of regulations.

DISCUSSION: Executive regulations are not a type of administrative rule or regulation.

Answer (A) is incorrect. Procedural rules govern the administrative agency's own conduct. **Answer (B) is incorrect.** Interpretive rules are statements by an agency that express the agency's understanding and interpretations of the statutes it administers. **Answer (C) is incorrect.** Legislative rules are those issued by an administrative agency under the authority delegated to it by Congress. These rules have the force of law and are binding on the agency, the courts, and the public.

10. Which of the following is an administrative authority of tax law?

A. Committee report.

B. Proposed regulation.

C. Tax treaty.

D. U.S. Tax Court.

Answer (B) is correct.

REQUIRED: The administrative authority of tax law.

DISCUSSION: Administrative authority is charged to the Treasury Department, which issues regulations as official interpretations of the IRC. Proposed regulations are the first classification of regulations. They are issued to elicit comments from the public. Public hearings are held if written requests are made. Proposed regulations might be used as somewhat of an authority for taking a tax position, but the regulations themselves do not state this and must be considered as a weak authority.

Answer (A) is incorrect. Committee reports are statutory authority. **Answer (C) is incorrect.** Tax treaties are statutory authority. **Answer (D) is incorrect.** U.S. Tax Courts are judicial authority.

11. Which of the following may be cited to sustain a position?

A. Private Letter Rulings.

B. Announcements.

C. Technical Advice Memoranda.

D. General Counsel Memoranda.

Answer (B) is correct.

REQUIRED: The precedential item.

DISCUSSION: Announcements are public pronouncements on matters of general interest, such as effective dates of temporary regulations, clarification of rulings, and form instructions. They are issued when guidance of a substantive or procedural nature is needed quickly. Announcements can be relied on to the same extent as revenue rulings and revenue procedures.

Answer (A) is incorrect. A Private Letter Ruling (PLR) represents the conclusion of the IRS for an individual taxpayer. **Answer (C) is incorrect.** Technical Advice Memoranda (TAMs) are binding on the IRS only in relation to the taxpayer who is the subject of the ruling. A TAM should not be applied or relied upon as a precedent in the disposition of other cases. **Answer (D) is incorrect.** Although General Counsel Memos (GCMs) contain legal analyses of substantive issues, they are not precedential guidance.

12. Which of the following is bound by Treasury Regulations?

A. U.S. Supreme Court.

B. U.S. Tax Court.

C. IRS Appeals Office.

D. U.S. District Court.

Answer (C) is correct.

REQUIRED: The institution bound by Treasury Regulations.

DISCUSSION: The IRS is bound by the regulations, whereas the courts are not.

Answer (A) is incorrect. The courts are not bound by Treasury Regulations. **Answer (B) is incorrect.** The courts are not bound by Treasury Regulations. **Answer (D) is incorrect.** The courts are not bound by Treasury Regulations.

6.3 The Court System (Judicial Law)

13. Which of the following statements best describes the applicability of a constitutionally valid Internal Revenue Code section on the various courts?

A. Only the Supreme Court is not bound to follow the Code section. All other courts are bound to the Code section.

B. Only the Tax Court is bound to the Code section. All other courts may waver from the Code section.

C. Only district, claims, and appellate courts are bound by the Code section. The Supreme and Tax Courts may waver from it.

D. All courts are bound by the Code section.

Answer (D) is correct.

REQUIRED: The statement that best describes the relationship between the Internal Revenue Code and the courts.

DISCUSSION: The Internal Revenue Code is the body of tax statutes enacted by Congress as the law of federal taxation. Because it is federal law, it is binding on all federal courts.

Answer (A) is incorrect. The Supreme Court is bound to a constitutionally valid Code section. **Answer (B) is incorrect.** No courts may waver from a constitutionally valid Code section. **Answer (C) is incorrect.** No courts may waver from a constitutionally valid Code section.

14. Which of the following statements is false?

A. The Tax Court will issue either a regular report or a memorandum decision depending upon the issues involved and the relative value of the decision being made.

B. The Commissioner of Internal Revenue may issue a public acquiescence or nonacquiescence on District Court or Court of Federal Claims cases.

C. Interpretative regulations are issued under the general authority of Internal Revenue Sec. 7805(a), and legislative regulations are issued under the authority of the specific Internal Revenue Code section to which they relate.

D. The government prints the regular and memorandum Tax Court decisions in bound volumes.

Answer (D) is correct.

REQUIRED: The false statement.

DISCUSSION: Only Tax Court regular decisions are printed by the government in bound volumes. A Tax Court memorandum decision is a report of a Tax Court decision thought to be of little value as a precedent because the issue has been decided one or more times before.

15. The Commissioner of Internal Revenue will NOT publicly announce acquiescence or nonacquiescence to the adverse regular decisions of which of the following courts?

A. United States Tax Court.

B. United States District Court.

C. United States Supreme Court.

D. United States Court of Federal Claims.

Answer (C) is correct.

REQUIRED: The court to whose adverse regular decisions the commissioner will not publicly announce acquiescence or nonacquiescence.

DISCUSSION: The commissioner may announce his or her acquiescence or nonacquiescence with regard to the regular, reported decisions of the courts other than the Supreme Court. Acquiescence is the commissioner's public endorsement of a court decision. In some cases, only specific issues are acquiesced, or the agreement may be in result only.

16. To research whether the Internal Revenue Service has announced an opinion on a Tax Court decision, refer to which of the following references for the original announcement?

A. Circular 230.

B. Federal Register.

C. Internal Revenue Bulletin.

D. Tax Court Reports.

Answer (C) is correct.

REQUIRED: The reference that contains the original announcement of an IRS opinion on a Tax Court decision.

DISCUSSION: The Internal Revenue Bulletin is published weekly and includes Treasury decisions, statutes, committee reports, U.S. Supreme Court decisions affecting the IRS, lists of the acquiescences and nonacquiescences of the IRS to decisions of the courts, and administrative rulings.

Answer (A) is incorrect. Circular 230 contains regulations governing practice before the IRS. It does not contain the original announcement of an IRS opinion on a Tax Court decision. **Answer (B) is incorrect.** The Federal Register publishes notices of proposed rulemaking. It does not contain the original announcement of an IRS opinion on a Tax Court decision. **Answer (D) is incorrect.** Tax Court Reports do not contain the original announcement of an IRS opinion on a Tax Court decision.

17. Decisions of which federal court require the IRS to alter its position for all taxpayers?

A. Tax Court.

B. District Court.

C. Circuit Court of Appeals.

D. Supreme Court.

Answer (D) is correct.

REQUIRED: The court that affects the IRS position for all taxpayers.

DISCUSSION: Decisions of the courts, other than the Supreme Court, are binding on the Commissioner only for the particular taxpayer and for the year litigated; thus, decisions of the lower courts do not require the IRS to alter its position for all taxpayers.

Answer (A) is incorrect. Decisions of the Tax Court only affect the IRS for the particular taxpayer and for the year litigated. **Answer (B) is incorrect.** Decisions of a district court only affect the IRS for the particular taxpayer and for the year litigated. **Answer (C) is incorrect.** Decisions of a circuit court of appeals only affect the IRS for the particular taxpayer and for the year litigated.

18. Which of the following is a list of courts that are referred to as courts of original jurisdiction, or trial courts, for tax matters?

A. The Tax Court, the U.S. District Courts, and the U.S. Court of Federal Claims.

B. The Tax Court, the U.S. District Courts, and the U.S. Supreme Court.

C. The Tax Court, the U.S. Court of Federal Claims, and the U.S. Court of Appeals.

D. The U.S. District Courts, the U.S. Court of Federal Claims, and the U.S. Court of Appeals.

Answer (A) is correct.

REQUIRED: The list of courts that are referred to as courts of original jurisdiction, or trial courts, for tax matters.

DISCUSSION: There are three levels of federal courts that hear tax cases: trial courts, appellate courts, and the high court. At the bottom of the hierarchy, there are several trial courts, including the Tax Court, the U.S. District Courts, and the U.S. Court of Federal Claims.

Answer (B) is incorrect. The U.S. Supreme Court is not a court of original jurisdiction in tax matters. **Answer (C) is incorrect.** The U.S. Court of Appeals is an appellate court, not a trial court. **Answer (D) is incorrect.** The U.S. Court of Appeals is an appellate court, not a trial court.

19. Which of the following statements is false with respect to court decisions?

A. Acquiescence by the Commissioner of Internal Revenue to regular Tax Court adverse decisions generally means that the IRS will follow the Tax Court decision in cases involving similar facts.

B. Petition to the Supreme Court to hear a case is by writ of certiorari, which is initially requested by the appealing party and is issued by the Supreme Court to the lower appellate court, requesting the record of a case for review.

C. A memorandum decision issued by the Tax Court is thought to be of little value as a precedent because the issue has been decided many times.

D. Dictum is the court's formal answer to the principal issue in litigation. It is legally binding and is enforceable by the authority of the courts.

Answer (D) is correct.

REQUIRED: The false statement regarding court decisions.

DISCUSSION: A dictum is a court's statement of opinion on a legal point not necessary for the decision of the case. Dictum is not controlling but may be persuasive to another court deciding the issue dealt with by the dictum.

20. Which of the following statements is true with respect to decisions by the Commissioner of the IRS on adverse regular decisions of the courts?

A. Acquiescence by the commissioner is intended as a substitute for a ruling or regulation program.

B. Acquiescence by the commissioner generally means that the IRS does not accept an adverse decision and will not follow it in cases on the same issue.

C. Acquiescence by the commissioner may not be subsequently revised by the commissioner.

D. Acquiescence by the commissioner generally means that the IRS will follow the court decision in cases involving similar facts.

Answer (D) is correct.

REQUIRED: The true statement with respect to decisions by the IRS Commissioner.

DISCUSSION: Acquiescence by the commissioner generally means that the IRS will follow the court decision in cases involving similar facts.

Answer (A) is incorrect. The acquiescence program is not intended as a substitute for a ruling or regulation program. However, acquiescence by the commissioner generally means that the IRS will follow the court decision in cases involving similar facts. **Answer (B) is incorrect.** Acquiescence by the commissioner generally means that the IRS will follow the court decision in cases involving similar facts. However, nonacquiescence by the commissioner generally means that the IRS does not accept an adverse decision and will not follow it in cases on the same issue. **Answer (C) is incorrect.** An acquiescence or a nonacquiescence may be subsequently revised by the commissioner. However, acquiescence by the commissioner generally means that the IRS will follow the court decision in cases involving similar facts.

21. Which of the following is a correct path for a tax case to reach the U.S. Supreme Court?

A. District Court, Court of Appeals for the Federal Circuit, Supreme Court.

B. Court of Federal Claims, Circuit Court of Appeals, Supreme Court.

C. Tax Court, Circuit Court of Appeals, Supreme Court.

D. District Court, Supreme Court.

Answer (C) is correct.

REQUIRED: The correct path, of those listed, for a tax case to reach the U.S. Supreme Court.

DISCUSSION: A case that first appears in a U.S. Tax or District Court may appeal to the U.S. Circuit Court of Appeals before reaching the U.S. Supreme Court. A case that first appears in a U.S. Court of Federal Claims may appeal to the U.S. Court of Appeals for the Federal Circuit before reaching the U.S. Supreme Court.

Answer (A) is incorrect. The Circuit Court of Appeals, not the Court of Appeals for the Federal Circuit, is the correct appellate court for a U.S. District Court case. **Answer (B) is incorrect.** The Court of Appeals for the Federal Circuit, not the Circuit Court of Appeals, is the correct appellate court for a claim out of a Court of Federal Claims. **Answer (D) is incorrect.** A U.S. District Court case must first appeal to the Circuit Court of Appeals before reaching the Supreme Court.

6.4 Tax Research

22. Which of the following is a primary tax source?

A. Tax services.

B. Newsletters.

C. Treaties.

D. Journals.

Answer (C) is correct.

REQUIRED: The primary tax source.

DISCUSSION: There are two classes of tax source materials: primary and secondary. Primary authorities consist of the law enacted by the legislature plus its official interpretation and indications of its meaning. Primary reference materials emanate from a branch of the government. Primary reference materials consist of the statutory law, administrative law, and judicial law. A tax treaty is an example of a primary authority.

23. Which of the following is NOT considered a primary authoritative source when conducting tax research?

A. Internal Revenue Code.

B. Tax Court cases.

C. IRS Publications.

D. Treasury Regulations.

Answer (C) is correct.

REQUIRED: The item not considered a primary authoritative source for tax matters.

DISCUSSION: IRS Publications are not binding on the IRS and do not necessarily cover all positions for a given issue. While a good source of general information, publications should not be cited to sustain a position. Therefore, IRS Publications are not considered a primary authoritative source.

Answer (A) is incorrect. The Internal Revenue Code is the primary source of federal tax law. It imposes income, estate, gift, employment, and miscellaneous excise taxes as well as provisions controlling the administration of federal taxation. **Answer (B) is incorrect.** Decisions of the Tax Court are binding on the Commissioner only for the particular taxpayer and for the year litigated; however, court cases are considered a primary authoritative source when conducting tax research. **Answer (D) is incorrect.** The Supreme Court has stated that "Treasury Regulations must be sustained unless unreasonable and plainly inconsistent with the revenue statutes." Therefore, Treasury Regulations are considered a primary authoritative source when conducting tax research.

STUDY UNIT SEVEN

RECORDKEEPING AND ELECTRONIC FILING

(18 pages of outline)

This study unit covers the topics of recordkeeping and electronic filing. The IRS has strict guidelines involving the type of records to be retained and the length of time that individuals and employers should retain certain records. The records are used to show proof of transactions in case of an IRS examination. Electronic filing is a method of filing a tax return. It involves far less paperwork and increases the speed and efficiency of the processing of a return.

7.1 RECORDKEEPING

Sufficient Records

1. Taxpayers must keep permanent books of account or records that are sufficient to support items shown on a return.
   a. The IRS recommends that taxpayers keep all sales slips, invoices, receipts, canceled checks, or other financial account statements relating to a particular transaction.
   b. A taxpayer may replace hard copies of books and records with electronic documents, provided the system is in compliance with IRS requirements.
   c. If a taxpayer cannot produce documents because of reasons beyond the taxpayer's control, the taxpayer may still reconstruct their records to prove a deduction.

Availability of Records

2. The records must be kept available at all times for inspection by IRS officers and designated employees and must be retained as long as they may be material. Since the IRS generally has 3 years from the date a return was due (or filed, if later) or 2 years from the date the tax was paid, whichever is later, to assess tax, a taxpayer must retain all records and forms until the later time.
   a. If the taxpayer does not report income that should be reported and it is more than 25% of the gross income on the return, the statute of limitations is 6 years.
   b. If the taxpayer overstates the basis of an asset by an amount that is more than 25% of the gross income on the return, the statute of limitations is 6 years.
   c. If the taxpayer files a fraudulent return, there is no statute of limitations on that return.
   d. If the taxpayer does not file a return, there is no statute of limitations on that return.
   e. If the taxpayer files for a credit or refund after a return is filed, the statute of limitations is the later of 3 years from the date the return was filed or 2 years after the tax was paid.
   f. If the taxpayer files a claim for a loss from worthless securities, the statute of limitations is 7 years.

Basis of Property

3. Records relating to the basis of property should be retained as long as they may be material.
   a. The basis of property is material until the statute of limitations expires for the year the property is sold.

Employment Taxes and Withholding

4. A person required to keep records relating to employment taxes and federal withholding taxes must keep them in a convenient and safe location accessible to the IRS, if requested.
   a. The records must be maintained for at least 4 years after the due date of the tax or the date such tax was paid, whichever is later.
   b. An employer required to withhold income tax on wages must keep records of all employee compensation. Specific records required to be kept for income tax withholding include
      1) The name, address, and Social Security number of the employee;
      2) The total amount and date of each payment of remuneration and the period of services covered by such payment;
      3) The amount of such remuneration payment that constitutes wages subject to withholding;
      4) The amount of tax collected with respect to such remuneration payment and, if collected at a time other than the time such payment was made, the date collected;
      5) The fair market value and date of each payment of noncash compensation made to a retail commission salesperson if no income tax was withheld;
      6) For health and accident plans, information about the amount of each payment;
      7) The withholding exemption certificate (Form W-4) filed with the employer by the employee; and,
      8) In the case of tips, copies of any statement furnished by the employee unless the information disclosed by such statements is recorded on another document retained by the employer.
   c. Employees are not required to keep additional records relating to employment taxes and withholding of income tax.

Business Travel and Meals

5. Taxpayers are required to substantiate business deductions for travel and deductible meals expenses.
   a. Substantiation of amount, time, place, business relationship, attendees, and business purpose is generally required.
      1) Documentary evidence is not required for expenses (other than lodging) that are less than $75.
   b. Business related expense reimbursements are treated as paid under an **accountable plan**. To be an accountable plan, the reimbursement agreement must take place within a reasonable time period. The rules for a reasonable time period are as follows:
      1) The advance is received within 30 days of the time the expense was incurred.
      2) Expenses are adequately accounted for within 60 days after paid or incurred.
      3) Excess reimbursement is returned within 120 days after the expense was paid or incurred.

Charitable Contributions

6. For cash contributions less than $250, a canceled check, bank/credit union/credit card statement, or receipt letter/other written communication from the donee is sufficient and permissible documentation.
   a. The documentation must show the name of the donee, date contributed, and amount contributed. In determining whether a contribution is $250 or more, do not combine separate contributions.
   b. Contributions of $250 or more require acknowledgment from the donee (i.e., a canceled check is insufficient).

Employers

7. Section 6060 states that a person who employs one or more income tax return preparers must make a return setting forth the name, identifying number, and place of work of each preparer and keep the records for up to 3 years.

Refusal to Submit Records/Information

8. No practitioner shall neglect or refuse to promptly submit records or information in any matter before the IRS upon proper and lawful request by an authorized IRS employee.
   a. A request can be refused if the tax preparer believes in good faith and on reasonable grounds that such record or information is privileged or that the request is of doubtful legality.
   b. Section 7525 states that the taxpayer has a privilege of confidentiality with his or her federally authorized tax preparer with regards to tax advice.
      1) This privilege can only be asserted in noncriminal hearings.
      2) This privilege does not apply to the determination of an item on an original income tax return or to any tax shelters.

Transcripts

9. A tax return preparer can obtain printouts of a taxpayer's account from the IRS.
10. Transcripts available from the IRS include the following:

Return Transcript

   a. A return transcript includes most of the line items of a tax return as filed with the IRS but is not a copy of the return. Transcripts are only available for the following returns: Form 1040 series, Form 1065, Form 1120, Form 1120-A, Form 1120-H, Form 1120-L, and Form 1120-S.

Account Transcript

   b. An account transcript contains information on the financial status of the account, such as payments made on the account, penalty assessments, and adjustments made by the taxpayer or the IRS after the return was filed.
      1) Return information is limited to such items as tax liability and estimated tax payments.
      2) Account transcripts are available for most returns.

Record of Account Transcript

c. A record of account transcript provides the most detailed information because it is a combination of the return transcript and the account transcript. It is available for the current year and 3 prior tax years.

Wage and Income Transcript

d. The IRS can provide a transcript that includes data from information returns such as Form W-2, Form 1099 series, Form 1098 series, or Form 5498 series.

1) State or local information is not included with the Form W-2 information.
2) The IRS may be able to provide this transcript information for up to 10 years.
3) Information for the current year may not be complete until July.

a) For example, W-2 information for 2021, filed in 2022, will generally not be available from the IRS until after July 2022.

Requesting Transcripts

e. e-Services is a suite of web-based tools that allows eligible individuals to complete transactions online with the IRS.

1) The tools include (a) Registration Services, (b) e-file Application, (c) Transcript Delivery System (TDS), and (d) Taxpayer Identification Number (TIN) Matching.
2) e-Services users must gain access via a two-factor authentication process (Secure Access).

f. The TDS is an e-service that assists tax practitioners working with the IRS on behalf of clients.

g. Tax practitioners can request transcripts of their clients' tax records and receive them within minutes using a secure online tool delivered through the IRS Business Systems Modernization program.

1) Paper requests for the same information can take days or weeks to complete.

h. Tax practitioners use transcripts when representing their clients before the IRS.

1) Transcripts are printouts of a taxpayer's account that show actions taken by the IRS or the taxpayer and any tax, penalties, or interest assessed.
2) Tax returns can also be printed as transcripts to show most of the numbers reported on the return and those from accompanying schedules or forms.
3) In many cases, transcripts are used instead of making copies of tax returns.

11. **Documentation**

a. Supporting tax documentation, such as receipts, W-2s, 1099s, canceled checks, and credit card statements, can generally be discarded 3 years after the return's due date. The 3-year retention rule applies to all documentation discussed in this subsection.

1) In some special circumstances, however, the taxpayer may need to hold on to tax documentation longer.

a) The IRS has 6 years, for example, to challenge a return if the taxpayer is suspected of underreporting income by 25% or more.
b) Copies of actual tax returns should be kept permanently.

b. Legal documents (e.g., birth certificates, divorce decrees, lawsuit settlements).

1) Proof of a live birth must be supported by an official document, such as a birth certificate.

2) Documentation requirements for proof of foreign status and for identification include a passport; U.S. Citizenship and Immigration Services (USCIS) photo identification; visa issued by the U.S. Department of State; U.S. driver's license; U.S. military identification card; foreign driver's license; foreign military identification card; national identification card (must be current and contain name, photograph, address, date of birth, and expiration date); U.S. state identification card; foreign voter's registration card; civil birth certificate; medical records (only for dependents under 6 years of age); school records (only valid for dependents under 18 years of age).

3) Reviews by the IRS of lawsuit settlements.

a) Information requested from the company paying the settlement:

i) Plaintiff's address, phone number, and Social Security number;

ii) Copies of the complaints, the settlement agreements, and/or waivers;

iii) The front and back of the checks; and

iv) Copies of any records documenting correspondence between the company and the plaintiffs with respect to negotiations affecting the outcome of the cases.

b) Information document request: Prior-year tax returns; original petition or claim filed; lawsuit settlement agreement; settlement checks or schedule of payments received; documentation of legal fees paid; disbursement schedule; and documentation from attorney indicating proceeds were not taxable.

4) Divorce decrees are needed for verification of support, alimony payments, filing status, etc.

Prior and Subsequent Tax Returns

c. General information includes employer or taxpayer addresses, identification numbers, birth dates, and names. This information can be used for subsequent return preparation. Use of prior-year information can allow for faster and more accurate preparation.

1) If an IRS agent is examining a tax return and determines that the taxpayer has deducted unallowable items as business expenses, (s)he will generally inspect prior years' returns to determine if the taxpayer has claimed the same types of expenses.

a) If the expenses are claimed and the amounts are material, the IRS agent has the authority to examine these returns for the purpose of making an adjustment.

Document Requirements for Tax Return Purposes

d. An income tax return preparer must furnish a completed copy of any tax return or refund claim that (s)he prepares for the taxpayer either before or at the same time as (s)he presents the return or claim to him or her for signing.

1) The preparer or the employer of the preparer must retain a completed copy of the return for a 3-year period.

Business Entity Supporting Documents

e. **Articles of incorporation** (sometimes referred to as a "charter") are formation documents and are filed with a government authority to legally document the creation of a corporation. The articles contain information that includes but is not limited to

1) Corporation name
2) Principal office and mailing address
3) Registered agent
4) Directors and officers
5) Authorized shares including class and par value

f. **Corporate bylaws**, generally, are created subsequent to filing articles of incorporation; however, it is not uncommon to find them within the articles. Bylaws stipulate a corporation's rules, how it will operate, and the responsibilities of the people who own and manage it.

g. A **partnership agreement** is a contract between two or more business partners that is used to stipulate the responsibilities and interest for each partner. Usually, the agreement includes rules for items such as

1) Capital contributed by each partner
2) Profit and loss distribution of each partner
3) Salaries and draws
4) Authority and decision-making powers
5) Admission and withdrawal of partners

NOTE: Items listed in e. through g. above represent examples of business entity supporting documents and are not an all-inclusive list.

Freedom of Information Act

12. All IRS records are subject to Freedom of Information Act (FOIA) requests.

a. However, FOIA does not require the IRS to release all documents that are subject to FOIA requests.

1) The IRS may withhold information pursuant to nine exemptions and three exclusions contained in the FOIA statute.

2) Documents must be made available electronically.

3) The IRS maintains two reading rooms:

a) The physical IRS Freedom of Information Reading Room is in Room 1621 of the IRS Headquarters building at 1111 Constitution Avenue NW in Washington, DC 20224.

b) The online Electronic Reading Room is located at www.irs.gov/privacy-disclosure/foia-library.

Identity Protection Personal Identification Number (IP PIN)

13. The IRS IP PIN is a 6-digit number assigned to eligible taxpayers to help prevent the misuse of their Social Security numbers on fraudulent federal income tax returns. The IP PIN helps the IRS verify a taxpayer's identity and accept his or her electronic or paper tax return.
    a. If a return is e-filed with the taxpayer's SSN and an incorrect or missing IP PIN, the IRS system will reject it until the return is submitted with the correct IP PIN or filed on paper. If the same conditions occur on a paper-filed return, the IRS will delay its processing and any refund that may be due for taxpayer protection while the IRS determines if the return is the taxpayer's.
    b. The Internal Revenue Service is expanding the Identity Protection PIN Opt-In Program to all taxpayers who can verify their identities. The Identity Protection PIN (IP PIN) is a six-digit code known only to the taxpayer and to the IRS. It helps prevent identity thieves from filing fraudulent tax returns using a taxpayer's personally identifiable information. Electronic returns that do not contain the correct IP PIN will be rejected, and paper returns will go through additional scrutiny for fraud. Taxpayers who want an IP PIN for 2021 should go to IRS.gov/IPPIN and use the Get an IP PIN tool. This online process will require taxpayers to verify their identities using the Secure Access authentication process if they do not already have an IRS account. An IP PIN is valid for one calendar year. A new IP PIN is generated each year for your account.

STOP AND REVIEW! **You have completed the outline for this subunit. Study multiple-choice questions 1 through 10 beginning on page 168.**

7.2 ELECTRONIC FILING

1. Tax return preparers who prepare income tax returns for individuals, trusts, and estates, such as Forms 1040 and 1041, and who reasonably expect to file 11 or more of these income tax returns in a calendar year are specified tax return preparers required to file these returns electronically.
   a. Tax return preparers who are members of a firm are specified tax return preparers and must electronically file the income tax returns they prepare and file if the firm's preparers, in the aggregate, expect to file 11 or more of these income tax returns in a calendar year.
   b. The e-file requirement does not apply to an individual income tax return when a tax return preparer's client chooses to have the return completed in paper format and the client, not the preparer, will file the paper return with the IRS.
      1) Preparers should document the client's choice to file in paper format and keep a signed copy on file. This documentation is completed by filing Form 8948 with the paper return.
2. Corporations with $10 million or more in total assets and that file 250 or more returns a year are required to file electronically.
3. Partnerships with more than 100 partners (Schedule K-1) are required to file their returns electronically.

E-File Provider

4. IRS e-file providers electronically file taxpayers' returns, including business, individual, and information returns.
   a. An authorized provider is a business or organization authorized by the IRS to participate in IRS e-file.
   b. A provider may be a sole proprietorship, partnership, corporation, or other entity.
5. Providers are described below and on the following pages. (Roles are not mutually exclusive.)

Electronic Return Originator (ERO)

   a. An ERO originates the electronic submission of tax returns to the IRS. The ERO is usually the first point of contact for most taxpayers filing a return using IRS e-file.
      1) Although an ERO also may engage in return preparation, that activity is separate and different from the origination of the electronic submission of the return to the IRS.
         a) After the taxpayer authorizes the filing of the return, an ERO originates the electronic submission of a return via IRS e-file.
         b) An ERO must originate the electronic submission only of returns that the ERO either prepared or collected from a taxpayer.

2) In originating the electronic submission of a return, the ERO has a variety of responsibilities, including, but not limited to,
    a) Timely originating the electronic submission of returns,
    b) Submitting any required supporting paper documents to the IRS,
    c) Providing copies to taxpayers,
    d) Retaining records and making records available to the IRS,
    e) Accepting returns only from taxpayers and authorized IRS e-file providers, and
    f) Having only one Electronic Filing Identification Number (EFIN) for the same firm for use at one location, unless the IRS issued more than one EFIN to the firm for the same location.
        i) For this purpose, the business entity is generally the entity that reports on its return the income derived from electronic filing.
        ii) The IRS may issue more than one EFIN to accommodate a high volume of returns or as it determines appropriate.

Intermediate Service Provider

b. An intermediate service provider assists with processing return information between the ERO (or from a taxpayer who files electronically using a personal computer, modem, and commercial tax preparation software) and a transmitter. An intermediate service provider's responsibilities include, but are not limited to,
    1) Including its EFIN and the ERO's EFIN with all return information it forwards to a transmitter;
    2) Serving as a contact point between its client EROs and the IRS, if requested;
    3) Providing the IRS with a list of each client ERO, if requested; and
    4) Adhering to all applicable rules that apply to transmitters.

Reporting Agent

c. A reporting agent originates the electronic submission of certain returns for its clients and/or transmits the returns to the IRS.
    1) A reporting agent must be an accounting service, franchiser, bank, or other person who complies with Rev. Proc. 2012-32.
    2) Form 8655, *Reporting Agent Authorization*, must be submitted before applying for e-file.

Software Developer

d. An e-file software developer creates software for the purposes of formatting electronic return information according to the IRS e-file specifications and/or transmitting electronic return information directly to the IRS.
    1) Software developers must pass what is referred to as either acceptance or assurance testing.
    2) A software developer's responsibilities include, but are not limited to,
        a) Promptly correcting any software error causing returns to reject and distributing the correction,
        b) Ensuring its software creates accurate returns, and
        c) Adhering to specifications published by the IRS.

Transmitter

e. A transmitter transmits electronic tax return information directly to the IRS. A bump-up service provider that increases the transmission rate or line speed of formatted or reformatted information sent to the IRS via a public switched telephone network is also a transmitter.

1) Prior to transmitting, testing to ensure the compatibility of the provider's system with that of the IRS must be completed. Transmitter responsibilities include, but are not limited to,

a) Ensuring EFINs of authorized e-file providers are included as required by IRS e-file specifications in the electronic return record of returns it transmits;

b) Timely transmitting returns to the IRS, retrieving acknowledgment files, and sending the acknowledgment file information to the ERO, intermediate service provider, or taxpayer (for Online Filing); and

c) Promptly correcting any transmission error that causes an electronic transmission to be rejected.

Online Provider

6. An online provider allows taxpayers to self-prepare returns by entering return data directly on commercially available software, software downloaded from an Internet site and prepared offline, or an online Internet site. An online provider also chooses another provider option (software developer, transmitter, or intermediate service provider) if being an online provider is a secondary activity.

a. Although an ERO also may use an Internet site to obtain information from taxpayers to subsequently originate the electronic submission of returns, the ERO is not an online provider.

b. The IRS has instructed online providers to use the following six security, privacy, and business standards:

1) Extended validation secure socket layer (SSL) certificate
2) External vulnerability scan
3) Information privacy and safeguard policies
4) Protection against bulk filing of fraudulent income tax returns
5) Public domain name registration
6) Reporting of security incidents

c. EROs, intermediate service providers, and online-provider transmitters must clearly display the firm's "doing business as" name at all locations and sites, including websites at which information from the taxpayers is obtained for electronic origination of returns by the ERO.

ACA (Affordable Care Act) Provider

7. An ACA provider is an organization engaged in manufacturing or importing branded prescription drugs sold to specified government programs ("covered entity"), a health insurance provider reporting net premiums written ("covered entity") that originates the electronic submission of its own information report(s), or a third party that will transmit report(s) on behalf of a covered entity.

E-File Provider Requirements

8. To become an IRS e-file provider, an applicant must (a) create an IRS e-Services account (i.e., Secure Access account), (b) submit an e-file application, and (c) pass a suitability check.
   a. An e-Services account facilitates electronic interaction with the IRS. When creating an e-Services account, the applicant must
      1) Provide the applicant's legal name, Social Security number, birth date, phone number, e-mail address, and home mailing address;
      2) Provide the applicant's adjusted gross income from the current or prior tax year;
      3) Create a username, a password, a PIN, and an answer to a reminder question for the username;
      4) Ensure every principal and responsible official in the applicant's firm signs up for e-Services; and
      5) Return to e-Services to confirm registration within 30 days of receipt of the confirmation code in the mail.
   b. Publication 1345, *Handbook for Authorized IRS e-file Providers of Individual Returns*, provides rules and requirements for participation in IRS e-file. Violation of a provision of this publication may subject an e-file provider to sanctions.
9. Each provider (principal or responsible official) must
   a. Be a U.S. citizen or an alien lawfully admitted for permanent residence,
   b. Be 18 years old as of the date of application,
   c. Meet applicable state and local licensing and/or bonding requirements for the preparation and collection of tax returns, and
   d. Submit fingerprints unless the individual provides evidence that (s)he is one of the following:
      1) Attorney
      2) Certified Public Accountant
      3) Enrolled Agent
      4) Officer of a publicly held corporation
      5) Banking official, bonded and fingerprinted within the last 2 years
10. The IRS will conduct a suitability check on the firm and each person listed on the application as a principal or responsible official.
    a. Suitability checks may include the following:
       1) A criminal background check
       2) A credit history check
       3) A tax compliance check to ensure that all required returns are filed and paid, and to identify assessed fraud penalties
       4) A check for prior noncompliance with IRS e-file requirements
    b. The IRS does not complete suitability checks on applicants only applying to be software developers.
    c. It can take the IRS 45 days to process the application and complete the suitability check.

11. The IRS assigns Electronic Filing Identification Numbers (EFINs) to all providers and assigns Electronic Transmission Identification Numbers (ETINs) to transmitters, software providers, and online providers.
12. Changes in situation that require revision of the IRS e-file application are as follows:
    a. A provider functioning solely as a software developer or reporting agent intends to do business as an ERO, intermediate service provider, or transmitter.
    b. An additional principal or responsible official (e.g., partner) of a firm needs to be added.
    c. A principal or responsible official changes.
    d. A principal or responsible official is being deleted.

    Providers must update their application information within 30 days of the date of any changes to the information on their current application.
13. Situations that require submission of a new IRS e-file application include but are not limited to the following:
    a. The provider wants to acquire a foreign EFIN.
    b. The provider acquires an existing IRS e-file business by purchase, transfer, or gift. The provider may not use the EFIN, other identification numbers, or passwords of the previous provider.
14. Providers must have security systems in place to prevent unauthorized access to taxpayer accounts and personal information.
    a. IRS Publication 4557 contains information to assist businesses and individuals with safeguarding taxpayer information.
    b. Providers must implement security and privacy practices that are appropriate for the size, complexity, nature, and scope of their business activities.
    c. Providers must register with the IRS all Internet websites from which information is collected from taxpayers (directly and indirectly) and used by the provider for federal returns that are filed electronically.

Form 8879

d. Form 8879, *IRS e-file Signature Authorization*, is the declaration document and signature authorization for a return e-filed by an ERO. This form is completed when the practitioner PIN method is used or when the taxpayer authorizes the ERO to enter or generate the taxpayer's PIN on the e-filed individual income tax return.
    1) The practitioner PIN method is an electronic signature option for taxpayers who use an ERO to e-file. The taxpayer creates a 5-digit PIN to use as the signature on the e-filed return.
        a) Form 8879 is not sent to the IRS unless requested.
        b) The completed form is retained for 3 years from the return due date or IRS received date, whichever is later.
        c) The form may be retained electronically.
    2) Taxpayers must sign Form 8879 by handwritten signature or electronic signature if supported by computer software.

Form 8453

e. Certain documentation is required to be mailed to the IRS. Form 8453, *U.S. Individual Income Tax Transmittal for an IRS e-file Return*, must accompany specific documentation mailed to the IRS.

1) If the taxpayer is required to mail any documentation not listed on Form 8453, the taxpayer cannot file the tax return electronically.

2) The ERO must mail Form 8453 to the IRS within 3 business days after receiving acknowledgment that the IRS has accepted the electronically filed tax return.

3) The forms and supporting documentation requiring Form 8453 are

a) Form 1098-C, *Contributions of Motor Vehicles, Boats, and Airplanes* (or equivalent contemporaneous written acknowledgment)

b) Form 2848, *Power of Attorney and Declaration of Representative* (or POA that states the agent is granted authority to sign the return)

c) Form 3115, *Application for Change in Accounting Method*

d) Form 3468, *Investment Credit* (attach copies of documentation related to proof of certified historic structures)

e) Form 4136, *Credit for Federal Tax Paid on Fuels* (attach certificate for biodiesel and other applicable statements/certificates)

f) Form 5713, *International Boycott Report*

g) Form 8283, *Noncash Charitable Contributions*, Section A or B, and any related attachments

h) Form 8332, *Release/Revocation of Release of Claim to Exemption for Child by Custodial Parent* (or certain pages from a divorce decree or separation agreement)

i) Form 8858, *Information Return of U.S. Persons With Respect to Foreign Disregarded Entities*

j) Form 8864, *Biodiesel and Renewable Diesel Fuels Credit* (attach the Certificate for Biodiesel and Statement of Biodiesel Reseller)

k) Form 8885, *Health Coverage Tax Credit*, and all required attachments

l) Form 8949, *Sales and Other Dispositions of Capital Assets*, or a statement with the same information, if electing not to report transactions electronically on Form 8949

f. IRS e-file returns have the same reporting requirements as paper returns.

1) A provider must retain a copy of any Form 8453 until the end of the calendar year (Publication 1345).

g. A taxpayer filing electronically may pay by electronic funds withdrawal, credit or debit card, check, money order, or electronic payment made by phone or online. Finally, taxpayers may request an installment agreement to pay their tax.

15. Filing individual income tax returns using IRS e-file is limited to tax returns with prescribed due dates in the current and 2 previous tax years, e.g., 2021 (current year), 2020 (1st prior year), and 2019 (2nd prior year).

a. The following returns are not processable by the IRS e-file program:

1) Tax returns with fiscal-year tax periods
2) Returns containing forms or schedules that cannot be processed by IRS e-file

Fees

16. If an ERO charges a fee for transmission of the electronic portion of a tax return, the fee may not be based on the time required to prepare the return, a percentage of the refund amount, or any other amount from the tax return (a contingent fee). An authorized ERO may not charge a separate fee for direct deposits.

Refund Options

17. EROs must advise taxpayers of the option to receive their refunds via either paper check or direct deposit.
    a. EROs must accept any direct deposit election to any eligible financial institution designated by the taxpayer and may not charge an additional fee for doing so.
    b. Direct deposits may be deposited into any qualified account, including checking, savings, share draft, IRA, or consumer asset accounts.
        1) The provider should caution the taxpayer that not all financial institutions will allow joint refunds into individual accounts.

Records

18. An ERO who is the paid preparer of an electronic tax return must also retain for the prescribed amount of time the materials described in Reg. 1.6107-1(b) that are required to be kept by an income tax return preparer.

Rejection of Return

19. If the IRS rejects the electronic portion of a taxpayer's return and the reason for the rejection cannot be rectified by the actions described in Rev. Proc. 98-50, the ERO must take reasonable steps to inform the taxpayer that the taxpayer's return has not been filed within 24 hours of receiving the rejection.
    a. When the ERO advises the taxpayer that the taxpayer's return has not been filed, the ERO must provide the taxpayer with
        1) The reject code(s),
        2) An explanation of the reject code(s), and
        3) The sequence number of each reject code.
    b. Rejected electronic return data can be corrected and retransmitted without new signatures or authorizations if changes are not more than $50 to "Total income" or "AGI" or more than $14 to "Total tax," "Federal income tax withheld," "Refund," or "Amount you owe." Taxpayers must be given paper copies of the new electronic return data.

Refund Anticipation Loan

20. A refund anticipation loan (RAL) is money borrowed by the taxpayer based on the taxpayer's anticipated income tax refund.
    a. A RAL is a contract between the taxpayer and the lender.
        1) The IRS has no involvement in RALs.
    b. All parties to the RAL must ensure the taxpayer understands that a RAL is not a substitute for a faster return.
    c. Any interest accrued as a result of a delay in the return of a refund is not the responsibility of the IRS since the IRS is not involved.
    d. An ERO may assist a taxpayer in applying for a RAL and may charge a flat fee for doing so.
        1) The fee must be identical for all of the ERO's customers and must not be related to the amount of the refund or RAL.
    e. An ERO that is also the return preparer and the financial institution that makes a RAL may not be related taxpayers.
    f. An authorized IRS e-file provider, who is also the return preparer, and the financial institution that makes a RAL may not be related taxpayers within the meaning of Sec. 267 or Sec. 707.
21. **Advertising Standards**
    a. A provider must comply with the advertising and solicitation provisions of Circular 230.
        1) This circular prohibits the use or participation in the use of any form of public communication containing a false, fraudulent, misleading, deceptive, unduly influencing, coercive, or unfair statement or claim.
        2) Any claims concerning faster refunds by virtue of electronic filing must be consistent with the language in official IRS publications.
    b. A provider must adhere to all relevant federal, state, and local consumer protection laws that relate to advertising and soliciting.
    c. A provider must not use "Internal Revenue Service" or "IRS" within a firm's name.
        1) However, once accepted to participate in IRS e-file, a participant may represent itself as an "Authorized IRS e-file Provider."
    d. Advertising for a cooperative electronic return filing project must clearly state the names of all cooperating parties.
    e. If a provider uses radio, television, Internet, signage, or other methods of communication to advertise IRS e-file, the provider must keep a copy and provide it to the IRS upon request, the text or, if prerecorded, the recorded advertisement.
        1) According to Sec. 10.30 of Circular 230, the provider must keep a copy of the advertisement for a period of at least 36 months from the date of the last transmission or use.
        2) Publication 3112 states that providers must retain copies until the end of the calendar year following the last transmission or use.

f. If a provider uses direct mail, e-mail, fax communications, or other distribution methods to advertise, the provider must retain a copy, as well as a list or other description of the firms, organizations, or individuals to whom the communication was sent.

1) According to Sec. 10.30 of Circular 230, the provider must keep a copy of the advertisement for a period of at least 36 months from the date of the last transmission or use.

2) Publication 3112 states that providers must retain the records until the end of the calendar year following the date sent and provide the records to the IRS upon request.

g. The IRS does not have a copyright for the IRS e-file logo. Use of the logo only indicates that a provider offers this service to taxpayers or has performed it on behalf of a taxpayer.

1) The logo must not be used to portray any other relationship between the IRS and any provider.

Business Taxpayers

22. For purposes of electronic filing, the IRS defines a **Large Taxpayer** as a business or other entity (excluding partnerships) with total assets of $10 million or more or a partnership with more than 100 partners (asset criteria does not apply to partnerships) that originates the electronic submission of its own return(s).

a. A Large Taxpayer may choose to electronically file its own **corporate return** or use an authorized IRS e-file provider.

b. Business taxpayers that do not meet the Large Taxpayer criteria must use an authorized IRS e-file provider.

c. A business or individual that has more than 250 information returns (including but not limited to various 1099s and W-2s) to file must do so electronically. The 250-or-more requirement applies separately to each type of form.

Electronic Payments

23. The Electronic Federal Tax Payment System (EFTPS) may be used to make electronic tax payments.

a. Individual taxpayers may enroll in EFTPS by phone or online.

1) Business taxpayers may use EFTPS directly or use a financial institution.

2) Access to EFTPS is via a taxpayer's Social Security number or other Taxpayer Identification Number, personal identification number (PIN) assigned upon enrollment, and an Internet password.

b. After a taxpayer has enrolled in EFTPS, (s)he may transfer funds from his or her personal accounts directly to the IRS.

1) When the taxpayer's information is accepted, the EFTPS system will provide the taxpayer with an Electronic Funds Transfer (EFT) Acknowledgment Number, which serves as a record of payment.

c. Transfers must be scheduled at least 1 day in advance of the tax due date.

d. EFTPS allows individual taxpayers to schedule payments up to a year in advance. Certain business taxpayers may schedule payments up to 120 days in advance.

e. EFTPS Direct vs. EFTPS via Financial Institution.

1) EFTPS-Direct: Similar to individual EFTPS. Taxpayers may pay taxes using a telephone, online, or with the IRS's PC software up to 1 day before the date the tax is due.

2) EFTPS-Through a Financial Institution: Taxpayers may pay taxes using the services of a financial institution. Taxpayers must initiate payment before the financial institution's processing deadline so that the financial institution can initiate the transfer up to 1 day before the tax is due.

3) Same-Day Payment: A service offered by some financial institutions, allowing taxpayers to pay taxes on the same day the taxes are due.

f. All taxpayers using EFTPS are responsible for ensuring that the tax payment is timely made, recording the EFTPS Acknowledgment Number, and making sure the account contains sufficient funds to cover the payment.

Sanctions

24. The IRS may impose a sanction on an electronic return originator for various infractions. These sanctions range from a written reprimand to expulsion. Sanctions are ranked on levels one through three. The IRS reserves the right to select the sanction it wishes to impose.

a. **Level one** infractions are violations that have **little or no adverse impact** on the quality of electronically filed returns or on IRS e-file.

1) A level one infraction may result in a written reprimand.

b. **Level two** infractions that have an **adverse impact** upon the quality of electronically filed returns or on IRS e-file may result in a restriction in participation in the IRS e-file Program or a 1-year suspension beginning with the effective date of suspension.

1) Level two infractions include continued level one infractions after the IRS has brought the level one infraction to the attention of the provider.

c. **Level three** infractions are violations that have a **significant adverse** impact on the quality of electronically filed returns or on IRS e-file.

1) Level three infractions include continued level two infractions after the IRS has brought the level two infraction to the attention of the provider.

2) A level three infraction may result in suspension from participation in IRS e-file for 2 years beginning with the effective date of the suspension year.

3) Depending on the severity of the infraction, such as identity theft, fraud, or criminal conduct, the infraction may result in expulsion without the opportunity for future participation.

4) The IRS reserves the right to suspend or expel a provider prior to administrative review for level three infractions.

Administrative Review

25. Most denied applicants and sanctioned providers are entitled to an administrative review. The administrative review is usually a two-step process.
    a. The denied applicant or sanctioned provider requests administrative review by the office that denied or sanctioned it.
    b. If the reviewing office affirms the denial or the sanction, the applicant or provider may request an appeal to the IRS appeals office unless the sanction was a written reprimand (i.e., level one).
        1) Failure to respond within 30 calendar days of the date of any denial letter or sanction letter irrevocably terminates an applicant's or provider's right to an administrative review or appeal.

EFIN Revocation

26. The IRS may revoke participation of an authorized IRS e-file provider, a principal, or a responsible official in IRS e-file if either (a) a federal court order enjoins the participant from filing returns or (b) the participant is prohibited by a federal or state legal action that would prohibit participation in e-file.
    a. Revoked providers are not entitled to an administrative review process for revocation of participation in IRS e-file if the IRS denies or revokes a firm, principal, or responsible official because of a federal court order enjoining filing of returns or a federal or state legal action that prohibits participation in filing of returns. If the injunction or other legal action expires or is reversed, the revoked provider may reapply to participate in IRS e-file after the injunction or other legal action expires or is reversed.

***STOP AND REVIEW!* You have completed the outline for this subunit. Study multiple-choice questions 11 through 25 beginning on page 172.**

QUESTIONS

7.1 Recordkeeping

1. Employers are required to keep records on employment taxes (income tax withholding, Social Security, Medicare, and federal unemployment tax) for

A. An indefinite time.

B. The statutory period for assessment of the employees' taxes.

C. At least 4 years after the date the tax becomes due or is paid, whichever is later.

D. At least 3 years after the due date of the return or 2 years after the date the tax was paid, whichever is later.

Answer (C) is correct.

REQUIRED: The length of time employers are required to keep employment tax records.

DISCUSSION: A person required to keep records relating to employment taxes and the collection of income tax must keep them at a convenient and safe location accessible to the IRS and available for inspection at all times. The records must be maintained for at least 4 years after the due date of the tax for the return period or the date such tax was paid, whichever is later.

2. Which of the following statements with respect to effective recordkeeping is false?

A. Records should identify the source of income in order to determine if an income item is taxable or nontaxable.

B. If an individual cannot provide a canceled check to prove payment of an expense item, (s)he may be able to prove it with certain financial account statements.

C. Records that support the basis of property should be kept until the statute of limitations expires for the year that the property was acquired.

D. Records should show how much of an individual's earnings is subject to self-employment tax.

Answer (C) is correct.

REQUIRED: The false statement with respect to effective recordkeeping.

DISCUSSION: Section 6001 requires every person liable for any tax imposed by the Internal Revenue Code to keep records sufficient to establish the amount of items required to be shown by such a person in any return of tax or information. Regulation 1.6001-1(a) provides that books of account or records should be sufficient to establish the amount of gross income, deductions, credits, or other matters required to be shown by such persons in any tax or information return.

Regulation 1.6001-1(e) provides that a taxpayer's records must be kept as long as the contents may be material in the administration of any Internal Revenue law. Records relating to the basis of property should be retained as long as they may be material [Reg. 1.6001-1(e)]. The basis of property is material until the statute of limitations expires for the year in which the property is sold.

Answer (A) is incorrect. Records should be sufficient to establish the amount of gross income, deductions, credits, or other matters required to be shown by such persons in any tax or information return, including the source of the income. **Answer (B) is incorrect.** The taxpayer's statement corroborated by financial account statements may suffice [Reg. 1.274-5(c)(3)]. **Answer (D) is incorrect.** Records should be sufficient to establish the amount of gross income, deductions, credits, or other matters required to be shown by such persons in any tax or information return, including what amount of an individual's earnings is subject to self-employment tax.

3. How long should you keep your records?

A. 3 years if you owe additional tax.

B. 7 years if you file a claim for a loss from worthless securities.

C. No limit if you do not file a return.

D. All of the answers are correct.

Answer (D) is correct.

REQUIRED: The amount of time a taxpayer should retain tax records.

DISCUSSION: Generally, tax records should be retained 3 years from the date a return was due or 2 years from the date the tax is paid, whichever is later. If a taxpayer owes additional tax, records should be retained for 3 years. If a taxpayer claims a loss from worthless securities, records should be kept for 7 years. If a taxpayer does not file a return, there is no limitation period. Therefore, records should be retained indefinitely (Publication 552).

4. With regard to expenses, the taxpayer should keep all of the following records EXCEPT

A. Canceled checks.

B. Cash register receipts.

C. Invoices.

D. Original copies of all records.

Answer (D) is correct.

REQUIRED: The documents that taxpayers must keep.

DISCUSSION: A taxpayer can replace hard copies of books and records using an electronic storage system provided the system is in compliance with IRS requirements.

Answer (A) is incorrect. Canceled checks should be kept to track cash outlays. **Answer (B) is incorrect.** Cash register receipts should be kept to track smaller purchases. **Answer (C) is incorrect.** Invoices should be kept to track purchases from certain vendors.

5. Bethany timely filed her 2018 1040 tax return and paid the $2,000 tax as shown on the return at the time of filing. The return was subsequently examined and Bethany signed an agreement form for the proposed changes on August 20, 2020. She paid the additional tax due of $5,000 on September 30, 2020. In 2021, Bethany located missing records, which she believes would make $3,000 of the additional assessment erroneous. Which of the following statements accurately states the date by which Bethany must file a claim for refund to get the $3,000 back?

A. August 20, 2022, 2 years from signing the agreement form.

B. April 15, 2022, 3 years from the due date of the original return.

C. September 30, 2022, 2 years from when the additional tax was paid.

D. No claim for refund can be filed since an examination agreement form was signed.

Answer (C) is correct.

REQUIRED: The date by which a claim for refund must be filed.

DISCUSSION: The records must be kept available at all times for inspection by IRS officers and designated employees and must be retained as long as they may be material. Since the IRS generally has 3 years from the date a return was due or filed or 2 years from the date the tax was paid, whichever is later, to assess tax, a taxpayer must retain all records and forms until the later time. If Bethany files for a credit or refund after she files her return, then the statute of limitations is the later of 3 years or 2 years after the tax was paid. Since she paid the most recent assessment on September 30, 2020, Bethany has until September 30, 2022, to file a claim for a refund.

Answer (A) is incorrect. It is 2 years from the date the tax is paid, not the date the agreement is signed. **Answer (B) is incorrect.** It is the later of 3 years from the date a return was due or filed or 2 years from the date the tax was paid. **Answer (D) is incorrect.** If evidence later arises that would support a claim or refund, the taxpayer may make a timely claim for refund.

6. Nancy, a calendar-year taxpayer, filed her federal income tax return for tax year 2019, which was due on April 15, 2020, on May 1, 2020. Nancy did not request and therefore did not receive an extension of time to file her 2019 federal income tax return. Nancy paid the amount due as shown on the 2019 return on June 30, 2020. Based on these facts, the last day for the IRS to assess additional tax with respect to Nancy's 2019 return is

A. June 20, 2022.

B. April 15, 2023.

C. May 1, 2023.

D. June 20, 2023.

Answer (C) is correct.

REQUIRED: The last day to assess additional tax.

DISCUSSION: The IRS generally has 3 years from the date a return was due or filed or 2 years from the date the tax was paid, whichever is later. Because Nancy filed her return on May 1, 2020, the 3-year period ending on May 1, 2023, is the time the IRS has to assess additional tax.

7. Which of the following is NOT a specific record required to be kept for income tax withholding?

A. Each employee's date of birth.

B. The fair market value and date of each payment of noncash compensation made to a retail commission salesperson if no income tax was withheld.

C. The total amount and date of each wage payment and the period of time the payment covers.

D. For accident or health plans, information about the amount of each payment.

Answer (A) is correct.

REQUIRED: The record that need not be maintained for income tax withholding.

DISCUSSION: Under Reg. 31.6001-5(a), every employer required to withhold income tax on wages must keep records of all remuneration paid to the employees. The list of items required to be shown in such records does not include each employee's date of birth.

8. With regard to effective recordkeeping, which of the following statements is false?

A. Records should show how much of an individual's earnings are subject to self-employment tax.

B. A canceled check always proves payment and establishes a tax deduction.

C. The invoice, paid receipt, or canceled check that supports an item of expense should be retained.

D. Records should identify the source of income in order to determine if an income item is taxable or nontaxable.

Answer (B) is correct.

REQUIRED: The false statement regarding recordkeeping.

DISCUSSION: The IRS recommends that taxpayers keep all sales slips, invoices, receipts, canceled checks, or other financial documents that prove the amounts shown on a return as income, deductions, and credits. Although a canceled check indicates payment, the IRS may require more substantive proof of payment in order for a deduction to be allowed.

9. Which of the following agencies must provide certain records upon request per the Freedom of Information Act?

A. Any state agency.

B. The U.S. Supreme Court.

C. Congress.

D. The IRS.

Answer (D) is correct.

REQUIRED: The scope of the Freedom of Information Act.

DISCUSSION: The FOIA was enacted in 1966 and generally provides that any person has the right to request access to federal agency records or information. All executive branch agencies must disclose any requested information outside of certain exceptions. State, legislative, and judicial agencies are not subject to the Act's requirements.

10. Regarding taxpayers' recordkeeping requirements, which of the following is true?

A. Taxpayers who store their documents electronically require written IRS approval in order to destroy original documents.

B. If a taxpayer does not have complete records, then deductions are not allowed.

C. If a taxpayer is missing documents due to events beyond their control, they can claim a deduction by reconstructing the records.

D. Taxpayers must keep original documents in addition to electronic documents.

Answer (C) is correct.

REQUIRED: The recordkeeping requirements of taxpayers.

DISCUSSION: If a taxpayer cannot produce a receipt because of reasons beyond the taxpayer's control (floods, fires, etc.), then the taxpayer can prove a deduction by reconstructing his or her records.

Answer (A) is incorrect. Provided the electronic system conforms to IRS guidelines, the original documentation can be destroyed. No written approval is required. **Answer (B) is incorrect.** Under certain circumstances, incomplete records do not eliminate all chances for deduction. **Answer (D) is incorrect.** Provided the electronic system conforms to IRS guidelines, the original documentation can be destroyed.

7.2 Electronic Filing

11. Samantha Sharp, an enrolled agent, prepares and electronically files Form 1040 tax returns. Samantha prepared the 2021 tax return for Tom, her client. Tom uses Form 8453 and attaches a Form 8332. On March 2, 2022, Samantha electronically filed Tom's tax return, which was a refund return. On March 3, Samantha received acknowledgment from the Internal Revenue Service that Tom's return had been accepted. On March 10, Tom received his refund. By what date must Samantha mail the executed Form 8453 to the IRS?

A. By March 13, 2022 (within 3 business days after Tom receives his refund).

B. By March 7, 2022 (within 5 business days after the return was electronically filed).

C. By March 6, 2022 (within 3 business days after the return is acknowledged as accepted by the IRS).

D. By March 31, 2022 (all Forms 8453 signed during the month must be sent to the IRS by the last day of the month).

Answer (C) is correct.

REQUIRED: The correct period for submitting Form 8453.

DISCUSSION: For a taxpayer submitting a Form 8453 and attaching certain documents for filing, the provider must submit Form 8453 within 3 business days after the return is acknowledged as accepted by the IRS.

12. Michael Young, an Authorized Internal Revenue Service e-file Provider, prepared and electronically transmitted the Form 1040 return of Vivian Blue to the Internal Revenue Service. The Internal Revenue Service notified Michael that the electronic portion of Vivian's return was rejected for processing. Which statement listed below best explains what Michael must do?

A. Michael must advise the taxpayer that the return may never be filed electronically. Vivian must return to the office, sign a paper copy of Form 1040, and mail it to the Service.

B. If Michael cannot correct the error with the information in his possession, he must take reasonable steps to inform the taxpayer of the rejection within 24 hours and provide the taxpayer with the reject code(s) accompanied by an explanation.

C. Michael must mail a paper copy of the return to the IRS with the original Form 8453 that Vivian signed.

D. If Michael cannot correct the error with the information in his possession, he must take reasonable steps to inform the taxpayer of the rejection by the return due date or within 1 week, whichever date is earlier.

Answer (B) is correct.

REQUIRED: The required actions when a taxpayer's return is rejected.

DISCUSSION: If the IRS rejects the electronic portion of a taxpayer's return and the reason for the rejection cannot be rectified by the actions described in the Rev. Proc. 98-50, the ERO must take reasonable steps to inform the taxpayer that the taxpayer's return has not been filed within 24 hours of receiving the rejection. When the ERO advises the taxpayer that the taxpayer's return has not been filed, the ERO must provide the taxpayer with the reject code(s), an explanation of the reject code(s), and the sequence number of each reject code.

Answer (A) is incorrect. A rejection does not necessarily mean that the taxpayer may never file electronically. **Answer (C) is incorrect.** Mailing a copy of Form 8453 is not an alternative for the ERO. **Answer (D) is incorrect.** Michael has 24 hours to inform the taxpayer.

13. Which fee arrangement described below is permissible for an electronic return originator (ERO)?

A. Fees based on AGI from the tax return.

B. Fees based on percent of refund.

C. Separate fees for direct deposits.

D. None of the answers are correct.

Answer (D) is correct.

REQUIRED: The fee arrangement permissible for an electronic return originator.

DISCUSSION: An ERO may not charge fees based on the refund amount or any other amount from the tax return. Furthermore, an ERO may not charge separate fees for direct deposits (Publication 1345).

14. If a taxpayer's return is rejected by the IRS and the ERO cannot fix the problem and retransmit the return in the time prescribed, the ERO must make reasonable attempts to notify the taxpayer of the reject. How long from the time the return is rejected does the ERO have to try to contact the taxpayer?

A. 12 hours.

B. 24 hours.

C. 48 hours.

D. 1 week.

Answer (B) is correct.

REQUIRED: The amount of time an ERO has to contact the taxpayer after a return is rejected.

DISCUSSION: If the IRS rejects the electronic portion of a taxpayer's return and the reason for the rejection cannot be rectified by the actions described in Rev. Proc. 98-50, the ERO, within 24 hours of receiving the rejection, must take reasonable steps to inform the taxpayer that the taxpayer's return has not been filed. When the ERO advises the taxpayer that the taxpayer's return has not been filed, the ERO must provide the taxpayer with the reject code(s), an explanation of the reject code(s), and the sequence number of each reject code.

15. The contractual agreement for a Refund Anticipation Loan (RAL) is between which of the following?

A. Taxpayer and lender.

B. Taxpayer and electronic filing provider.

C. Electronic filing provider and the lender.

D. IRS and the taxpayer.

Answer (A) is correct.

REQUIRED: The parties that form contractual agreements for Refund Anticipation Loans.

DISCUSSION: A refund anticipation loan (RAL) is money borrowed by a taxpayer that is based on a taxpayer's anticipated income tax refund. The IRS has no involvement in RALs. A RAL is a contract between the taxpayer and the lender. A refund anticipation loan indicator must be included in the electronic return data transmission to the IRS.

Answer (B) is incorrect. The electronic provider cannot be a party to a RAL. **Answer (C) is incorrect.** The taxpayer, not the electronic filing provider, is the party with the lender to a RAL. **Answer (D) is incorrect.** The IRS has no involvement with RALs.

16. Which of the following statements is true regarding electronically filed returns?

A. A return for a deceased taxpayer may be electronically filed.

B. U.S. Individual Income Tax Return for tax year 2021 may not be electronically filed after April 15, 2022.

C. For tax year 2021, current- and prior-year tax returns may not be electronically filed.

D. For tax year 2021, all electronically filed returns require a separate signature document to be submitted to the appropriate Internal Revenue Service Center.

Answer (A) is correct.

REQUIRED: The true statement regarding electronically filed returns.

DISCUSSION: Decedent's tax returns are permitted to be electronically filed (Publication 559).

Answer (B) is incorrect. Individual income tax returns may be electronically filed year-round, e.g., after April 15, 2022. **Answer (C) is incorrect.** Current- and prior-year tax returns are permitted to be electronically filed. **Answer (D) is incorrect.** Signatures for electronically filed returns are provided through electronic signatures.

17. Which of the following is an acceptable method of computation for an Electronic Return Originator (ERO) fee?

A. Fees based on time required for preparation.

B. Fees based on AGI from the tax return.

C. Fees based on percent of refund.

D. Flat fee identical for all customers.

Answer (D) is correct.

REQUIRED: The most accurate statement regarding an ERO fee.

DISCUSSION: If an Electronic Return Originator charges a fee for the transmission of the electronic portion of a tax return, the fee may not be based on a percentage of the refund or any other amount from the tax return. An authorized ERO may not charge a separate fee for direct deposits. Therefore, a flat fee for all customers is an acceptable method of computing an Electronic Return Originator fee (Publication 1345).

Answer (A) is incorrect. ERO fees are not allowed to be based on the amount of time it takes to prepare a tax return. **Answer (B) is incorrect.** Basing ERO fees on AGI from the tax return is not allowed. **Answer (C) is incorrect.** The amount of the refund is based on the tax return and is not allowed.

18. A Refund Anticipation Loan (RAL) is money borrowed by a taxpayer from a lender based on the taxpayer's anticipated income tax refund. Which of the statements below is true?

A. All parties to Refund Anticipation Loan agreements, including Electronic Return Originators (EROs), must ensure that taxpayers understand that Refund Anticipation Loans are interest bearing loans and not substitutes for a faster way of receiving a refund.

B. The IRS has minimal involvement and responsibility for Refund Anticipation Loans.

C. The Electronic Return Originator should advise the taxpayer that if a direct deposit is not received within the expected time frame, the IRS may be liable to the lender for additional interest on the Refund Anticipation Loan.

D. The IRS is responsible for ensuring that Refund Anticipation Loan indicators are included in the electronic return data that is transmitted to the IRS.

Answer (A) is correct.

REQUIRED: The true statement regarding a Refund Anticipation Loan.

DISCUSSION: A Refund Anticipation Loan (RAL) is money borrowed by a taxpayer that is based on a taxpayer's anticipated income tax refund. The IRS has no involvement in RALs. A RAL is a contract between the taxpayer and the lender. A refund anticipation loan indicator must be included in the electronic return data transmitted to the IRS. All parties to the RAL must ensure that the taxpayer understands that a RAL is not a substitute for a faster way of receiving a refund. In addition, any interest accrued as a result of a delay in the return of a refund is not the responsibility of the IRS, since it is not involved.

Answer (B) is incorrect. The IRS has no involvement in RALs. **Answer (C) is incorrect.** The IRS has no involvement in RALs and thus would not be responsible for accrued interest in the event of a delayed refund. **Answer (D) is incorrect.** The IRS has no involvement in RALs. The ERO is responsible for ensuring that RAL indicators are included in the electronic return.

19. Taxpayers often elect the direct deposit option because it is the fastest way of receiving refunds. The Electronic Return Originator should advise the taxpayer of the option to receive his or her refund by direct deposit or paper check. Select the statement below that is true with respect to direct deposit.

A. The Electronic Return Originator does not have to accept a direct deposit election to a financial institution designated by the taxpayer.

B. Refunds may be direct deposited to credit card accounts.

C. The Electronic Return Originator may make a separate charge of only $15 or less as a processing fee if the taxpayer elects direct deposit.

D. The Electronic Return Originator should caution taxpayers that some financial institutions do not permit the deposit of joint refunds into individual accounts.

Answer (D) is correct.

REQUIRED: The true statement regarding the direct deposit of a refund.

DISCUSSION: Publication 1345 addresses the relevant information regarding electronic filing. This publication discusses the responsibilities of the Electronic Return Originator (ERO) to inform the taxpayer of important information regarding the direct deposit. Direct deposits may be deposited into any qualified account, including checking, savings, share draft, or consumer asset accounts. However, the taxpayer cannot deposit these funds onto a credit card. The ERO should caution the taxpayer that not all financial institutions will allow joint refunds into individual accounts. In addition, the ERO must accept any direct deposit election and may not charge an additional fee for doing so.

Answer (A) is incorrect. The ERO must accept any direct deposit election. **Answer (B) is incorrect.** Refunds may not be direct deposited onto credit card accounts. **Answer (C) is incorrect.** The ERO cannot charge a separate fee for a direct deposit election.

20. According to Circular 230, which of the following applies to radio or television broadcasting regarding advertisement of electronic filing?

A. The broadcast must be preapproved by the IRS.

B. The broadcast must be prerecorded.

C. The broadcast advertisement must be kept for a period of 36 months from the date of the last transmission or use.

D. The broadcast must be prerecorded, and the broadcast advertisement must be kept for a period of 36 months from the date of the last transmission or use.

Answer (D) is correct.

REQUIRED: The statement that applies to radio or television broadcasting regarding advertisement of electronic filing.

DISCUSSION: If an ERO uses radio or television broadcasting to advertise, the broadcast must be prerecorded. The ERO must keep a copy of the prerecorded advertisement for a period of at least 36 months from the date of the last transmission or use.

Publication 3112, *IRS e-file Application and Participation*, states that copies must be retained until the end of the calendar year following the last transmission or use.

Answer (A) is incorrect. The broadcast need not be preapproved by the IRS. **Answer (B) is incorrect.** Although the broadcast must be prerecorded, it is also required that a copy of the advertisement be kept for a period of at least 36 months from the date of the last transmission or use. **Answer (C) is incorrect.** The broadcast must be prerecorded.

21. By which means can Form 8453, *U.S. Individual Income Tax Transmittal for an IRS e-file Return*, be sent to the IRS?

A. Mail.

B. Email.

C. Fax.

D. All of the answers are correct.

Answer (A) is correct.

REQUIRED: The transmission and usage of Form 8453.

DISCUSSION: Form 8453 must be mailed with all required attachments. It cannot be filed electronically.

Answer (B) is incorrect. Form 8453 cannot be emailed or filed electronically. **Answer (C) is incorrect.** Form 8453 cannot be faxed. **Answer (D) is incorrect.** Form 8453 requires a specific channel of transmission.

22. A Form 1065, *U.S. Partnership Return*, must be filed electronically if the number of partners exceeds

A. 50

B. 75

C. 100

D. 250

Answer (C) is correct.

REQUIRED: The number of partners that determines if Form 1065 must be electronically filed.

DISCUSSION: Partnerships with more than 100 partners are required to file Form 1065 electronically if not specifically exempted (e.g., partnerships that use a fiscal year).

23. The Internal Revenue Service monitors and performs annual suitability checks on authorized IRS electronic filing providers for compliance with the revenue procedure and program requirements. Violations may result in a variety of sanctions. Which statement is true with respect to sanctions the IRS may impose on an electronic filing provider?

A. The IRS may issue a letter of reprimand or a 1-year suspension as a sanction for a level one infraction in the electronic filing program.

B. The IRS may impose a period of suspension that includes the remainder of the calendar year in which the suspension occurs, plus the next 2 calendar years, for a level two infraction in the electronic filing program.

C. The IRS may suspend or expel an authorized IRS electronic return originator prior to administrative review for a level three infraction in the electronic filing program.

D. The IRS may not impose a sanction that is greater than a 1-year suspension from the electronic filing program.

Answer (C) is correct.

REQUIRED: The true statement regarding sanctions on electronic filing providers.

DISCUSSION: The IRS may impose a sanction on an electronic return originator for various infractions. These sanctions range from a written reprimand to expulsion (Publication 3112). These sanctions rank on levels one through three. A level one infraction may result in a written reprimand. A level two infraction may result in a restriction in participation in the IRS e-file Program or a 1-year suspension, in addition to the rest of the calendar year. A level three infraction may result in a suspension from participation in the IRS e-file Program for 2 years in addition to the rest of the calendar year or an expulsion from the program. The IRS reserves the right to select the sanction they wish to impose.

Answer (A) is incorrect. The IRS cannot suspend a participant in the IRS e-file Program for a level one infraction. **Answer (B) is incorrect.** A participant in the IRS e-file Program who receives a level two infraction will only be suspended for 1 year in addition to the rest of the current calendar year. **Answer (D) is incorrect.** The IRS also may issue a sanction for 2 years or an expulsion from the program.

24. Regarding entities that are required to file tax returns electronically, which of the following is false?

A. Partnerships with greater than 50 partners must file Form 1065 electronically.

B. Tax-exempt organizations are required to file Form 990 electronically if they own more than $10 million in assets and file at least 250 returns annually.

C. Corporations are required to file Form 1120, 1120-S, and 1120-F electronically if they own more than $10 million in assets and file at least 250 returns annually.

D. Charitable trusts and private foundations must file Form 990-PF electronically if they file at least 250 returns annually, regardless of their assets.

Answer (A) is correct.

REQUIRED: The forced e-filing requirements.

DISCUSSION: The e-file requirement applies to partnerships with greater than 100 partners, not 50 partners.

25. Form 8453 must be used to send additional documentation to the IRS when a tax return is filed electronically. All of the following forms must be sent with Form 8453 EXCEPT

A. Form 8283, *Noncash Charitable Contributions*, Section A or B, and any related attachments.

B. Form 2848, *Power of Attorney and Declaration of Representative* (or POA that states the agent is granted authority to sign the return).

C. Form 8379, *Injured Spouse Allocation*.

D. Form 1098-C, *Contributions of Motor Vehicles, Boats, and Airplanes* (or equivalent contemporaneous written acknowledgment).

Answer (C) is correct.

REQUIRED: The scope and usage of Form 8453.

DISCUSSION: Form 8453 is used to send additional required paper documents to the IRS when a tax return is otherwise filed electronically. Form 8379 can be filed electronically and is not required to be sent separately with Form 8453.

APPENDIX A
CIRCULAR NO. 230 REPRINT (REV. 6-2014)

We have reproduced the full text of Treasury Department Circular No. 230 below and on the following pages. Please refer to it as needed and be familiar with its contents.

NOTE: Circular No. 230 was last released in June 2014. There have been multiple changes that make it outdated. These changes are reflected in our outlines. Major changes include

- The Registered Tax Return Preparer designation is no longer applicable.
- The IRS does not have the ability to regulate the process of preparing tax returns.
- The Annual Filing Season Program was created to replace the Registered Tax Return Preparer designation. Participants in the AFSP have limited rights to practice before the IRS in certain situations.
- For returns filed after December 31, 2015, unenrolled preparers cannot practice before the IRS unless they are specifically allowed, even if they prepared the tax return. Previously, these preparers had limited ability to represent their clients before the IRS if they prepared the tax return.

Title 31 Code of Federal Regulations, Subtitle A, Part 10, published (June 12, 2014)

31 U.S.C. §330. Practice before the Department

(a) Subject to section 500 of title 5, the Secretary of the Treasury may —

(1) regulate the practice of representatives of persons before the Department of the Treasury; and

(2) before admitting a representative to practice, require that the representative demonstrate

(A) good character;

(B) good reputation;

(C) necessary qualifications to enable the representative to provide to persons valuable service; and

(D) competency to advise and assist persons in presenting their cases.

(b) After notice and opportunity for a proceeding, the Secretary may suspend or disbar from practice before the Department, or censure, a representative who —

(1) is incompetent;

(2) is disreputable;

(3) violates regulations prescribed under this section; or

(4) with intent to defraud, willfully and knowingly misleads or threatens the person being represented or a prospective person to be represented.

The Secretary may impose a monetary penalty on any representative described in the preceding sentence. If the representative was acting on behalf of an employer or any firm or other entity in connection with the conduct giving rise to such penalty, the Secretary may impose a monetary penalty on such employer, firm, or entity if it knew, or reasonably should have known, of such conduct. Such penalty shall not exceed the gross income derived (or to be derived) from the conduct giving rise to the penalty and may be in addition to, or in lieu of, any suspension, disbarment, or censure of the representative.

(c) After notice and opportunity for a hearing to any appraiser, the Secretary may —

(1) provide that appraisals by such appraiser shall not have any probative effect in any administrative proceeding before the Department of the Treasury or the Internal Revenue Service, and

(2) bar such appraiser from presenting evidence or testimony in any such proceeding.

(d) Nothing in this section or in any other provision of law shall be construed to limit the authority of the Secretary of the Treasury to impose standards applicable to the rendering of written advice with respect to any entity, transaction plan or arrangement, or other plan or arrangement, which is of a type which the Secretary determines as having a potential for tax avoidance or evasion.

(Pub. L. 97–258, Sept. 13, 1982, 96 Stat. 884; Pub. L. 98–369, div. A, title I, §156(a), July 18, 1984, 98 Stat. 695; Pub. L. 99–514, §2, Oct. 22, 1986, 100 Stat. 2095; Pub. L. 108–357, title VIII, §822(a)(1), (b), Oct. 22, 2004, 118 Stat. 1586, 1587; Pub. L. 109–280, title XII, §1219(d), Aug. 17, 2006, 120 Stat. 1085.)

Part 10 -- PRACTICE BEFORE THE INTERNAL REVENUE SERVICE

Paragraph 1

Sec.

Subpart C -- Sanctions for Violation of the Regulations

Subpart D -- Rules Applicable to Disciplinary Proceedings

Subpart E -- General Provisions

Paragraph 1. The authority citation for 31 CFR, part 10 continues to read as follows:

Authority: Sec. 3, 23 Stat. 258, secs. 2-12, 60 Stat. 237 et. seq.; 5 U.S.C. 301, 500, 551-559; 31 U.S.C. 321; 31 U.S.C. 330; Reorg. Plan No. 26 of 1950, 15 FR 4935, 64 Stat. 1280, 3 CFR, 1949-1953 Comp., p. 1017.

§ 10.0 Scope of part.

(a) This part contains rules governing the recognition of attorneys, certified public accountants, enrolled agents, enrolled retirement plan agents, registered tax return preparers, and other persons representing taxpayers before the Internal Revenue Service. Subpart A of this part sets forth rules relating to the authority to practice before the Internal Revenue Service; subpart B of this part prescribes the duties and restrictions relating to such practice; subpart C of this part prescribes the sanctions for violating the regulations; subpart D of this part contains the rules applicable to disciplinary proceedings; and subpart E of this part contains general provisions relating to the availability of official records.

(b) *Effective/applicability date*. This section is applicable beginning August 2, 2011.

Subpart A -- Rules Governing Authority to Practice

§ 10.1 Offices.

(a) *Establishment of office(s)*. The Commissioner shall establish the Office of Professional Responsibility and any other office(s) within the Internal Revenue Service necessary to administer and enforce this part. The Commissioner shall appoint the Director of the Office of Professional Responsibility and any other Internal Revenue official(s) to manage and direct any office(s) established to administer or enforce this part. Offices established under this part include, but are not limited to:

(1) The Office of Professional Responsibility, which shall generally have responsibility for matters related to practitioner conduct and shall have exclusive responsibility for discipline, including disciplinary proceedings and sanctions; and

(2) An office with responsibility for matters related to authority to practice before the Internal Revenue Service, including acting on applications for enrollment to practice before the Internal Revenue Service and administering competency testing and continuing education.

(b) Officers and employees within any office established under this part may perform acts necessary or appropriate to carry out the responsibilities of their office(s) under this part or as otherwise prescribed by the Commissioner.

(c) *Acting*. The Commissioner will designate an officer or employee of the Internal Revenue Service to perform the duties of an individual appointed under paragraph (a) of this section in the absence of that officer or employee or during a vacancy in that office.

(d) *Effective/applicability date*. This section is applicable beginning August 2, 2011, except that paragraph (a)(1) is applicable beginning June 12, 2014.

§ 10.2 Definitions.

(a) As used in this part, except where the text provides otherwise —

(1) *Attorney* means any person who is a member in good standing of the bar of the highest court of any state, territory, or possession of the United States, including a Commonwealth, or the District of Columbia.

(2) *Certified Public Accountant* means any person who is duly qualified to practice as a certified public accountant in any state, territory, or possession of the United States, including a Commonwealth, or the District of Columbia.

(3) *Commissioner* refers to the Commissioner of Internal Revenue.

(4) *Practice before the Internal Revenue Service* comprehends all matters connected with a presentation to the Internal Revenue Service or any of its officers or employees relating to a taxpayer's rights, privileges, or liabilities under laws or regulations administered by the Internal Revenue Service. Such presentations include, but are not limited to, preparing documents; filing documents; corresponding and communicating with the Internal Revenue Service; rendering written advice with respect to any entity, transaction, plan or arrangement, or other plan or arrangement having a potential for tax avoidance or evasion; and representing a client at conferences, hearings, and meetings.

(5) *Practitioner* means any individual described in paragraphs (a), (b), (c), (d), (e), or (f) of §10.3.

(6) A *tax return* includes an amended tax return and a claim for refund.

(7) *Service* means the Internal Revenue Service.

(8) *Tax return preparer* means any individual within the meaning of section 7701(a)(36) and 26 CFR 301.7701-15.

(b) *Effective/applicability date.* This section is applicable on August 2, 2011.

§ 10.3 Who may practice.

(a) *Attorneys.* Any attorney who is not currently under suspension or disbarment from practice before the Internal Revenue Service may practice before the Internal Revenue Service by filing with the Internal Revenue Service a written declaration that the attorney is currently qualified as an attorney and is authorized to represent the party or parties. Notwithstanding the preceding sentence, attorneys who are not currently under suspension or disbarment from practice before the Internal Revenue Service are not required to file a written declaration with the IRS before rendering written advice covered under §10.37, but their rendering of this advice is practice before the Internal Revenue Service.

(b) *Certified public accountants.* Any certified public accountant who is not currently under suspension or disbarment from practice before the Internal Revenue Service may practice before the Internal Revenue Service by filing with the Internal Revenue Service a written declaration that the certified public accountant is currently qualified as a certified public accountant and is authorized to represent the party or parties. Notwithstanding the preceding sentence, certified public accountants who are not currently under suspension or disbarment from practice before the Internal Revenue Service are not required to file a written declaration with the IRS before rendering written advice covered under §10.37, but their rendering of this advice is practice before the Internal Revenue Service.

(c) *Enrolled agents.* Any individual enrolled as an agent pursuant to this part who is not currently under suspension or disbarment from practice before the Internal Revenue Service may practice before the Internal Revenue Service.

(d) *Enrolled actuaries.*

(1) Any individual who is enrolled as an actuary by the Joint Board for the Enrollment of Actuaries pursuant to 29 U.S.C. 1242 who is not currently under suspension or disbarment from practice before the Internal Revenue Service may practice before the Internal Revenue Service by filing with the Internal Revenue Service a written declaration stating that he or she is currently qualified as an enrolled actuary and is authorized to represent the party or parties on whose behalf he or she acts.

(2) Practice as an enrolled actuary is limited to representation with respect to issues involving the following statutory provisions in title 26 of the United States Code: sections 401 (relating to qualification of employee plans), 403(a) (relating to whether an annuity plan meets the requirements of section 404(a) (2)), 404 (relating to deductibility of employer contributions), 405 (relating to qualification of bond purchase plans), 412 (relating to funding requirements for certain employee plans), 413 (relating to application of qualification requirements to collectively bargained plans and to plans maintained by more than one employer), 414 (relating to definitions and special rules with respect to the employee plan area), 419 (relating to treatment of funded welfare benefits), 419A (relating to qualified asset accounts), 420 (relating to transfers of excess pension assets to retiree health accounts), 4971 (relating to excise taxes payable as a result of an accumulated funding deficiency under section 412), 4972 (relating to tax on nondeductible contributions to qualified employer plans), 4976 (relating to taxes with respect to funded welfare benefit plans), 4980 (relating to tax on reversion of qualified plan assets to employer), 6057 (relating to annual registration of plans), 6058 (relating to information required in connection with certain plans of deferred compensation), 6059 (relating to periodic report of actuary), 6652(e) (relating to the failure to file annual registration and other notifications by pension plan), 6652(f) (relating to the failure to file information required in connection with certain plans of deferred compensation), 6692 (relating to the failure to file actuarial report), 7805(b) (relating to the extent to which an Internal Revenue Service ruling or determination letter coming under the statutory provisions listed here will be applied without retroactive effect); and 29 U.S.C. § 1083 (relating to the waiver of funding for nonqualified plans).

(3) An individual who practices before the Internal Revenue Service pursuant to paragraph (d)(1) of this section is subject to the provisions of this part in the same manner as attorneys, certified public accountants, enrolled agents, enrolled retirement plan agents, and registered tax return preparers.

(e) *Enrolled retirement plan agents* —

(1) Any individual enrolled as a retirement plan agent pursuant to this part who is not currently under suspension or disbarment from practice before the Internal Revenue Service may practice before the Internal Revenue Service.

(2) Practice as an enrolled retirement plan agent is limited to representation with respect to issues involving the following programs: Employee Plans Determination Letter program; Employee Plans Compliance Resolution System; and Employee Plans Master and Prototype and Volume Submitter program. In addition, enrolled retirement plan agents are generally permitted to represent taxpayers with respect to IRS forms under the 5300 and 5500 series which are filed by retirement plans and plan sponsors, but not with respect to actuarial forms or schedules.

(3) An individual who practices before the Internal Revenue Service pursuant to paragraph (e)(1) of this section is subject to the provisions of this part in the same manner as attorneys, certified public accountants, enrolled agents, enrolled actuaries, and registered tax return preparers.

(f) *Registered tax return preparers.*

(1) Any individual who is designated as a registered tax return preparer pursuant to §10.4(c) of this part who is not currently under suspension or disbarment from practice before the Internal Revenue Service may practice before the Internal Revenue Service.

(2) Practice as a registered tax return preparer is limited to preparing and signing tax returns and claims for refund, and other documents for submission to the Internal Revenue Service. A registered tax return preparer may prepare all or substantially all of a tax return or claim for refund of tax. The Internal Revenue Service will prescribe by forms, instructions, or other appropriate guidance the tax returns and claims for refund that a registered tax return preparer may prepare and sign.

(3) A registered tax return preparer may represent taxpayers before revenue agents, customer service representatives, or similar officers and employees of the Internal Revenue Service (including the Taxpayer Advocate Service) during an examination if the registered tax return preparer signed the tax return or claim for refund for the taxable year or period under examination. Unless otherwise prescribed by regulation or notice, this right does not permit such individual to represent the taxpayer, regardless of the circumstances requiring representation, before appeals officers, revenue officers, Counsel or similar officers or employees of the Internal Revenue Service or the Treasury Department. A registered tax return preparer's authorization to practice under this part also does not include the authority to provide tax advice to a client or another person except as necessary to prepare a tax return, claim for refund, or other document intended to be submitted to the Internal Revenue Service.

(4) An individual who practices before the Internal Revenue Service pursuant to paragraph (f)(1) of this section is subject to the provisions of this part in the same manner as attorneys, certified public accountants, enrolled agents, enrolled retirement plan agents, and enrolled actuaries.

(g) *Others.* Any individual qualifying under paragraph §10.5(e) or §10.7 is eligible to practice before the Internal Revenue Service to the extent provided in those sections.

(h) *Government officers and employees, and others.* An individual, who is an officer or employee of the executive, legislative, or judicial branch of the United States Government; an officer or employee of the District of Columbia; a Member of Congress; or a Resident Commissioner may not practice before the Internal Revenue Service if such practice violates 18 U.S.C. §§ 203 or 205.

(i) *State officers and employees.* No officer or employee of any State, or subdivision of any State, whose duties require him or her to pass upon, investigate, or deal with tax matters for such State or subdivision, may practice before the Internal Revenue Service, if such employment may disclose facts or information applicable to Federal tax matters.

(j) *Effective/applicability date.* Paragraphs (a), (b), and (g) of this section are applicable beginning June 12, 2014. Paragraphs (c) through (f), (h), and (i) of this section are applicable beginning August 2, 2011.

§ 10.4 Eligibility to become an enrolled agent, enrolled retirement plan agent, or registered tax return preparer.

(a) *Enrollment as an enrolled agent upon examination.* The Commissioner, or delegate, will grant enrollment as an enrolled agent to an applicant eighteen years of age or older who demonstrates special competence in tax matters by written examination administered by, or administered under the oversight of, the Internal Revenue Service, who possesses a current or otherwise valid preparer tax identification number or other prescribed identifying number, and who has not engaged in any conduct that would justify the suspension or disbarment of any practitioner under the provisions of this part.

(b) *Enrollment as a retirement plan agent upon examination.* The Commissioner, or delegate, will grant enrollment as an enrolled retirement plan agent to an applicant eighteen years of age or older who demonstrates special competence in qualified retirement plan matters by written examination administered by, or administered under the oversight of, the Internal Revenue Service, who possesses a current or otherwise valid preparer tax identification number or other prescribed identifying number, and who has not engaged in any conduct that would justify the suspension or disbarment of any practitioner under the provisions of this part.

(c) *Designation as a registered tax return preparer.* The Commissioner, or delegate, may designate an individual eighteen years of age or older as a registered tax return preparer provided an applicant demonstrates competence in Federal tax return preparation matters by written examination administered by, or administered under the oversight of, the Internal Revenue Service, or otherwise meets the requisite standards prescribed by the Internal Revenue Service, possesses a current or otherwise valid preparer tax identification number or other prescribed identifying number, and has not engaged in any conduct that would justify the suspension or disbarment of any practitioner under the provisions of this part.

(d) *Enrollment of former Internal Revenue Service employees.* The Commissioner, or delegate, may grant enrollment as an enrolled agent or enrolled retirement plan agent to an applicant who, by virtue of past service and technical experience in the Internal Revenue Service, has qualified for such enrollment and who has not engaged in any conduct that would justify the suspension or disbarment of any practitioner under the provisions of this part, under the following circumstances:

(1) The former employee applies for enrollment on an Internal Revenue Service form and supplies the information requested on the form and such other information regarding the experience and training of the applicant as may be relevant.

(2) The appropriate office of the Internal Revenue Service provides a detailed report of the nature and rating of the applicant's work while employed by the Internal Revenue Service and a recommendation whether such employment qualifies the applicant technically or otherwise for the desired authorization.

(3) Enrollment as an enrolled agent based on an applicant's former employment with the Internal Revenue Service may be of unlimited scope or it may be limited to permit the presentation of matters only of the particular specialty or only before the particular unit or division of the Internal Revenue Service for which the applicant's former employment has qualified the applicant. Enrollment as an enrolled retirement plan agent based on an applicant's former employment with the Internal Revenue Service will be limited to permit the presentation of matters only with respect to qualified retirement plan matters.

(4) Application for enrollment as an enrolled agent or enrolled retirement plan agent based on an applicant's former employment with the Internal Revenue Service must be made within three years from the date of separation from such employment.

(5) An applicant for enrollment as an enrolled agent who is requesting such enrollment based on former employment with the Internal Revenue Service must have had a minimum of five years continuous employment with the Internal Revenue Service during which the applicant must have been regularly engaged in applying and interpreting the provisions of the Internal Revenue Code and the regulations relating to income, estate, gift, employment, or excise taxes.

(6) An applicant for enrollment as an enrolled retirement plan agent who is requesting such enrollment based on former employment with the Internal Revenue Service must have had a minimum of five years continuous employment with the Internal Revenue Service during which the applicant must have been regularly engaged in applying and interpreting the provisions of the Internal Revenue Code and the regulations relating to qualified retirement plan matters.

(7) For the purposes of paragraphs (d)(5) and (6) of this section, an aggregate of 10 or more years of employment in positions involving the application and interpretation of the provisions of the Internal Revenue Code, at least three of which occurred within the five years preceding the date of application, is the equivalent of five years continuous employment.

(e) *Natural persons*. Enrollment to practice may be granted only to natural persons.

(f) *Effective/applicability date*. This section is applicable beginning August 2, 2011.

§ 10.5 Application to become an enrolled agent, enrolled retirement plan agent, or registered tax return preparer.

(a) *Form; address*. An applicant to become an enrolled agent, enrolled retirement plan agent, or registered tax return preparer must apply as required by forms or procedures established and published by the Internal Revenue Service, including proper execution of required forms under oath or affirmation. The address on the application will be the address under which a successful applicant is enrolled or registered and is the address to which all correspondence concerning enrollment or registration will be sent.

(b) *Fee*. A reasonable nonrefundable fee may be charged for each application to become an enrolled agent, enrolled retirement plan agent, or registered tax return preparer. See 26 CFR part 300.

(c) *Additional information; examination*. The Internal Revenue Service may require the applicant, as a condition to consideration of an application, to file additional information and to submit to any written or oral examination under oath or otherwise. Upon the applicant's written request, the Internal Revenue Service will afford the applicant the opportunity to be heard with respect to the application.

(d) *Compliance and suitability checks*.

(1) As a condition to consideration of an application, the Internal Revenue Service may conduct a Federal tax compliance check and suitability check. The tax compliance check will be limited to an inquiry regarding whether an applicant has filed all required individual or business tax returns and whether the applicant has failed to pay, or make proper arrangements with the Internal Revenue Service for payment of, any Federal tax debts. The suitability check will be limited to an inquiry regarding whether an applicant has engaged in any conduct that would justify suspension or disbarment of any practitioner under the provisions of this part on the date the application is submitted, including whether the applicant has engaged in disreputable conduct as defined in §10.51. The application will be denied only if the results of the compliance or suitability check are sufficient to establish that the practitioner engaged in conduct subject to sanctions under §§10.51 and 10.52.

(2) If the applicant does not pass the tax compliance or suitability check, the applicant will not be issued an enrollment or registration card or certificate pursuant to §10.6(b) of this part. An applicant who is initially denied enrollment or registration for failure to pass a tax compliance check may reapply after the initial denial if the applicant becomes current with respect to the applicant's tax liabilities.

(e) *Temporary recognition*. On receipt of a properly executed application, the Commissioner, or delegate, may grant the applicant temporary recognition to practice pending a determination as to whether status as an enrolled agent, enrolled retirement plan agent, or registered tax return preparer should be granted. Temporary recognition will be granted only in unusual circumstances and it will not be granted, in any circumstance, if the application is not regular on its face, if the information stated in the application, if true, is not sufficient to warrant granting the application to practice, or the Commissioner, or delegate, has information indicating that the statements in the application are untrue or that the applicant would not otherwise qualify to become an enrolled agent, enrolled retirement plan agent, or registered tax return preparer. Issuance of temporary recognition does not constitute either a designation or a finding of eligibility as an enrolled agent, enrolled retirement plan agent, or registered tax return preparer, and the temporary recognition may be withdrawn at any time.

(f) *Protest of application denial.* The applicant will be informed in writing as to the reason(s) for any denial of an application. The applicant may, within 30 days after receipt of the notice of denial of the application, file a written protest of the denial as prescribed by the Internal Revenue Service in forms, guidance, or other appropriate guidance. A protest under this section is not governed by subpart D of this part.

(g) *Effective/applicability date.* This section is applicable to applications received on or after August 2, 2011.

§ 10.6 Term and renewal of status as an enrolled agent, enrolled retirement plan agent, or registered tax return preparer.

(a) *Term.* Each individual authorized to practice before the Internal Revenue Service as an enrolled agent, enrolled retirement plan agent, or registered tax return preparer will be accorded active enrollment or registration status subject to renewal of enrollment or registration as provided in this part.

(b) *Enrollment or registration card or certificate.* The Internal Revenue Service will issue an enrollment or registration card or certificate to each individual whose application to practice before the Internal Revenue Service is approved. Each card or certificate will be valid for the period stated on the card or certificate. An enrolled agent, enrolled retirement plan agent, or registered tax return preparer may not practice before the Internal Revenue Service if the card or certificate is not current or otherwise valid. The card or certificate is in addition to any notification that may be provided to each individual who obtains a preparer tax identification number.

(c) *Change of address.* An enrolled agent, enrolled retirement plan agent, or registered tax return preparer must send notification of any change of address to the address specified by the Internal Revenue Service within 60 days of the change of address. This notification must include the enrolled agent's, enrolled retirement plan agent's, or registered tax return preparer's name, prior address, new address, tax identification number(s) (including preparer tax identification number), and the date the change of address is effective. Unless this notification is sent, the address for purposes of any correspondence from the appropriate Internal Revenue Service office responsible for administering this part shall be the address reflected on the practitioner's most recent application for enrollment or registration, or application for renewal of enrollment or registration. A practitioner's change of address notification under this part will not constitute a change of the practitioner's last known address for purposes of section 6212 of the Internal Revenue Code and regulations thereunder.

(d) *Renewal.*

(1) *In general.* Enrolled agents, enrolled retirement plan agents, and registered tax return preparers must renew their status with the Internal Revenue Service to maintain eligibility to practice before the Internal Revenue Service. Failure to receive notification from the Internal Revenue Service of the renewal requirement will not be justification for the individual's failure to satisfy this requirement.

(2) *Renewal period for enrolled agents.*

(i) All enrolled agents must renew their preparer tax identification number as prescribed by forms, instructions, or other appropriate guidance.

(ii) Enrolled agents who have a social security number or tax identification number that ends with the numbers 0, 1, 2, or 3, except for those individuals who received their initial enrollment after November 1, 2003, must apply for renewal between November 1, 2003, and January 31, 2004. The renewal will be effective April 1, 2004.

(iii) Enrolled agents who have a social security number or tax identification number that ends with the numbers 4, 5, or 6, except for those individuals who received their initial enrollment after November 1, 2004, must apply for renewal between November 1, 2004, and January 31, 2005. The renewal will be effective April 1, 2005.

(iv) Enrolled agents who have a social security number or tax identification number that ends with the numbers 7, 8, or 9, except for those individuals who received their initial enrollment after November 1, 2005, must apply for renewal between November 1, 2005, and January 31, 2006. The renewal will be effective April 1, 2006.

(v) Thereafter, applications for renewal as an enrolled agent will be required between November 1 and January 31 of every subsequent third year as specified in paragraph (d)(2)(i), (d)(2)(ii), or (d)(2)(iii) of this section according to the last number of the individual's social security number or tax identification number. Those individuals who receive initial enrollment as an enrolled agent after November 1 and before April 2 of the applicable renewal period will not be required to renew their enrollment before the first full renewal period following the receipt of their initial enrollment.

(3) *Renewal period for enrolled retirement plan agents*.

(i) All enrolled retirement plan agents must renew their preparer tax identification number as prescribed by the Internal Revenue Service in forms, instructions, or other appropriate guidance.

(ii) Enrolled retirement plan agents will be required to renew their status as enrolled retirement plan agents between April 1 and June 30 of every third year subsequent to their initial enrollment.

(4) *Renewal period for registered tax return preparers*. Registered tax return preparers must renew their preparer tax identification number and their status as a registered tax return preparer as prescribed by the Internal Revenue Service in forms, instructions, or other appropriate guidance.

(5) *Notification of renewal*. After review and approval, the Internal Revenue Service will notify the individual of the renewal and will issue the individual a card or certificate evidencing current status as an enrolled agent, enrolled retirement plan agent, or registered tax return preparer.

(6) *Fee*. A reasonable nonrefundable fee may be charged for each application for renewal filed. See 26 CFR part 300.

(7) *Forms*. Forms required for renewal may be obtained by sending a written request to the address specified by the Internal Revenue Service or from such other source as the Internal Revenue Service will publish in the Internal Revenue Bulletin (see 26 CFR 601.601(d)(2)(ii)(b)) and on the Internal Revenue Service webpage (www.irs.gov).

(e) *Condition for renewal*: continuing education. In order to qualify for renewal as an enrolled agent, enrolled retirement plan agent, or registered tax return preparer, an individual must certify, in the manner prescribed by the Internal Revenue Service, that the individual has satisfied the requisite number of continuing education hours.

(1) *Definitions*. For purposes of this section —

(i) *Enrollment year* means January 1 to December 31 of each year of an enrollment cycle.

(ii) *Enrollment cycle* means the three successive enrollment years preceding the effective date of renewal.

(iii) *Registration year* means each 12-month period the registered tax return preparer is authorized to practice before the Internal Revenue Service.

(iv) *The effective date of renewal* is the first day of the fourth month following the close of the period for renewal described in paragraph (d) of this section.

(2) *For renewed enrollment as an enrolled agent or enrolled retirement plan agent* —

(i) *Requirements for enrollment cycle*. A minimum of 72 hours of continuing education credit, including six hours of ethics or professional conduct, must be completed during each enrollment cycle.

(ii) *Requirements for enrollment year*. A minimum of 16 hours of continuing education credit, including two hours of ethics or professional conduct, must be completed during each enrollment year of an enrollment cycle.

(iii) *Enrollment during enrollment cycle* —

(A) *In general*. Subject to paragraph (e)(2)(iii)(B) of this section, an individual who receives initial enrollment during an enrollment cycle must complete two hours of qualifying continuing education credit for each month enrolled during the enrollment cycle. Enrollment for any part of a month is considered enrollment for the entire month.

(B) *Ethics*. An individual who receives initial enrollment during an enrollment cycle must complete two hours of ethics or professional conduct for each enrollment year during the enrollment cycle. Enrollment for any part of an enrollment year is considered enrollment for the entire year.

(3) *Requirements for renewal as a registered tax return preparer*. A minimum of 15 hours of continuing education credit, including two hours of ethics or professional conduct, three hours of Federal tax law updates, and 10 hours of Federal tax law topics, must be completed during each registration year.

(f) *Qualifying continuing education* —

(1) *General* —

(i) *Enrolled agents*. To qualify for continuing education credit for an enrolled agent, a course of learning must —

(A) Be a qualifying continuing education program designed to enhance professional knowledge in Federal taxation or Federal tax related matters (programs comprised of current subject matter in Federal taxation or Federal tax related matters, including accounting, tax return preparation software, taxation, or ethics); and

(B) Be a qualifying continuing education program consistent with the Internal Revenue Code and effective tax administration.

(ii) *Enrolled retirement plan agents*. To qualify for continuing education credit for an enrolled retirement plan agent, a course of learning must —

(A) Be a qualifying continuing education program designed to enhance professional knowledge in qualified retirement plan matters; and

(B) Be a qualifying continuing education program consistent with the Internal Revenue Code and effective tax administration.

(iii) *Registered tax return preparers*. To qualify for continuing education credit for a registered tax return preparer, a course of learning must —

(A) Be a qualifying continuing education program designed to enhance professional knowledge in Federal taxation or Federal tax related matters (programs comprised of current subject matter in Federal taxation or Federal tax related matters, including accounting, tax return preparation software, taxation, or ethics); and

(B) Be a qualifying continuing education program consistent with the Internal Revenue Code and effective tax administration.

(2) *Qualifying programs* —

(i) *Formal programs*. A formal program qualifies as a continuing education program if it —

(A) Requires attendance and provides each attendee with a certificate of attendance;

(B) Is conducted by a qualified instructor, discussion leader, or speaker (in other words, a person whose background, training, education, and experience is appropriate for instructing or leading a discussion on the subject matter of the particular program);

(C) Provides or requires a written outline, textbook, or suitable electronic educational materials; and

(D) Satisfies the requirements established for a qualified continuing education program pursuant to §10.9.

(ii) *Correspondence or individual study programs (including taped programs).* Qualifying continuing education programs include correspondence or individual study programs that are conducted by continuing education providers and completed on an individual basis by the enrolled individual. The allowable credit hours for such programs will be measured on a basis comparable to the measurement of a seminar or course for credit in an accredited educational institution. Such programs qualify as continuing education programs only if they —

(A) Require registration of the participants by the continuing education provider;

(B) Provide a means for measuring successful completion by the participants (for example, a written examination), including the issuance of a certificate of completion by the continuing education provider;

(C) Provide a written outline, textbook, or suitable electronic educational materials; and

(D) Satisfy the requirements established for a qualified continuing education program pursuant to §10.9.

(iii) *Serving as an instructor, discussion leader or speaker.*

(A) One hour of continuing education credit will be awarded for each contact hour completed as an instructor, discussion leader, or speaker at an educational program that meets the continuing education requirements of paragraph (f) of this section.

(B) A maximum of two hours of continuing education credit will be awarded for actual subject preparation time for each contact hour completed as an instructor, discussion leader, or speaker at such programs. It is the responsibility of the individual claiming such credit to maintain records to verify preparation time.

(C) The maximum continuing education credit for instruction and preparation may not exceed four hours annually for registered tax return preparers and six hours annually for enrolled agents and enrolled retirement plan agents.

(D) An instructor, discussion leader, or speaker who makes more than one presentation on the same subject matter during an enrollment cycle or registration year will receive continuing education credit for only one such presentation for the enrollment cycle or registration year.

(3) *Periodic examination.* Enrolled Agents and Enrolled Retirement Plan Agents may establish eligibility for renewal of enrollment for any enrollment cycle by —

(i) Achieving a passing score on each part of the Special Enrollment Examination administered under this part during the three year period prior to renewal; and

(ii) Completing a minimum of 16 hours of qualifying continuing education during the last year of an enrollment cycle.

(g) *Measurement of continuing education coursework.*

(1) All continuing education programs will be measured in terms of contact hours. The shortest recognized program will be one contact hour.

(2) A contact hour is 50 minutes of continuous participation in a program. Credit is granted only for a full contact hour, which is 50 minutes or multiples thereof. For example, a program lasting more than 50 minutes but less than 100 minutes will count as only one contact hour.

(3) Individual segments at continuous conferences, conventions and the like will be considered one total program. For example, two 90-minute segments (180 minutes) at a continuous conference will count as three contact hours.

(4) For university or college courses, each semester hour credit will equal 15 contact hours and a quarter hour credit will equal 10 contact hours.

(h) *Recordkeeping requirements*.

(1) Each individual applying for renewal must retain for a period of four years following the date of renewal the information required with regard to qualifying continuing education credit hours. Such information includes —

(i) The name of the sponsoring organization;

(ii) The location of the program;

(iii) The title of the program, qualified program number, and description of its content;

(iv) Written outlines, course syllabi, textbook, and/or electronic materials provided or required for the course;

(v) The dates attended;

(vi) The credit hours claimed;

(vii) The name(s) of the instructor(s), discussion leader(s), or speaker(s), if appropriate; and

(viii) The certificate of completion and/or signed statement of the hours of attendance obtained from the continuing education provider.

(2) To receive continuing education credit for service completed as an instructor, discussion leader, or speaker, the following information must be maintained for a period of four years following the date of renewal —

(i) The name of the sponsoring organization;
(ii) The location of the program;
(iii) The title of the program and copy of its content;
(iv) The dates of the program; and
(v) The credit hours claimed.

(i) *Waivers*.

(1) Waiver from the continuing education requirements for a given period may be granted for the following reasons —

(i) Health, which prevented compliance with the continuing education requirements;

(ii) Extended active military duty;

(iii) Absence from the United States for an extended period of time due to employment or other reasons, provided the individual does not practice before the Internal Revenue Service during such absence; and

(iv) Other compelling reasons, which will be considered on a case-by-case basis.

(2) A request for waiver must be accompanied by appropriate documentation. The individual is required to furnish any additional documentation or explanation deemed necessary. Examples of appropriate documentation could be a medical certificate or military orders.

(3) A request for waiver must be filed no later than the last day of the renewal application period.

(4) If a request for waiver is not approved, the individual will be placed in inactive status. The individual will be notified that the waiver was not approved and that the individual has been placed on a roster of inactive enrolled agents, enrolled retirement plan agents, or registered tax return preparers.

(5) If the request for waiver is not approved, the individual may file a protest as prescribed by the Internal Revenue Service in forms, instructions, or other appropriate guidance. A protest filed under this section is not governed by subpart D of this part.

(6) If a request for waiver is approved, the individual will be notified and issued a card or certificate evidencing renewal.

(7) Those who are granted waivers are required to file timely applications for renewal of enrollment or registration.

(j) *Failure to comply*.

(1) Compliance by an individual with the requirements of this part is determined by the Internal Revenue Service. The Internal Revenue Service will provide notice to any individual who fails to meet the continuing education and fee requirements of eligibility for renewal. The notice will state the basis for the determination of noncompliance and will provide the individual an opportunity to furnish the requested information in writing relating to the matter within 60 days of the date of the notice. Such information will be considered in making a final determination as to eligibility for renewal. The individual must be informed of the reason(s) for any denial of a renewal. The individual may, within 30 days after receipt of the notice of denial of renewal, file a written protest of the denial as prescribed by the Internal Revenue Service in forms, instructions, or other appropriate guidance. A protest under this section is not governed by subpart D of this part.

(2) The continuing education records of an enrolled agent, enrolled retirement plan agent, or registered tax return preparer may be reviewed to determine compliance with the requirements and standards for renewal as provided in paragraph (f) of this section. As part of this review, the enrolled agent, enrolled retirement plan agent or registered tax return preparer may be required to provide the Internal Revenue Service with copies of any continuing education records required to be maintained under this part. If the enrolled agent, enrolled retirement plan agent or registered tax return preparer fails to comply with this requirement, any continuing education hours claimed may be disallowed.

(3) An individual who has not filed a timely application for renewal, who has not made a timely response to the notice of noncompliance with the renewal requirements, or who has not satisfied the requirements of eligibility for renewal will be placed on a roster of inactive enrolled individuals or inactive registered individuals. During this time, the individual will be ineligible to practice before the Internal Revenue Service.

(4) Individuals placed in inactive status and individuals ineligible to practice before the Internal Revenue Service may not state or imply that they are eligible to practice before the Internal Revenue Service, or use the terms enrolled agent, enrolled retirement plan agent, or registered tax return preparer, the designations "EA" or "ERPA" or other form of reference to eligibility to practice before the Internal Revenue Service.

(5) An individual placed in inactive status may be reinstated to an active status by filing an application for renewal and providing evidence of the completion of all required continuing education hours for the enrollment cycle or registration year. Continuing education credit under this paragraph (j)(5) may not be used to satisfy the requirements of the enrollment cycle or registration year in which the individual has been placed back on the active roster.

(6) An individual placed in inactive status must file an application for renewal and satisfy the requirements for renewal as set forth in this section within three years of being placed in inactive status. Otherwise, the name of such individual will be removed from the inactive status roster and the individual's status as an enrolled agent, enrolled retirement plan agent, or registered tax return preparer will terminate. Future eligibility for active status must then be reestablished by the individual as provided in this section.

(7) Inactive status is not available to an individual who is the subject of a pending disciplinary matter before the Internal Revenue Service.

(k) *Inactive retirement status*. An individual who no longer practices before the Internal Revenue Service may request to be placed in an inactive retirement status at any time and such individual will be placed in an inactive retirement status. The individual will be ineligible to practice before the Internal Revenue Service. An individual who is placed in an inactive retirement status may be reinstated to an active status by filing an application for renewal and providing evidence of the completion of the required continuing education hours for the enrollment cycle or registration year. Inactive retirement status is not available to an individual who is ineligible to practice before the Internal Revenue Service or an individual who is the subject of a pending disciplinary matter under this part.

(l) *Renewal while under suspension or disbarment*. An individual who is ineligible to practice before the Internal Revenue Service by virtue of disciplinary action under this part is required to conform to the requirements for renewal of enrollment or registration before the individual's eligibility is restored.

(m) *Enrolled actuaries*. The enrollment and renewal of enrollment of actuaries authorized to practice under paragraph (d) of §10.3 are governed by the regulations of the Joint Board for the Enrollment of Actuaries at 20 CFR 901.1 through 901.72.

(n) *Effective/applicability date*. This section is applicable to enrollment or registration effective beginning August 2, 2011.

§ 10.7 Representing oneself; participating in rulemaking; limited practice; and special appearances.

(a) *Representing oneself*. Individuals may appear on their own behalf before the Internal Revenue Service provided they present satisfactory identification.

(b) *Participating in rulemaking*. Individuals may participate in rulemaking as provided by the Administrative Procedure Act. See 5 U.S.C. § 553.

(c) *Limited practice* —

(1) *In general*. Subject to the limitations in paragraph (c)(2) of this section, an individual who is not a practitioner may represent a taxpayer before the Internal Revenue Service in the circumstances described in this paragraph (c)(1), even if the taxpayer is not present, provided the individual presents satisfactory identification and proof of his or her authority to represent the taxpayer. The circumstances described in this paragraph (c)(1) are as follows:

(i) An individual may represent a member of his or her immediate family.

(ii) A regular full-time employee of an individual employer may represent the employer.

(iii) A general partner or a regular full-time employee of a partnership may represent the partnership.

(iv) A bona fide officer or a regular full-time employee of a corporation (including a parent, subsidiary, or other affiliated corporation), association, or organized group may represent the corporation, association, or organized group.

(v) A regular full-time employee of a trust, receivership, guardianship, or estate may represent the trust, receivership, guardianship, or estate.

(vi) An officer or a regular employee of a governmental unit, agency, or authority may represent the governmental unit, agency, or authority in the course of his or her official duties.

(vii) An individual may represent any individual or entity, who is outside the United States, before personnel of the Internal Revenue Service when such representation takes place outside the United States.

(2) *Limitations*.

(i) An individual who is under suspension or disbarment from practice before the Internal Revenue Service may not engage in limited practice before the Internal Revenue Service under paragraph (c)(1) of this section.

(ii) The Commissioner, or delegate, may, after notice and opportunity for a conference, deny eligibility to engage in limited practice before the Internal Revenue Service under paragraph (c)(1) of this section to any individual who has engaged in conduct that would justify a sanction under §10.50.

(iii) An individual who represents a taxpayer under the authority of paragraph (c)(1) of this section is subject, to the extent of his or her authority, to such rules of general applicability regarding standards of conduct and other matters as prescribed by the Internal Revenue Service.

(d) *Special appearances*. The Commissioner, or delegate, may, subject to conditions deemed appropriate, authorize an individual who is not otherwise eligible to practice before the Internal Revenue Service to represent another person in a particular matter.

(e) *Fiduciaries*. For purposes of this part, a fiduciary (for example, a trustee, receiver, guardian, personal representative, administrator, or executor) is considered to be the taxpayer and not a representative of the taxpayer.

(f) *Effective/applicability date*. This section is applicable beginning August 2, 2011.

§ 10.8 Return preparation and application of rules to other individuals.

(a) *Preparing all or substantially all of a tax return.* Any individual who for compensation prepares or assists with the preparation of all or substantially all of a tax return or claim for refund must have a preparer tax identification number. Except as otherwise prescribed in forms, instructions, or other appropriate guidance, an individual must be an attorney, certified public accountant, enrolled agent, or registered tax return preparer to obtain a preparer tax identification number. Any individual who for compensation prepares or assists with the preparation of all or substantially all of a tax return or claim for refund is subject to the duties and restrictions relating to practice in subpart B, as well as subject to the sanctions for violation of the regulations in subpart C.

(b) *Preparing a tax return and furnishing information.* Any individual may for compensation prepare or assist with the preparation of a tax return or claim for refund (provided the individual prepares less than substantially all of the tax return or claim for refund), appear as a witness for the taxpayer before the Internal Revenue Service, or furnish information at the request of the Internal Revenue Service or any of its officers or employees.

(c) *Application of rules to other individuals.* Any individual who for compensation prepares, or assists in the preparation of, all or a substantial portion of a document pertaining to any taxpayer's tax liability for submission to the Internal Revenue Service is subject to the duties and restrictions relating to practice in subpart B, as well as subject to the sanctions for violation of the regulations in subpart C. Unless otherwise a practitioner, however, an individual may not for compensation prepare, or assist in the preparation of, all or substantially all of a tax return or claim for refund, or sign tax returns and claims for refund. For purposes of this paragraph, an individual described in 26 CFR 301.7701-15(f) is not treated as having prepared all or a substantial portion of the document by reason of such assistance.

(d) *Effective/applicability date.* This section is applicable beginning August 2, 2011.

§ 10.9 Continuing education providers and continuing education programs.

(a) *Continuing education providers* —

(1) *In general.* Continuing education providers are those responsible for presenting continuing education programs. A continuing education provider must —

(i) Be an accredited educational institution;

(ii) Be recognized for continuing education purposes by the licensing body of any State, territory, or possession of the United States, including a Commonwealth, or the District of Columbia;

(iii) Be recognized and approved by a qualifying organization as a provider of continuing education on subject matters within §10.6(f) of this part. The Internal Revenue Service may, at its discretion, identify a professional organization, society or business entity that maintains minimum education standards comparable to those set forth in this part as a qualifying organization for purposes of this part in appropriate forms, instructions, and other appropriate guidance; or

(iv) Be recognized by the Internal Revenue Service as a professional organization, society, or business whose programs include offering continuing professional education opportunities in subject matters within §10.6(f) of this part. The Internal Revenue Service, at its discretion, may require such professional organizations, societies, or businesses to file an agreement and/or obtain Internal Revenue Service approval of each program as a qualified continuing education program in appropriate forms, instructions or other appropriate guidance.

(2) *Continuing education provider numbers* —

(i) *In general.* A continuing education provider is required to obtain a continuing education provider number and pay any applicable user fee.

(ii) *Renewal.* A continuing education provider maintains its status as a continuing education provider during the continuing education provider cycle by renewing its continuing education provider number as prescribed by forms, instructions or other appropriate guidance and paying any applicable user fee.

(3) *Requirements for qualified continuing education programs.* A continuing education provider must ensure the qualified continuing education program complies with all the following requirements —

(i) Programs must be developed by individual(s) qualified in the subject matter;

(ii) Program subject matter must be current;

(iii) Instructors, discussion leaders, and speakers must be qualified with respect to program content;

(iv) Programs must include some means for evaluation of the technical content and presentation to be evaluated;

(v) Certificates of completion bearing a current qualified continuing education program number issued by the Internal Revenue Service must be provided to the participants who successfully complete the program; and

(vi) Records must be maintained by the continuing education provider to verify the participants who attended and completed the program for a period of four years following completion of the program. In the case of continuous conferences, conventions, and the like, records must be maintained to verify completion of the program and attendance by each participant at each segment of the program.

(4) *Program numbers* —

(i) *In general.* Every continuing education provider is required to obtain a continuing education provider program number and pay any applicable user fee for each program offered. Program numbers shall be obtained as prescribed by forms, instructions or other appropriate guidance. Although, at the discretion of the Internal Revenue Service, a continuing education provider may be required to demonstrate that the program is designed to enhance professional knowledge in Federal taxation or Federal tax related matters (programs comprised of current subject matter in Federal taxation or Federal tax related matters, including accounting, tax return preparation software, taxation, or ethics) and complies with the requirements in paragraph (a)(2) of this section before a program number is issued.

(ii) *Update programs.* Update programs may use the same number as the program subject to update. An update program is a program that instructs on a change of existing law occurring within one year of the update program offering. The qualifying education program subject to update must have been offered within the two year time period prior to the change in existing law.

(iii) *Change in existing law.* A change in existing law means the effective date of the statute or regulation, or date of entry of judicial decision, that is the subject of the update.

(b) *Failure to comply.* Compliance by a continuing education provider with the requirements of this part is determined by the Internal Revenue Service. A continuing education provider who fails to meet the requirements of this part will be notified by the Internal Revenue Service. The notice will state the basis for the determination of noncompliance and will provide the continuing education provider an opportunity to furnish the requested information in writing relating to the matter within 60 days of the date of the notice. The continuing education provider may, within 30 days after receipt of the notice of denial, file a written protest as prescribed by the Internal Revenue Service in forms, instructions, or other appropriate guidance. A protest under this section is not governed by subpart D of this part.

(c) *Effective/applicability date.* This section is applicable beginning August 2, 2011.

Subpart B -- Duties and Restrictions Relating to Practice Before the Internal Revenue Service

§ 10.20 Information to be furnished.

(a) *To the Internal Revenue Service.*

(1) A practitioner must, on a proper and lawful request by a duly authorized officer or employee of the Internal Revenue Service, promptly submit records or information in any matter before the Internal Revenue Service unless the practitioner believes in good faith and on reasonable grounds that the records or information are privileged.

(2) Where the requested records or information are not in the possession of, or subject to the control of, the practitioner or the practitioner's client, the practitioner must promptly notify the requesting Internal Revenue Service officer or employee and the practitioner must provide any information that the practitioner has regarding the identity of any person who the practitioner believes may have possession or control of the requested records or information. The practitioner must make reasonable inquiry of his or her client regarding the identity of any person who may have possession or control of the requested records or information, but the practitioner is not required to make inquiry of any other person or independently verify any information provided by the practitioner's client regarding the identity of such persons.

(3) When a proper and lawful request is made by a duly authorized officer or employee of the Internal Revenue Service, concerning an inquiry into an alleged violation of the regulations in this part, a practitioner must provide any information the practitioner has concerning the alleged violation and testify regarding this information in any proceeding instituted under this part, unless the practitioner believes in good faith and on reasonable grounds that the information is privileged.

(b) *Interference with a proper and lawful request for records or information*. A practitioner may not interfere, or attempt to interfere, with any proper and lawful effort by the Internal Revenue Service, its officers or employees, to obtain any record or information unless the practitioner believes in good faith and on reasonable grounds that the record or information is privileged.

(c) *Effective/applicability date*. This section is applicable beginning August 2, 2011.

§ 10.21 Knowledge of client's omission.

A practitioner who, having been retained by a client with respect to a matter administered by the Internal Revenue Service, knows that the client has not complied with the revenue laws of the United States or has made an error in or omission from any return, document, affidavit, or other paper which the client submitted or executed under the revenue laws of the United States, must advise the client promptly of the fact of such noncompliance, error, or omission. The practitioner must advise the client of the consequences as provided under the Code and regulations of such noncompliance, error, or omission.

§ 10.22 Diligence as to accuracy.

(a) *In general*. A practitioner must exercise due diligence —

(1) In preparing or assisting in the preparation of, approving, and filing tax returns, documents, affidavits, and other papers relating to Internal Revenue Service matters;

(2) In determining the correctness of oral or written representations made by the practitioner to the Department of the Treasury; and

(3) In determining the correctness of oral or written representations made by the practitioner to clients with reference to any matter administered by the Internal Revenue Service.

(b) *Reliance on others*. Except as modified by §§ 10.34 and 10.37, a practitioner will be presumed to have exercised due diligence for purposes of this section if the practitioner relies on the work product of another person and the practitioner used reasonable care in engaging, supervising, training, and evaluating the person, taking proper account of the nature of the relationship between the practitioner and the person.

(c) *Effective/applicability date*. Paragraph (a) of this section is applicable on September 26, 2007. Paragraph (b) of this section is applicable beginning June 12, 2014.

§ 10.23 Prompt disposition of pending matters.

A practitioner may not unreasonably delay the prompt disposition of any matter before the Internal Revenue Service.

§ 10.24 Assistance from or to disbarred or suspended persons and former Internal Revenue Service employees.

A practitioner may not, knowingly and directly or indirectly:

(a) Accept assistance from or assist any person who is under disbarment or suspension from practice before the Internal Revenue Service if the assistance relates to a matter or matters constituting practice before the Internal Revenue Service.

(b) Accept assistance from any former government employee where the provisions of § 10.25 or any Federal law would be violated.

§ 10.25 Practice by former government employees, their partners and their associates.

(a) *Definitions*. For purposes of this section —

(1) *Assist* means to act in such a way as to advise, furnish information to, or otherwise aid another person, directly, or indirectly.

(2) *Government employee* is an officer or employee of the United States or any agency of the United States, including a special Government employee as defined in *18 U.S.C. 202(a)*, or of the District of Columbia, or of any State, or a member of Congress or of any State legislature.

(3) *Member of a firm* is a sole practitioner or an employee or associate thereof, or a partner, stockholder, associate, affiliate or employee of a partnership, joint venture, corporation, professional association or other affiliation of two or more practitioners who represent nongovernmental parties.

(4) *Particular matter involving specific parties* is defined at 5 CFR 2637.201(c), or superseding post-employment regulations issued by the U.S. Office of Government Ethics.

(5) *Rule* includes Treasury regulations, whether issued or under preparation for issuance as notices of proposed rulemaking or as Treasury decisions, revenue rulings, and revenue procedures published in the Internal Revenue Bulletin (see *26 CFR 601.601(d)(2)(ii)(b))*.

(b) *General rules* —

(1) No former Government employee may, subsequent to Government employment, represent anyone in any matter administered by the Internal Revenue Service if the representation would violate *18 U.S.C. 207* or any other laws of the United States.

(2) No former Government employee who personally and substantially participated in a particular matter involving specific parties may, subsequent to Government employment, represent or knowingly assist, in that particular matter, any person who is or was a specific party to that particular matter.

(3) A former Government employee who within a period of one year prior to the termination of Government employment had official responsibility for a particular matter involving specific parties may not, within two years after Government employment is ended, represent in that particular matter any person who is or was a specific party to that particular matter.

(4) No former Government employee may, within one year after Government employment is ended, communicate with or appear before, with the intent to influence, any employee of the Treasury Department in connection with the publication, withdrawal, amendment, modification, or interpretation of a rule the development of which the former Government employee participated in, or for which, within a period of one year prior to the termination of Government employment, the former government employee had official responsibility. This paragraph (b)(4) does not, however, preclude any former employee from appearing on one's own behalf or from representing a taxpayer before the Internal Revenue Service in connection with a particular matter involving specific parties involving the application or interpretation of a rule with respect to that particular matter, provided that the representation is otherwise consistent with the other provisions of this section and the former employee does not utilize or disclose any confidential information acquired by the former employee in the development of the rule.

(c) *Firm representation* —

(1) No member of a firm of which a former Government employee is a member may represent or knowingly assist a person who was or is a specific party in any particular matter with respect to which the restrictions of paragraph (b)(2) of this section apply to the former Government employee, in that particular matter, unless the firm isolates the former Government employee in such a way to ensure that the former Government employee cannot assist in the representation.

(2) When isolation of a former Government employee is required under paragraph (c)(1) of this section, a statement affirming the fact of such isolation must be executed under oath by the former Government employee and by another member of the firm acting on behalf of the firm. The statement must clearly identify the firm, the former Government employee, and the particular matter(s) requiring isolation. The statement must be retained by the firm and, upon request, provided to the office(s) of the Internal Revenue Service administering or enforcing this part.

(d) *Pending representation*. The provisions of this regulation will govern practice by former Government employees, their partners and associates with respect to representation in particular matters involving specific parties where actual representation commenced before the effective date of this regulation.

(e) *Effective/applicability date*. This section is applicable beginning August 2, 2011.

§ 10.26 Notaries.

A practitioner may not take acknowledgments, administer oaths, certify papers, or perform any official act as a notary public with respect to any matter administered by the Internal Revenue Service and for which he or she is employed as counsel, attorney, or agent, or in which he or she may be in any way interested.

§ 10.27 Fees.

(a) *In general*. A practitioner may not charge an unconscionable fee in connection with any matter before the Internal Revenue Service.

(b) *Contingent fees* —

(1) Except as provided in paragraphs (b)(2), (3), and (4) of this section, a practitioner may not charge a contingent fee for services rendered in connection with any matter before the Internal Revenue Service.

(2) A practitioner may charge a contingent fee for services rendered in connection with the Service's examination of, or challenge to —

(i) An original tax return; or

(ii) An amended return or claim for refund or credit where the amended return or claim for refund or credit was filed within 120 days of the taxpayer receiving a written notice of the examination of, or a written challenge to the original tax return.

(3) A practitioner may charge a contingent fee for services rendered in connection with a claim for credit or refund filed solely in connection with the determination of statutory interest or penalties assessed by the Internal Revenue Service.

(4) A practitioner may charge a contingent fee for services rendered in connection with any judicial proceeding arising under the Internal Revenue Code.

(c) *Definitions*. For purposes of this section —

(1) *Contingent fee* is any fee that is based, in whole or in part, on whether or not a position taken on a tax return or other filing avoids challenge by the Internal Revenue Service or is sustained either by the Internal Revenue Service or in litigation. A contingent fee includes a fee that is based on a percentage of the refund reported on a return, that is based on a percentage of the taxes saved, or that otherwise depends on the specific result attained. A contingent fee also includes any fee arrangement in which the practitioner will reimburse the client for all or a portion of the client's fee in the event that a position taken on a tax return or other filing is challenged by the Internal Revenue Service or is not sustained, whether pursuant to an indemnity agreement, a guarantee, rescission rights, or any other arrangement with a similar effect.

(2) *Matter before the Internal Revenue Service* includes tax planning and advice, preparing or filing or assisting in preparing or filing returns or claims for refund or credit, and all matters connected with a presentation to the Internal Revenue Service or any of its officers or employees relating to a taxpayer's rights, privileges, or liabilities under laws or regulations administered by the Internal Revenue Service. Such presentations include, but are not limited to, preparing and filing documents, corresponding and communicating with the Internal Revenue Service, rendering written advice with respect to any entity, transaction, plan or arrangement, and representing a client at conferences, hearings, and meetings.

(d) *Effective/applicability date*. This section is applicable for fee arrangements entered into after March 26, 2008.

§ 10.28 Return of client's records.

(a) In general, a practitioner must, at the request of a client, promptly return any and all records of the client that are necessary for the client to comply with his or her Federal tax obligations. The practitioner may retain copies of the records returned to a client. The existence of a dispute over fees generally does not relieve the practitioner of his or her responsibility under this section. Nevertheless, if applicable state law allows or permits the retention of a client's records by a practitioner in the case of a dispute over fees for services rendered, the practitioner need only return those records that must be attached to the taxpayer's return. The practitioner, however, must provide the client with reasonable access to review and copy any additional records of the client retained by the practitioner under state law that are necessary for the client to comply with his or her Federal tax obligations.

(b) For purposes of this section — Records of the client include all documents or written or electronic materials provided to the practitioner, or obtained by the practitioner in the course of the practitioner's representation of the client, that preexisted the retention of the practitioner by the client. The term also includes materials that were prepared by the client or a third party (not including an employee or agent of the practitioner) at any time and provided to the practitioner with respect to the subject matter of the representation. The term also includes any return, claim for refund, schedule, affidavit, appraisal or any other document prepared by the practitioner, or his or her employee or agent, that was presented to the client with respect to a prior representation if such document is necessary for the taxpayer to comply with his or her current Federal tax obligations. The term does not include any return, claim for refund, schedule, affidavit, appraisal or any other document prepared by the practitioner or the practitioner's firm, employees or agents if the practitioner is withholding such document pending the client's performance of its contractual obligation to pay fees with respect to such document.

§ 10.29 Conflicting interests.

(a) Except as provided by paragraph (b) of this section, a practitioner shall not represent a client before the Internal Revenue Service if the representation involves a conflict of interest. A conflict of interest exists if —

(1) The representation of one client will be directly adverse to another client; or

(2) There is a significant risk that the representation of one or more clients will be materially limited by the practitioner's responsibilities to another client, a former client or a third person, or by a personal interest of the practitioner.

(b) Notwithstanding the existence of a conflict of interest under paragraph (a) of this section, the practitioner may represent a client if —

(1) The practitioner reasonably believes that the practitioner will be able to provide competent and diligent representation to each affected client;

(2) The representation is not prohibited by law; and

(3) Each affected client waives the conflict of interest and gives informed consent, confirmed in writing by each affected client, at the time the existence of the conflict of interest is known by the practitioner. The confirmation may be made within a reasonable period of time after the informed consent, but in no event later than 30 days.

(c) Copies of the written consents must be retained by the practitioner for at least 36 months from the date of the conclusion of the representation of the affected clients, and the written consents must be provided to any officer or employee of the Internal Revenue Service on request.

(d) *Effective/applicability date*. This section is applicable on September 26, 2007.

§ 10.30 Solicitation.

(a) *Advertising and solicitation restrictions.*

(1) A practitioner may not, with respect to any Internal Revenue Service matter, in any way use or participate in the use of any form of public communication or private solicitation containing a false, fraudulent, or coercive statement or claim; or a misleading or deceptive statement or claim. Enrolled agents, enrolled retirement plan agents, or registered tax return preparers, in describing their professional designation, may not utilize the term "certified" or imply an employer/employee relationship with the Internal Revenue Service. Examples of acceptable descriptions for enrolled agents are "enrolled to represent taxpayers before the Internal Revenue Service," "enrolled to practice before the Internal Revenue Service," and "admitted to practice before the Internal Revenue Service." Similarly, examples of acceptable descriptions for enrolled retirement plan agents are "enrolled to represent taxpayers before the Internal Revenue Service as a retirement plan agent" and "enrolled to practice before the Internal Revenue Service as a retirement plan agent." An example of an acceptable description for registered tax return preparers is "designated as a registered tax return preparer by the Internal Revenue Service."

(2) A practitioner may not make, directly or indirectly, an uninvited written or oral solicitation of employment in matters related to the Internal Revenue Service if the solicitation violates Federal or State law or other applicable rule, e.g., attorneys are precluded from making a solicitation that is prohibited by conduct rules applicable to all attorneys in their State(s) of licensure. Any lawful solicitation made by or on behalf of a practitioner eligible to practice before the Internal Revenue Service must, nevertheless, clearly identify the solicitation as such and, if applicable, identify the source of the information used in choosing the recipient.

(b) *Fee information.*

(1) (i) A practitioner may publish the availability of a written schedule of fees and disseminate the following fee information —

(A) Fixed fees for specific routine services.
(B) Hourly rates.
(C) Range of fees for particular services.
(D) Fee charged for an initial consultation.

(ii) Any statement of fee information concerning matters in which costs may be incurred must include a statement disclosing whether clients will be responsible for such costs.

(2) A practitioner may charge no more than the rate(s) published under paragraph (b)(1) of this section for at least 30 calendar days after the last date on which the schedule of fees was published.

(c) *Communication of fee information*. Fee information may be communicated in professional lists, telephone directories, print media, mailings, and electronic mail, facsimile, hand delivered flyers, radio, television, and any other method. The method chosen, however, must not cause the communication to become untruthful, deceptive, or otherwise in violation of this part. A practitioner may not persist in attempting to contact a prospective client if the prospective client has made it known to the practitioner that he or she does not desire to be solicited. In the case of radio and television broadcasting, the broadcast must be recorded and the practitioner must retain a recording of the actual transmission. In the case of direct mail and e-commerce communications, the practitioner must retain a copy of the actual communication, along with a list or other description of persons to whom the communication was mailed or otherwise distributed. The copy must be retained by the practitioner for a period of at least 36 months from the date of the last transmission or use.

(d) *Improper associations*. A practitioner may not, in matters related to the Internal Revenue Service, assist, or accept assistance from, any person or entity who, to the knowledge of the practitioner, obtains clients or otherwise practices in a manner forbidden under this section.

(e) *Effective/applicability date*. This section is applicable beginning August 2, 2011.

(Approved by the Office of Management and Budget under Control No. 1545-1726)

§ 10.31 Negotiation of taxpayer checks.

(a) A practitioner may not endorse or otherwise negotiate any check (including directing or accepting payment by any means, electronic or otherwise, into an account owned or controlled by the practitioner or any firm or other entity with whom the practitioner is associated) issued to a client by the government in respect of a Federal tax liability.

(b) *Effective/applicability date*. This section is applicable beginning June 12, 2014.

§ 10.32 Practice of law.

Nothing in the regulations in this part may be construed as authorizing persons not members of the bar to practice law.

§ 10.33 Best practices for tax advisors.

(a) *Best practices*. Tax advisors should provide clients with the highest quality representation concerning Federal tax issues by adhering to best practices in providing advice and in preparing or assisting in the preparation of a submission to the Internal Revenue Service. In addition to compliance with the standards of practice provided elsewhere in this part, best practices include the following:

(1) Communicating clearly with the client regarding the terms of the engagement. For example, the advisor should determine the client's expected purpose for and use of the advice and should have a clear understanding with the client regarding the form and scope of the advice or assistance to be rendered.

(2) Establishing the facts, determining which facts are relevant, evaluating the reasonableness of any assumptions or representations, relating the applicable law (including potentially applicable judicial doctrines) to the relevant facts, and arriving at a conclusion supported by the law and the facts.

(3) Advising the client regarding the import of the conclusions reached, including, for example, whether a taxpayer may avoid accuracy-related penalties under the Internal Revenue Code if a taxpayer acts in reliance on the advice.

(4) Acting fairly and with integrity in practice before the Internal Revenue Service.

(b) *Procedures to ensure best practices for tax advisors*. Tax advisors with responsibility for overseeing a firm's practice of providing advice concerning Federal tax issues or of preparing or assisting in the preparation of submissions to the Internal Revenue Service should take reasonable steps to ensure that the firm's procedures for all members, associates, and employees are consistent with the best practices set forth in paragraph (a) of this section.

(c) *Applicability date*. This section is effective after June 20, 2005.

§ 10.34 Standards with respect to tax returns and documents, affidavits and other papers.

(a) *Tax returns*.

(1) A practitioner may not willfully, recklessly, or through gross incompetence —

(i) Sign a tax return or claim for refund that the practitioner knows or reasonably should know contains a position that —

(A) Lacks a reasonable basis;

(B) Is an unreasonable position as described in section 6694(a)(2) of the Internal Revenue Code (Code) (including the related regulations and other published guidance); or

(C) Is a willful attempt by the practitioner to understate the liability for tax or a reckless or intentional disregard of rules or regulations by the practitioner as described in section 6694(b)(2) of the Code (including the related regulations and other published guidance).

(ii) Advise a client to take a position on a tax return or claim for refund, or prepare a portion of a tax return or claim for refund containing a position, that —

(A) Lacks a reasonable basis;

(B) Is an unreasonable position as described in section 6694(a)(2) of the Code (including the related regulations and other published guidance); or

(C) Is a willful attempt by the practitioner to understate the liability for tax or a reckless or intentional disregard of rules or regulations by the practitioner as described in section 6694(b)(2) of the Code (including the related regulations and other published guidance).

(2) A pattern of conduct is a factor that will be taken into account in determining whether a practitioner acted willfully, recklessly, or through gross incompetence.

(b) *Documents, affidavits and other papers* —

(1) A practitioner may not advise a client to take a position on a document, affidavit or other paper submitted to the Internal Revenue Service unless the position is not frivolous.

(2) A practitioner may not advise a client to submit a document, affidavit or other paper to the Internal Revenue Service —

(i) The purpose of which is to delay or impede the administration of the Federal tax laws;

(ii) That is frivolous; or

(iii) That contains or omits information in a manner that demonstrates an intentional disregard of a rule or regulation unless the practitioner also advises the client to submit a document that evidences a good faith challenge to the rule or regulation.

(c) *Advising clients on potential penalties* —

(1) A practitioner must inform a client of any penalties that are reasonably likely to apply to the client with respect to —

(i) A position taken on a tax return if —

(A) The practitioner advised the client with respect to the position; or

(B) The practitioner prepared or signed the tax return; and

(ii) Any document, affidavit or other paper submitted to the Internal Revenue Service.

(2) The practitioner also must inform the client of any opportunity to avoid any such penalties by disclosure, if relevant, and of the requirements for adequate disclosure.

(3) This paragraph (c) applies even if the practitioner is not subject to a penalty under the Internal Revenue Code with respect to the position or with respect to the document, affidavit or other paper submitted.

(d) *Relying on information furnished by clients*. A practitioner advising a client to take a position on a tax return, document, affidavit or other paper submitted to the Internal Revenue Service, or preparing or signing a tax return as a preparer, generally may rely in good faith without verification upon information furnished by the client. The practitioner may not, however, ignore the implications of information furnished to, or actually known by, the practitioner, and must make reasonable inquiries if the information as furnished appears to be incorrect, inconsistent with an important fact or another factual assumption, or incomplete.

(e) *Effective/applicability date*. Paragraph (a) of this section is applicable for returns or claims for refund filed, or advice provided, beginning August 2, 2011. Paragraphs (b) through (d) of this section are applicable to tax returns, documents, affidavits, and other papers filed on or after September 26, 2007.

§ 10.35 Competence.

(a) A practitioner must possess the necessary competence to engage in practice before the Internal Revenue Service. Competent practice requires the appropriate level of knowledge, skill, thoroughness, and preparation necessary for the matter for which the practitioner is engaged. A practitioner may become competent for the matter for which the practitioner has been engaged through various methods, such as consulting with experts in the relevant area or studying the relevant law.

(b) *Effective/applicability date*. This section is applicable beginning June 12, 2014.

§10.36 Procedures to ensure compliance.

(a) Any individual subject to the provisions of this part who has (or individuals who have or share) principal authority and responsibility for overseeing a firm's practice governed by this part, including the provision of advice concerning Federal tax matters and preparation of tax returns, claims for refund, or other documents for submission to the Internal Revenue Service, must take reasonable steps to ensure that the firm has adequate procedures in effect for all members, associates, and employees for purposes of complying with subparts A, B, and C of this part, as applicable. In the absence of a person or persons identified by the firm as having the principal authority and responsibility described in this paragraph, the Internal Revenue Service may identify one or more individuals subject to the provisions of this part responsible for compliance with the requirements of this section.

(b) Any such individual who has (or such individuals who have or share) principal authority as described in paragraph (a) of this section will be subject to discipline for failing to comply with the requirements of this section if—

(1) The individual through willfulness, recklessness, or gross incompetence does not take reasonable steps to ensure that the firm has adequate procedures to comply with this part, as applicable, and one or more individuals who are members of, associated with, or employed by, the firm are, or have, engaged in a pattern or practice, in connection with their practice with the firm, of failing to comply with this part, as applicable;

(2) The individual through willfulness, recklessness, or gross incompetence does not take reasonable steps to ensure that firm procedures in effect are properly followed, and one or more individuals who are members of, associated with, or employed by, the firm are, or have, engaged in a pattern or practice, in connection with their practice with the firm, of failing to comply with this part, as applicable; or

(3) The individual knows or should know that one or more individuals who are members of, associated with, or employed by, the firm are, or have, engaged in a pattern or practice, in connection with their practice with the firm, that does not comply with this part, as applicable, and the individual, through willfulness, recklessness, or gross incompetence fails to take prompt action to correct the noncompliance.

(c) *Effective/applicability date*. This section is applicable beginning June 12, 2014.

§10.37 Requirements for other written advice.

(a) *Requirements.*

(1) A practitioner may give written advice (including by means of electronic communication) concerning one or more Federal tax matters subject to the requirements in paragraph (a)(2) of this section. Government submissions on matters of general policy are not considered written advice on a Federal tax matter for purposes of this section. Continuing education presentations provided to an audience solely for the purpose of enhancing practitioners' professional knowledge on Federal tax matters are not considered written advice on a Federal tax matter for purposes of this section. The preceding sentence does not apply to presentations marketing or promoting transactions.

(2) The practitioner must—

(i) Base the written advice on reasonable factual and legal assumptions (including assumptions as to future events);

(ii) Reasonably consider all relevant facts and circumstances that the practitioner knows or reasonably should know;

(iii) Use reasonable efforts to identify and ascertain the facts relevant to written advice on each Federal tax matter;

(iv) Not rely upon representations, statements, findings, or agreements (including projections, financial forecasts, or appraisals) of the taxpayer or any other person if reliance on them would be unreasonable;

(v) Relate applicable law and authorities to facts; and

(vi) Not, in evaluating a Federal tax matter, take into account the possibility that a tax return will not be audited or that a matter will not be raised on audit.

(3) Reliance on representations, statements, findings, or agreements is unreasonable if the practitioner knows or reasonably should know that one or more representations or assumptions on which any representation is based are incorrect, incomplete, or inconsistent.

(b) *Reliance on advice of others.* A practitioner may only rely on the advice of another person if the advice was reasonable and the reliance is in good faith considering all the facts and circumstances. Reliance is not reasonable when—

(1) The practitioner knows or reasonably should know that the opinion of the other person should not be relied on;

(2) The practitioner knows or reasonably should know that the other person is not competent or lacks the necessary qualifications to provide the advice; or

(3) The practitioner knows or reasonably should know that the other person has a conflict of interest in violation of the rules described in this part.

(c) *Standard of review.*

(1) In evaluating whether a practitioner giving written advice concerning one or more Federal tax matters complied with the requirements of this section, the Commissioner, or delegate, will apply a reasonable practitioner standard, considering all facts and circumstances, including, but not limited to, the scope of the engagement and the type and specificity of the advice sought by the client.

(2) In the case of an opinion the practitioner knows or has reason to know will be used or referred to by a person other than the practitioner (or a person who is a member of, associated with, or employed by the practitioner's firm) in promoting, marketing, or recommending to one or more taxpayers a partnership or other entity, investment plan or arrangement a significant purpose of which is the avoidance or evasion of any tax imposed by the Internal Revenue Code, the Commissioner, or delegate, will apply a reasonable practitioner standard, considering all facts and circumstances, with emphasis given to the additional risk caused by the practitioner's lack of knowledge of the taxpayer's particular circumstances, when determining whether a practitioner has failed to comply with this section.

(d) *Federal tax matter.* A Federal tax matter, as used in this section, is any matter concerning the application or interpretation of---

(1) A revenue provision as defined in section 6110(i)(1)(B) of the Internal Revenue Code;

(2) Any provision of law impacting a person's obligations under the internal revenue laws and regulations, including but not limited to the person's liability to pay tax or obligation to file returns; or

(3) Any other law or regulation administered by the Internal Revenue Service.

(e) *Effective/applicability date.* This section is applicable to written advice rendered after June 12, 2014.

§10.38 Establishment of advisory committees.

(a) *Advisory committees.* To promote and maintain the public's confidence in tax advisors, the Internal Revenue Service is authorized to establish one or more advisory committees composed of at least six individuals authorized to practice before the Internal Revenue Service. Membership of an advisory committee must be balanced among those who practice as attorneys, accountants, enrolled agents, enrolled actuaries, enrolled retirement plan agents, and registered tax return preparers. Under procedures prescribed by the Internal Revenue Service, an advisory committee may review and make general recommendations regarding the practices, procedures, and policies of the offices described in §10.1.

(b) *Effective date.* This section is applicable beginning August 2, 2011.

Subpart C -- Sanctions for Violation of the Regulations

§10.50 Sanctions.

(a) *Authority to censure, suspend, or disbar*. The Secretary of the Treasury, or delegate, after notice and an opportunity for a proceeding, may censure, suspend, or disbar any practitioner from practice before the Internal Revenue Service if the practitioner is shown to be incompetent or disreputable (within the meaning of §10.51), fails to comply with any regulation in this part (under the prohibited conduct standards of §10.52), or with intent to defraud, willfully and knowingly misleads or threatens a client or prospective client. Censure is a public reprimand.

(b) *Authority to disqualify*. The Secretary of the Treasury, or delegate, after due notice and opportunity for hearing, may disqualify any appraiser for a violation of these rules as applicable to appraisers.

(1) If any appraiser is disqualified pursuant to this subpart C, the appraiser is barred from presenting evidence or testimony in any administrative proceeding before the Department of Treasury or the Internal Revenue Service, unless and until authorized to do so by the Internal Revenue Service pursuant to §10.81, regardless of whether the evidence or testimony would pertain to an appraisal made prior to or after the effective date of disqualification.

(2) Any appraisal made by a disqualified appraiser after the effective date of disqualification will not have any probative effect in any administrative proceeding before the Department of the Treasury or the Internal Revenue Service. An appraisal otherwise barred from admission into evidence pursuant to this section may be admitted into evidence solely for the purpose of determining the taxpayer's reliance in good faith on such appraisal.

(c) *Authority to impose monetary penalty* —

(1) *In general.*

(i) The Secretary of the Treasury, or delegate, after notice and an opportunity for a proceeding, may impose a monetary penalty on any practitioner who engages in conduct subject to sanction under paragraph (a) of this section.

(ii) If the practitioner described in paragraph (c)(1)(i) of this section was acting on behalf of an employer or any firm or other entity in connection with the conduct giving rise to the penalty, the Secretary of the Treasury, or delegate, may impose a monetary penalty on the employer, firm, or entity if it knew, or reasonably should have known of such conduct.

(2) *Amount of penalty*. The amount of the penalty shall not exceed the gross income derived (or to be derived) from the conduct giving rise to the penalty.

(3) *Coordination with other sanctions*. Subject to paragraph (c)(2) of this section —

(i) Any monetary penalty imposed on a practitioner under this paragraph (c) may be in addition to or in lieu of any suspension, disbarment or censure and may be in addition to a penalty imposed on an employer, firm or other entity under paragraph (c)(1)(ii) of this section.

(ii) Any monetary penalty imposed on an employer, firm or other entity may be in addition to or in lieu of penalties imposed under paragraph (c)(1)(i) of this section.

(d) *Authority to accept a practitioner's consent to sanction*. The Internal Revenue Service may accept a practitioner's offer of consent to be sanctioned under §10.50 in lieu of instituting or continuing a proceeding under §10.60(a).

(e) *Sanctions to be imposed*. The sanctions imposed by this section shall take into account all relevant facts and circumstances.

(f) *Effective/applicability date*. This section is applicable to conduct occurring on or after August 2, 2011, except that paragraphs (a), (b)(2), and (e) apply to conduct occurring on or after September 26, 2007, and paragraph (c) applies to prohibited conduct that occurs after October 22, 2004.

§10.51 Incompetence and disreputable conduct.

(a) *Incompetence and disreputable conduct.* Incompetence and disreputable conduct for which a practitioner may be sanctioned under §10.50 includes, but is not limited to —

(1) Conviction of any criminal offense under the Federal tax laws.

(2) Conviction of any criminal offense involving dishonesty or breach of trust.

(3) Conviction of any felony under Federal or State law for which the conduct involved renders the practitioner unfit to practice before the Internal Revenue Service.

(4) Giving false or misleading information, or participating in any way in the giving of false or misleading information to the Department of the Treasury or any officer or employee thereof, or to any tribunal authorized to pass upon Federal tax matters, in connection with any matter pending or likely to be pending before them, knowing the information to be false or misleading. Facts or other matters contained in testimony, Federal tax returns, financial statements, applications for enrollment, affidavits, declarations, and any other document or statement, written or oral, are included in the term "information."

(5) Solicitation of employment as prohibited under §10.30, the use of false or misleading representations with intent to deceive a client or prospective client in order to procure employment, or intimating that the practitioner is able improperly to obtain special consideration or action from the Internal Revenue Service or any officer or employee thereof.

(6) Willfully failing to make a Federal tax return in violation of the Federal tax laws, or willfully evading, attempting to evade, or participating in any way in evading or attempting to evade any assessment or payment of any Federal tax.

(7) Willfully assisting, counseling, encouraging a client or prospective client in violating, or suggesting to a client or prospective client to violate, any Federal tax law, or knowingly counseling or suggesting to a client or prospective client an illegal plan to evade Federal taxes or payment thereof.

(8) Misappropriation of, or failure properly or promptly to remit, funds received from a client for the purpose of payment of taxes or other obligations due the United States.

(9) Directly or indirectly attempting to influence, or offering or agreeing to attempt to influence, the official action of any officer or employee of the Internal Revenue Service by the use of threats, false accusations, duress or coercion, by the offer of any special inducement or promise of an advantage or by the bestowing of any gift, favor or thing of value.

(10) Disbarment or suspension from practice as an attorney, certified public accountant, public accountant, or actuary by any duly constituted authority of any State, territory, or possession of the United States, including a Commonwealth, or the District of Columbia, any Federal court of record or any Federal agency, body or board.

(11) Knowingly aiding and abetting another person to practice before the Internal Revenue Service during a period of suspension, disbarment or ineligibility of such other person.

(12) Contemptuous conduct in connection with practice before the Internal Revenue Service, including the use of abusive language, making false accusations or statements, knowing them to be false, or circulating or publishing malicious or libelous matter.

(13) Giving a false opinion, knowingly, recklessly, or through gross incompetence, including an opinion which is intentionally or recklessly misleading, or engaging in a pattern of providing incompetent opinions on questions arising under the Federal tax laws. False opinions described in this paragraph (a)(l3) include those which reflect or result from a knowing misstatement of fact or law, from an assertion of a position known to be unwarranted under existing law, from counseling or assisting in conduct known to be illegal or fraudulent, from concealing matters required by law to be revealed, or from consciously disregarding information indicating that material facts expressed in the opinion or offering material are false or misleading. For purposes of this paragraph (a)(13), reckless conduct is a highly unreasonable omission or misrepresentation involving an extreme departure from the standards of ordinary care that a practitioner should observe under the circumstances. A pattern of conduct is a factor that will be taken into account in determining whether a practitioner acted knowingly, recklessly, or through gross incompetence. Gross incompetence includes conduct that reflects gross indifference, preparation which is grossly inadequate under the circumstances, and a consistent failure to perform obligations to the client.

(14) Willfully failing to sign a tax return prepared by the practitioner when the practitioner's signature is required by Federal tax laws unless the failure is due to reasonable cause and not due to willful neglect.

(15) Willfully disclosing or otherwise using a tax return or tax return information in a manner not authorized by the Internal Revenue Code, contrary to the order of a court of competent jurisdiction, or contrary to the order of an administrative law judge in a proceeding instituted under §10.60.

(16) Willfully failing to file on magnetic or other electronic media a tax return prepared by the practitioner when the practitioner is required to do so by the Federal tax laws unless the failure is due to reasonable cause and not due to willful neglect.

(17) Willfully preparing all or substantially all of, or signing, a tax return or claim for refund when the practitioner does not possess a current or otherwise valid preparer tax identification number or other prescribed identifying number.

(18) Willfully representing a taxpayer before an officer or employee of the Internal Revenue Service unless the practitioner is authorized to do so pursuant to this part.

(b) *Effective/applicability date*. This section is applicable beginning August 2, 2011.

§10.52 Violations subject to sanction.

(a) A practitioner may be sanctioned under §10.50 if the practitioner —

(1) Willfully violates any of the regulations (other than §10.33) contained in this part; or

(2) Recklessly or through gross incompetence (within the meaning of §10.51(a)(13)) violates §§ 10.34, 10.35, 10.36 or 10.37.

(b) *Effective/applicability date*. This section is applicable to conduct occurring on or after September 26, 2007.

§10.53 Receipt of information concerning practitioner.

(a) *Officer or employee of the Internal Revenue Service*. If an officer or employee of the Internal Revenue Service has reason to believe a practitioner has violated any provision of this part, the officer or employee will promptly make a written report of the suspected violation. The report will explain the facts and reasons upon which the officer's or employee's belief rests and must be submitted to the office(s) of the Internal Revenue Service responsible for administering or enforcing this part.

(b) *Other persons*. Any person other than an officer or employee of the Internal Revenue Service having information of a violation of any provision of this part may make an oral or written report of the alleged violation to the office(s) of the Internal Revenue Service responsible for administering or enforcing this part or any officer or employee of the Internal Revenue Service. If the report is made to an officer or employee of the Internal Revenue Service, the officer or employee will make a written report of the suspected violation and submit the report to the office(s) of the Internal Revenue Service responsible for administering or enforcing this part.

(c) *Destruction of report*. No report made under paragraph (a) or (b) of this section shall be maintained unless retention of the report is permissible under the applicable records control schedule as approved by the National Archives and Records Administration and designated in the Internal Revenue Manual. Reports must be destroyed as soon as permissible under the applicable records control schedule.

(d) *Effect on proceedings under subpart D*. The destruction of any report will not bar any proceeding under subpart D of this part, but will preclude the use of a copy of the report in a proceeding under subpart D of this part.

(e) *Effective/applicability date*. This section is applicable beginning August 2, 2011.

Subpart D -- Rules Applicable to Disciplinary Proceedings

§10.60 Institution of proceeding.

(a) Whenever it is determined that a practitioner (or employer, firm or other entity, if applicable) violated any provision of the laws governing practice before the Internal Revenue Service or the regulations in this part, the practitioner may be reprimanded or, in accordance with §10.62, subject to a proceeding for sanctions described in §10.50.

(b) Whenever a penalty has been assessed against an appraiser under the Internal Revenue Code and an appropriate officer or employee in an office established to enforce this part determines that the appraiser acted willfully, recklessly, or through gross incompetence with respect to the proscribed conduct, the appraiser may be reprimanded or, in accordance with §10.62, subject to a proceeding for disqualification. A proceeding for disqualification of an appraiser is instituted by the filing of a complaint, the contents of which are more fully described in §10.62.

(c) Except as provided in §10.82, a proceeding will not be instituted under this section unless the proposed respondent previously has been advised in writing of the law, facts and conduct warranting such action and has been accorded an opportunity to dispute facts, assert additional facts, and make arguments (including an explanation or description of mitigating circumstances).

(d) *Effective/applicability date*. This section is applicable beginning August 2, 2011.

§10.61 Conferences.

(a) *In general*. The Commissioner, or delegate, may confer with a practitioner, employer, firm or other entity, or an appraiser concerning allegations of misconduct irrespective of whether a proceeding has been instituted. If the conference results in a stipulation in connection with an ongoing proceeding in which the practitioner, employer, firm or other entity, or appraiser is the respondent, the stipulation may be entered in the record by either party to the proceeding.

(b) *Voluntary sanction* —

(1) *In general*. In lieu of a proceeding being instituted or continued under §10.60(a), a practitioner or appraiser (or employer, firm or other entity, if applicable) may offer a consent to be sanctioned under §10.50.

(2) *Discretion; acceptance or declination*. The Commissioner, or delegate, may accept or decline the offer described in paragraph (b)(1) of this section. When the decision is to decline the offer, the written notice of declination may state that the offer described in paragraph (b)(1) of this section would be accepted if it contained different terms. The Commissioner, or delegate, has the discretion to accept or reject a revised offer submitted in response to the declination or may counteroffer and act upon any accepted counteroffer.

(c) *Effective/applicability date*. This section is applicable beginning August 2, 2011.

§10.62 Contents of complaint.

(a) *Charges*. A complaint must name the respondent, provide a clear and concise description of the facts and law that constitute the basis for the proceeding, and be signed by an authorized representative of the Internal Revenue Service under §10.69(a)(1). A complaint is sufficient if it fairly informs the respondent of the charges brought so that the respondent is able to prepare a defense.

(b) *Specification of sanction*. The complaint must specify the sanction sought against the practitioner or appraiser. If the sanction sought is a suspension, the duration of the suspension sought must be specified.

(c) *Demand for answer*. The respondent must be notified in the complaint or in a separate paper attached to the complaint of the time for answering the complaint, which may not be less than 30 days from the date of service of the complaint, the name and address of the Administrative Law Judge with whom the answer must be filed, the name and address of the person representing the Internal Revenue Service to whom a copy of the answer must be served, and that a decision by default may be rendered against the respondent in the event an answer is not filed as required.

(d) *Effective/applicability date*. This section is applicable beginning August 2, 2011.

§10.63 Service of complaint; service of other papers; service of evidence in support of complaint; filing of papers.

(a) *Service of complaint.*

(1) *In general.* The complaint or a copy of the complaint must be served on the respondent by any manner described in paragraphs (a) (2) or (3) of this section.

(2) *Service by certified or first class mail.*

(i) Service of the complaint may be made on the respondent by mailing the complaint by certified mail to the last known address (as determined under section 6212 of the Internal Revenue Code and the regulations thereunder) of the respondent. Where service is by certified mail, the returned post office receipt duly signed by the respondent will be proof of service.

(ii) If the certified mail is not claimed or accepted by the respondent, or is returned undelivered, service may be made on the respondent, by mailing the complaint to the respondent by first class mail. Service by this method will be considered complete upon mailing, provided the complaint is addressed to the respondent at the respondent's last known address as determined under section 6212 of the Internal Revenue Code and the regulations thereunder.

(3) *Service by other than certified or first class mail.*

(i) Service of the complaint may be made on the respondent by delivery by a private delivery service designated pursuant to section 7502(f) of the Internal Revenue Code to the last known address (as determined under section 6212 of the Internal Revenue Code and the regulations there under) of the respondent. Service by this method will be considered complete, provided the complaint is addressed to the respondent at the respondent's last known address as determined under section 6212 of the Internal Revenue Code and the regulations thereunder.

(ii) Service of the complaint may be made in person on, or by leaving the complaint at the office or place of business of, the respondent. Service by this method will be considered complete and proof of service will be a written statement, sworn or affirmed by the person who served the complaint, identifying the manner of service, including the recipient, relationship of recipient to respondent, place, date and time of service.

(iii) Service may be made by any other means agreed to by the respondent. Proof of service will be a written statement, sworn or affirmed by the person who served the complaint, identifying the manner of service, including the recipient, relationship of recipient to respondent, place, date and time of service.

(4) For purposes of this section, *respondent* means the practitioner, employer, firm or other entity, or appraiser named in the complaint or any other person having the authority to accept mail on behalf of the practitioner, employer, firm or other entity or appraiser.

(b) *Service of papers other than complaint.* Any paper other than the complaint may be served on the respondent, or his or her authorized representative under §10.69(a)(2) by:

(1) mailing the paper by first class mail to the last known address (as determined under section 6212 of the Internal Revenue Code and the regulations thereunder) of the respondent or the respondent's authorized representative,

(2) delivery by a private delivery service designated pursuant to section 7502(f) of the Internal Revenue Code to the last known address (as determined under section 6212 of the Internal Revenue Code and the regulations thereunder) of the respondent or the respondent's authorized representative, or

(3) as provided in paragraphs (a)(3)(ii) and (a)(3)(iii) of this section.

(c) *Service of papers on the Internal Revenue Service.* Whenever a paper is required or permitted to be served on the Internal Revenue Service in connection with a proceeding under this part, the paper will be served on the Internal Revenue Service's authorized representative under §10.69(a)(1) at the address designated in the complaint, or at an address provided in a notice of appearance. If no address is designated in the complaint or provided in a notice of appearance, service will be made on the office(s) established to enforce this part under the authority of §10.1, Internal Revenue Service, 1111 Constitution Avenue, NW, Washington, DC 20224.

(d) *Service of evidence in support of complaint*. Within 10 days of serving the complaint, copies of the evidence in support of the complaint must be served on the respondent in any manner described in paragraphs (a)(2) and (3) of this section.

(e) *Filing of papers*. Whenever the filing of a paper is required or permitted in connection with a proceeding under this part, the original paper, plus one additional copy, must be filed with the Administrative Law Judge at the address specified in the complaint or at an address otherwise specified by the Administrative Law Judge. All papers filed in connection with a proceeding under this part must be served on the other party, unless the Administrative Law Judge directs otherwise. A certificate evidencing such must be attached to the original paper filed with the Administrative Law Judge.

(f) *Effective/applicability date*. This section is applicable beginning August 2, 2011.

§10.64 Answer; default.

(a) *Filing*. The respondent's answer must be filed with the Administrative Law Judge, and served on the Internal Revenue Service, within the time specified in the complaint unless, on request or application of the respondent, the time is extended by the Administrative Law Judge.

(b) *Contents*. The answer must be written and contain a statement of facts that constitute the respondent's grounds of defense. General denials are not permitted. The respondent must specifically admit or deny each allegation set forth in the complaint, except that the respondent may state that the respondent is without sufficient information to admit or deny a specific allegation. The respondent, nevertheless, may not deny a material allegation in the complaint that the respondent knows to be true, or state that the respondent is without sufficient information to form a belief, when the respondent possesses the required information. The respondent also must state affirmatively any special matters of defense on which he or she relies.

(c) *Failure to deny or answer allegations in the complaint*. Every allegation in the complaint that is not denied in the answer is deemed admitted and will be considered proved; no further evidence in respect of such allegation need be adduced at a hearing.

(d) *Default*. Failure to file an answer within the time prescribed (or within the time for answer as extended by the Administrative Law Judge), constitutes an admission of the allegations of the complaint and a waiver of hearing, and the Administrative Law Judge may make the decision by default without a hearing or further procedure. A decision by default constitutes a decision under §10.76.

(e) *Signature*. The answer must be signed by the respondent or the respondent's authorized representative under §10.69(a)(2) and must include a statement directly above the signature acknowledging that the statements made in the answer are true and correct and that knowing and willful false statements may be punishable under 18 U.S.C. §1001.

(f) *Effective/applicability date*. This section is applicable beginning August 2, 2011.

§10.65 Supplemental charges.

(a) *In general*. Supplemental charges may be filed against the respondent by amending the complaint with the permission of the Administrative Law Judge if, for example —

(1) It appears that the respondent, in the answer, falsely and in bad faith, denies a material allegation of fact in the complaint or states that the respondent has insufficient knowledge to form a belief, when the respondent possesses such information; or

(2) It appears that the respondent has knowingly introduced false testimony during the proceedings against the respondent.

(b) *Hearing*. The supplemental charges may be heard with other charges in the case, provided the respondent is given due notice of the charges and is afforded a reasonable opportunity to prepare a defense to the supplemental charges.

(c) *Effective/applicability date*. This section is applicable beginning August 2, 2011.

§10.66 Reply to answer.

(a) The Internal Revenue Service may file a reply to the respondent's answer, but unless otherwise ordered by the Administrative Law Judge, no reply to the respondent's answer is required. If a reply is not filed, new matter in the answer is deemed denied.

(b) *Effective/applicability date*. This section is applicable beginning August 2, 2011.

§10.67 Proof; variance; amendment of pleadings.

In the case of a variance between the allegations in pleadings and the evidence adduced in support of the pleadings, the Administrative Law Judge, at any time before decision, may order or authorize amendment of the pleadings to conform to the evidence. The party who would otherwise be prejudiced by the amendment must be given a reasonable opportunity to address the allegations of the pleadings as amended and the Administrative Law Judge must make findings on any issue presented by the pleadings as amended.

§10.68 Motions and requests.

(a) *Motions* —

(1) *In general*. At any time after the filing of the complaint, any party may file a motion with the Administrative Law Judge. Unless otherwise ordered by the Administrative Law Judge, motions must be in writing and must be served on the opposing party as provided in §10.63(b). A motion must concisely specify its grounds and the relief sought, and, if appropriate, must contain a memorandum of facts and law in support.

(2) *Summary adjudication*. Either party may move for a summary adjudication upon all or any part of the legal issues in controversy. If the non-moving party opposes summary adjudication in the moving party's favor, the non-moving party must file a written response within 30 days unless ordered otherwise by the Administrative Law Judge.

(3) *Good Faith*. A party filing a motion for extension of time, a motion for postponement of a hearing, or any other non-dispositive or procedural motion must first contact the other party to determine whether there is any objection to the motion, and must state in the motion whether the other party has an objection.

(b) *Response*. Unless otherwise ordered by the Administrative Law Judge, the nonmoving party is not required to file a response to a motion. If the Administrative Law Judge does not order the nonmoving party to file a response, and the nonmoving party files no response, the nonmoving party is deemed to oppose the motion. If a nonmoving party does not respond within 30 days of the filing of a motion for decision by default for failure to file a timely answer or for failure to prosecute, the nonmoving party is deemed not to oppose the motion.

(c) *Oral motions; oral argument* —

(1) The Administrative Law Judge may, for good cause and with notice to the parties, permit oral motions and oral opposition to motions.

(2) The Administrative Law Judge may, within his or her discretion, permit oral argument on any motion.

(d) *Orders*. The Administrative Law Judge should issue written orders disposing of any motion or request and any response thereto.

(e) *Effective/applicability date*. This section is applicable on September 26, 2007.

§10.69 Representation; ex parte communication.

(a) *Representation*.

(1) The Internal Revenue Service may be represented in proceedings under this part by an attorney or other employee of the Internal Revenue Service. An attorney or an employee of the Internal Revenue Service representing the Internal Revenue Service in a proceeding under this part may sign the complaint or any document required to be filed in the proceeding on behalf of the Internal Revenue Service.

(2) A respondent may appear in person, be represented by a practitioner, or be represented by an attorney who has not filed a declaration with the Internal Revenue Service pursuant to §10.3. A practitioner or an attorney representing a respondent or proposed respondent may sign the answer or any document required to be filed in the proceeding on behalf of the respondent.

(b) *Ex parte communication*. The Internal Revenue Service, the respondent, and any representatives of either party, may not attempt to initiate or participate in ex parte discussions concerning a proceeding or potential proceeding with the Administrative Law Judge (or any person who is likely to advise the Administrative Law Judge on a ruling or decision) in the proceeding before or during the pendency of the proceeding. Any memorandum, letter or other communication concerning the merits of the proceeding, addressed to the Administrative Law Judge, by or on behalf of any party shall be regarded as an argument in the proceeding and shall be served on the other party.

(c) *Effective/applicability date*. This section is applicable beginning August 2, 2011.

§10.70 Administrative Law Judge.

(a) *Appointment*. Proceedings on complaints for the sanction (as described in §10.50) of a practitioner, employer, firm or other entity, or appraiser will be conducted by an Administrative Law Judge appointed as provided by *5 U.S.C. 3105*.

(b) *Powers of the Administrative Law Judge*. The Administrative Law Judge, among other powers, has the authority, in connection with any proceeding under §10.60 assigned or referred to him or her, to do the following:

(1) Administer oaths and affirmations;

(2) Make rulings on motions and requests, which rulings may not be appealed prior to the close of a hearing except in extraordinary circumstances and at the discretion of the Administrative Law Judge;

(3) Determine the time and place of hearing and regulate its course and conduct;

(4) Adopt rules of procedure and modify the same from time to time as needed for the orderly disposition of proceedings;

(5) Rule on offers of proof, receive relevant evidence, and examine witnesses;

(6) Take or authorize the taking of depositions or answers to requests for admission;

(7) Receive and consider oral or written argument on facts or law;

(8) Hold or provide for the holding of conferences for the settlement or simplification of the issues with the consent of the parties;

(9) Perform such acts and take such measures as are necessary or appropriate to the efficient conduct of any proceeding; and

(10) Make decisions.

(c) *Effective/applicability date*. This section is applicable on September 26, 2007.

§10.71 Discovery.

(a) *In general*. Discovery may be permitted, at the discretion of the Administrative Law Judge, only upon written motion demonstrating the relevance, materiality and reasonableness of the requested discovery and subject to the requirements of §10.72(d)(2) and (3). Within 10 days of receipt of the answer, the Administrative Law Judge will notify the parties of the right to request discovery and the timeframe for filing a request. A request for discovery, and objections, must be filed in accordance with §10.68. In response to a request for discovery, the Administrative Law Judge may order —

(1) Depositions upon oral examination; or

(2) Answers to requests for admission.

(b) *Depositions upon oral examination* —

(1) A deposition must be taken before an officer duly authorized to administer an oath for general purposes or before an officer or employee of the Internal Revenue Service who is authorized to administer an oath in Federal tax law matters.

(2) In ordering a deposition, the Administrative Law Judge will require reasonable notice to the opposing party as to the time and place of the deposition. The opposing party, if attending, will be provided the opportunity for full examination and cross-examination of any witness.

(3) Expenses in the reporting of depositions shall be borne by the party at whose instance the deposition is taken. Travel expenses of the deponent shall be borne by the party requesting the deposition, unless otherwise authorized by Federal law or regulation.

(c) *Requests for admission*. Any party may serve on any other party a written request for admission of the truth of any matters which are not privileged and are relevant to the subject matter of this proceeding. Requests for admission shall not exceed a total of 30 (including any subparts within a specific request) without the approval from the Administrative Law Judge.

(d) *Limitations*. Discovery shall not be authorized if —

(1) The request fails to meet any requirement set forth in paragraph (a) of this section;

(2) It will unduly delay the proceeding;

(3) It will place an undue burden on the party required to produce the discovery sought;

(4) It is frivolous or abusive;

(5) It is cumulative or duplicative;

(6) The material sought is privileged or otherwise protected from disclosure by law;

(7) The material sought relates to mental impressions, conclusions, of legal theories of any party, attorney, or other representative, or a party prepared in the anticipation of a proceeding; or

(8) The material sought is available generally to the public, equally to the parties, or to the party seeking the discovery through another source.

(e) *Failure to comply*. Where a party fails to comply with an order of the Administrative Law Judge under this section, the Administrative Law Judge may, among other things, infer that the information would be adverse to the party failing to provide it, exclude the information from evidence or issue a decision by default.

(f) *Other discovery*. No discovery other than that specifically provided for in this section is permitted.

(g) *Effective/applicability date*. This section is applicable to proceedings initiated on or after September 26, 2007.

§10.72 Hearings.

(a) *In general* —

(1) *Presiding officer*. An Administrative Law Judge will preside at the hearing on a complaint filed under §10.60 for the sanction of a practitioner, employer, firm or other entity, or appraiser.

(2) *Time for hearing*. Absent a determination by the Administrative Law Judge that, in the interest of justice, a hearing must be held at a later time, the Administrative Law Judge should, on notice sufficient to allow proper preparation, schedule the hearing to occur no later than 180 days after the time for filing the answer.

(3) *Procedural requirements*.

(i) Hearings will be stenographically recorded and transcribed and the testimony of witnesses will be taken under oath or affirmation.

(ii) Hearings will be conducted pursuant to *5 U.S.C. 556*.

(iii) A hearing in a proceeding requested under §10.82(g) will be conducted de novo.

(iv) An evidentiary hearing must be held in all proceedings prior to the issuance of a decision by the Administrative Law Judge unless —

(A) The Internal Revenue Service withdraws the complaint;

(B) A decision is issued by default pursuant to §10.64(d);

(C) A decision is issued under §10.82 (e);

(D) The respondent requests a decision on the written record without a hearing; or

(E) The Administrative Law Judge issues a decision under §10.68(d) or rules on another motion that disposes of the case prior to the hearing.

(b) *Cross-examination*. A party is entitled to present his or her case or defense by oral or documentary evidence, to submit rebuttal evidence, and to conduct cross-examination, in the presence of the Administrative Law Judge, as may be required for a full and true disclosure of the facts. This paragraph (b) does not limit a party from presenting evidence contained within a deposition when the Administrative Law Judge determines that the deposition has been obtained in compliance with the rules of this subpart D.

(c) *Prehearing memorandum*. Unless otherwise ordered by the Administrative Law Judge, each party shall file, and serve on the opposing party or the opposing party's representative, prior to any hearing, a prehearing memorandum containing —

(1) A list (together with a copy) of all proposed exhibits to be used in the party's case in chief;

(2) A list of proposed witnesses, including a synopsis of their expected testimony, or a statement that no witnesses will be called;

(3) Identification of any proposed expert witnesses, including a synopsis of their expected testimony and a copy of any report prepared by the expert or at his or her direction; and

(4) A list of undisputed facts.

(d) *Publicity* —

(1) *In general*. All reports and decisions of the Secretary of the Treasury, or delegate, including any reports and decisions of the Administrative Law Judge, under this subpart D are, subject to the protective measures in paragraph (d)(4) of this section, public and open to inspection within 30 days after the agency's decision becomes final.

(2) *Request for additional publicity*. The Administrative Law Judge may grant a request by a practitioner or appraiser that all the pleadings and evidence of the disciplinary proceeding be made available for inspection where the parties stipulate in advance to adopt the protective measures in paragraph (d)(4) of this section.

(3) *Returns and return information* —

(i) *Disclosure to practitioner or appraiser*. Pursuant to *section 6103(l)(4) of the Internal Revenue Code*, the Secretary of the Treasury, or delegate, may disclose returns and return information to any practitioner or appraiser, or to the authorized representative of the practitioner or appraiser, whose rights are or may be affected by an administrative action or proceeding under this subpart D, but solely for use in the action or proceeding and only to the extent that the Secretary of the Treasury, or delegate, determines that the returns or return information are or may be relevant and material to the action or proceeding.

(ii) *Disclosure to officers and employees of the Department of the Treasury*. Pursuant to *section 6103(l)(4)(B) of the Internal Revenue Code* the Secretary of the Treasury, or delegate, may disclose returns and return information to officers and employees of the Department of the Treasury for use in any action or proceeding under this subpart D, to the extent necessary to advance or protect the interests of the United States.

(iii) *Use of returns and return information*. Recipients of returns and return information under this paragraph (d)(3) may use the returns or return information solely in the action or proceeding, or in preparation for the action or proceeding, with respect to which the disclosure was made.

(iv) *Procedures for disclosure of returns and return information.* When providing returns or return information to the practitioner or appraiser, or authorized representative, the Secretary of the Treasury, or delegate, will —

(A) Redact identifying information of any third party taxpayers and replace it with a code;

(B) Provide a key to the coded information; and

(C) Notify the practitioner or appraiser, or authorized representative, of the restrictions on the use and disclosure of the returns and return information, the applicable damages remedy under *section 7431 of the Internal Revenue Code*, and that unauthorized disclosure of information provided by the Internal Revenue Service under this paragraph (d)(3) is also a violation of this part.

(4) *Protective measures* —

(i) *Mandatory protection order.* If redaction of names, addresses, and other identifying information of third party taxpayers may still permit indirect identification of any third party taxpayer, the Administrative Law Judge will issue a protective order to ensure that the identifying information is available to the parties and the Administrative Law Judge for purposes of the proceeding, but is not disclosed to, or open to inspection by, the public.

(ii) *Authorized orders.*

(A) Upon motion by a party or any other affected person, and for good cause shown, the Administrative Law Judge may make any order which justice requires to protect any person in the event disclosure of information is prohibited by law, privileged, confidential, or sensitive in some other way, including, but not limited to, one or more of the following —

(*1*) That disclosure of information be made only on specified terms and conditions, including a designation of the time or place;

(*2*) That a trade secret or other information not be disclosed, or be disclosed only in a designated way.

(iii) *Denials.* If a motion for a protective order is denied in whole or in part, the Administrative Law Judge may, on such terms or conditions as the Administrative Law Judge deems just, order any party or person to comply with, or respond in accordance with, the procedure involved.

(iv) *Public inspection of documents.* The Secretary of the Treasury, or delegate, shall ensure that all names, addresses or other identifying details of third party taxpayers are redacted and replaced with the code assigned to the corresponding taxpayer in all documents prior to public inspection of such documents.

(e) *Location.* The location of the hearing will be determined by the agreement of the parties with the approval of the Administrative Law Judge, but, in the absence of such agreement and approval, the hearing will be held in Washington, D.C.

(f) *Failure to appear.* If either party to the proceeding fails to appear at the hearing, after notice of the proceeding has been sent to him or her, the party will be deemed to have waived the right to a hearing and the Administrative Law Judge may make his or her decision against the absent party by default.

(g) *Effective/applicability date.* This section is applicable beginning August 2, 2011.

§10.73 Evidence.

(a) *In general.* The rules of evidence prevailing in courts of law and equity are not controlling in hearings or proceedings conducted under this part. The Administrative Law Judge may, however, exclude evidence that is irrelevant, immaterial, or unduly repetitious.

(b) *Depositions.* The deposition of any witness taken pursuant to §10.71 may be admitted into evidence in any proceeding instituted under §10.60.

(c) *Requests for admission.* Any matter admitted in response to a request for admission under §10.71 is conclusively established unless the Administrative Law Judge on motion permits withdrawal or modification of the admission. Any admission made by a party is for the purposes of the pending action only and is not an admission by a party for any other purpose, nor may it be used against a party in any other proceeding.

(d) *Proof of documents.* Official documents, records, and papers of the Internal Revenue Service and the Office of Professional Responsibility are admissible in evidence without the production of an officer or employee to authenticate them. Any documents, records, and papers may be evidenced by a copy attested to or identified by an officer or employee of the Internal Revenue Service or the Treasury Department, as the case may be.

(e) *Withdrawal of exhibits.* If any document, record, or other paper is introduced in evidence as an exhibit, the Administrative Law Judge may authorize the withdrawal of the exhibit subject to any conditions that he or she deems proper.

(f) *Objections.* Objections to evidence are to be made in short form, stating the grounds for the objection. Except as ordered by the Administrative Law Judge, argument on objections will not be recorded or transcribed. Rulings on objections are to be a part of the record, but no exception to a ruling is necessary to preserve the rights of the parties.

(g) *Effective/applicability date.* This section is applicable on September 26, 2007.

§10.74 Transcript.

In cases where the hearing is stenographically reported by a Government contract reporter, copies of the transcript may be obtained from the reporter at rates not to exceed the maximum rates fixed by contract between the Government and the reporter. Where the hearing is stenographically reported by a regular employee of the Internal Revenue Service, a copy will be supplied to the respondent either without charge or upon the payment of a reasonable fee. Copies of exhibits introduced at the hearing or at the taking of depositions will be supplied to the parties upon the payment of a reasonable fee (Sec. 501, Public Law 82-137) (65 Stat. 290) (31 U.S.C. § 483a).

§10.75 Proposed findings and conclusions.

Except in cases where the respondent has failed to answer the complaint or where a party has failed to appear at the hearing, the parties must be afforded a reasonable opportunity to submit proposed findings and conclusions and their supporting reasons to the Administrative Law Judge.

§10.76 Decision of Administrative Law Judge.

(a) *In general* —

(1) *Hearings.* Within 180 days after the conclusion of a hearing and the receipt of any proposed findings and conclusions timely submitted by the parties, the Administrative Law Judge should enter a decision in the case. The decision must include a statement of findings and conclusions, as well as the reasons or basis for making such findings and conclusions, and an order of censure, suspension, disbarment, monetary penalty, disqualification, or dismissal of the complaint.

(2) *Summary adjudication.* In the event that a motion for summary adjudication is filed, the Administrative Law Judge should rule on the motion for summary adjudication within 60 days after the party in opposition files a written response, or if no written response is filed, within 90 days after the motion for summary adjudication is filed. A decision shall thereafter be rendered if the pleadings, depositions, admissions, and any other admissible evidence show that there is no genuine issue of material fact and that a decision may be rendered as a matter of law. The decision must include a statement of conclusions, as well as the reasons or basis for making such conclusions, and an order of censure, suspension, disbarment, monetary penalty, disqualification, or dismissal of the complaint.

(3) *Returns and return information.* In the decision, the Administrative Law Judge should use the code assigned to third party taxpayers (described in §10.72(d)).

(b) *Standard of proof.* If the sanction is censure or a suspension of less than six months' duration, the Administrative Law Judge, in rendering findings and conclusions, will consider an allegation of fact to be proven if it is established by the party who is alleging the fact by a preponderance of the evidence in the record. If the sanction is a monetary penalty, disbarment or a suspension of six months or longer duration, an allegation of fact that is necessary for a finding against the practitioner must be proven by clear and convincing evidence in the record. An allegation of fact that is necessary for a finding of disqualification against an appraiser must be proved by clear and convincing evidence in the record.

(c) *Copy of decision.* The Administrative Law Judge will provide the decision to the Internal Revenue Service's authorized representative, and a copy of the decision to the respondent or the respondent's authorized representative.

(d) *When final.* In the absence of an appeal to the Secretary of the Treasury or delegate, the decision of the Administrative Law Judge will, without further proceedings, become the decision of the agency 30 days after the date of the Administrative Law Judge's decision.

(e) *Effective/applicability date.* This section is applicable beginning August 2, 2011.

§10.77 Appeal of decision of Administrative Law Judge.

(a) *Appeal.* Any party to the proceeding under this subpart D may appeal the decision of the Administrative Law Judge by filing a notice of appeal with the Secretary of the Treasury, or delegate deciding appeals. The notice of appeal must include a brief that states exceptions to the decision of Administrative Law Judge and supporting reasons for such exceptions.

(b) *Time and place for filing of appeal.* The notice of appeal and brief must be filed, in duplicate, with the Secretary of the Treasury, or delegate deciding appeals, at an address for appeals that is identified to the parties with the decision of the Administrative Law Judge. The notice of appeal and brief must be filed within 30 days of the date that the decision of the Administrative Law Judge is served on the parties. The appealing party must serve a copy of the notice of appeal and the brief to any non appealing party or, if the party is represented, the non-appealing party's representative.

(c) *Response.* Within 30 days of receiving the copy of the appellant's brief, the other party may file a response brief with the Secretary of the Treasury, or delegate deciding appeals, using the address identified for appeals. A copy of the response brief must be served at the same time on the opposing party or, if the party is represented, the opposing party's representative.

(d) *No other briefs, responses or motions as of right.* Other than the appeal brief and response brief, the parties are not permitted to file any other briefs, responses or motions, except on a grant of leave to do so after a motion demonstrating sufficient cause, or unless otherwise ordered by the Secretary of the Treasury, or delegate deciding appeals.

(e) *Additional time for briefs and responses.* Notwithstanding the time for filing briefs and responses provided in paragraphs (b) and (c) of this section, the Secretary of the Treasury, or delegate deciding appeals, may, for good cause, authorize additional time for filing briefs and responses upon a motion of a party or upon the initiative of the Secretary of the Treasury, or delegate deciding appeals.

(f) *Effective/applicability date.* This section is applicable beginning August 2, 2011.

§10.78 Decision on review.

(a) *Decision on review.* On appeal from or review of the decision of the Administrative Law Judge, the Secretary of the Treasury, or delegate, will make the agency decision. The Secretary of the Treasury, or delegate, should make the agency decision within 180 days after receipt of the appeal.

(b) *Standard of review.* The decision of the Administrative Law Judge will not be reversed unless the appellant establishes that the decision is clearly erroneous in light of the evidence in the record and applicable law. Issues that are exclusively matters of law will be reviewed de novo. In the event that the Secretary of the Treasury, or delegate, determines that there are unresolved issues raised by the record, the case may be remanded to the Administrative Law Judge to elicit additional testimony or evidence.

(c) *Copy of decision on review*. The Secretary of the Treasury, or delegate, will provide copies of the agency decision to the authorized representative of the Internal Revenue Service and the respondent or the respondent's authorized representative.

(d) *Effective/applicability date*. This section is applicable beginning August 2, 2011.

§10.79 Effect of disbarment, suspension, or censure.

(a) *Disbarment*. When the final decision in a case is against the respondent (or the respondent has offered his or her consent and such consent has been accepted by the Internal Revenue Service) and such decision is for disbarment, the respondent will not be permitted to practice before the Internal Revenue Service unless and until authorized to do so by the Internal Revenue Service pursuant to §10.81.

(b) *Suspension*. When the final decision in a case is against the respondent (or the respondent has offered his or her consent and such consent has been accepted by the Internal Revenue Service) and such decision is for suspension, the respondent will not be permitted to practice before the Internal Revenue Service during the period of suspension. For periods after the suspension, the practitioner's future representations may be subject to conditions as authorized by paragraph (d) of this section.

(c) *Censure*. When the final decision in the case is against the respondent (or the Internal Revenue Service has accepted the respondent's offer to consent, if such offer was made) and such decision is for censure, the respondent will be permitted to practice before the Internal Revenue Service, but the respondent's future representations may be subject to conditions as authorized by paragraph (d) of this section.

(d) *Conditions*. After being subject to the sanction of either suspension or censure, the future representations of a practitioner so sanctioned shall be subject to specified conditions designed to promote high standards of conduct. These conditions can be imposed for a reasonable period in light of the gravity of the practitioner's violations. For example, where a practitioner is censured because the practitioner failed to advise the practitioner's clients about a potential conflict of interest or failed to obtain the clients' written consents, the practitioner may be required to provide the Internal Revenue Service with a copy of all consents obtained by the practitioner for an appropriate period following censure, whether or not such consents are specifically requested.

(e) *Effective/applicability date*. This section is applicable beginning August 2, 2011.

§10.80 Notice of disbarment, suspension, censure, or disqualification.

(a) *In general*. On the issuance of a final order censuring, suspending, or disbarring a practitioner or a final order disqualifying an appraiser, notification of the censure, suspension, disbarment or disqualification will be given to appropriate officers and employees of the Internal Revenue Service and interested departments and agencies of the Federal government. The Internal Revenue Service may determine the manner of giving notice to the proper authorities of the State by which the censured, suspended, or disbarred person was licensed to practice.

(b) *Effective/applicability date*. This section is applicable beginning August 2, 2011.

§10.81 Petition for reinstatement.

(a) *In general*. A practitioner disbarred or suspended under §10.60, or suspended under §10.82, or a disqualified appraiser may petition for reinstatement before the Internal Revenue Service after the expiration of 5 years following such disbarment, suspension, or disqualification (or immediately following the expiration of the suspension or disqualification period, if shorter than 5 years). Reinstatement will not be granted unless the Internal Revenue Service is satisfied that the petitioner is not likely to engage thereafter in conduct contrary to the regulations in this part, and that granting such reinstatement would not be contrary to the public interest.

(b) *Effective/applicability date*. This section is applicable beginning June 12, 2014.

§10.82 Expedited suspension.

(a) *When applicable*. Whenever the Commissioner, or delegate, determines that a practitioner is described in paragraph (b) of this section, the expedited procedures described in this section may be used to suspend the practitioner from practice before the Internal Revenue Service.

(b) *To whom applicable*. This section applies to any practitioner who, within 5 years prior to the date that a show cause order under this section's expedited suspension procedures is served:

(1) Has had a license to practice as an attorney, certified public accountant, or actuary suspended or revoked for cause (not including a failure to pay a professional licensing fee) by any authority or court, agency, body, or board described in §10.51(a)(10).

(2) Has, irrespective of whether an appeal has been taken, been convicted of any crime under title 26 of the United States Code, any crime involving dishonesty or breach of trust, or any felony for which the conduct involved renders the practitioner unfit to practice before the Internal Revenue Service.

(3) Has violated conditions imposed on the practitioner pursuant to §10.79(d).

(4) Has been sanctioned by a court of competent jurisdiction, whether in a civil or criminal proceeding (including suits for injunctive relief), relating to any taxpayer's tax liability or relating to the practitioner's own tax liability, for —

(i) Instituting or maintaining proceedings primarily for delay;
(ii) Advancing frivolous or groundless arguments; or
(iii) Failing to pursue available administrative remedies.

(5) Has demonstrated a pattern of willful disreputable conduct by—

(i) Failing to make an annual Federal tax return, in violation of the Federal tax laws, during 4 of the 5 tax years immediately preceding the institution of a proceeding under paragraph (c) of this section and remains noncompliant with any of the practitioner's Federal tax filing obligations at the time the notice of suspension is issued under paragraph (f) of this section; or

(ii) Failing to make a return required more frequently than annually, in violation of the Federal tax laws, during 5 of the 7 tax periods immediately preceding the institution of a proceeding under paragraph (c) of this section and remains noncompliant with any of the practitioner's Federal tax filing obligations at the time the notice of suspension is issued under paragraph (f) of this section.

(c) *Expedited suspension procedures*. A suspension under this section will be proposed by a show cause order that names the respondent, is signed by an authorized representative of the Internal Revenue Service under §10.69(a)(1), and served according to the rules set forth in §10.63(a). The show cause order must give a plain and concise description of the allegations that constitute the basis for the proposed suspension. The show cause order must notify the respondent —

(1) Of the place and due date for filing a response;

(2) That an expedited suspension decision by default may be rendered if the respondent fails to file a response as required;

(3) That the respondent may request a conference to address the merits of the show cause order and that any such request must be made in the response; and

(4) That the respondent may be suspended either immediately following the expiration of the period within which a response must be filed or, if a conference is requested, immediately following the conference.

(d) *Response*. The response to the show cause order described in this section must be filed no later than 30 calendar days following the date the show cause order is served, unless the time for filing is extended. The response must be filed in accordance with the rules set forth for answers to a complaint in §10.64, except as otherwise provided in this section. The response must include a request for a conference, if a conference is desired. The respondent is entitled to the conference only if the request is made in a timely filed response.

(e) *Conference.* An authorized representative of the Internal Revenue Service will preside at a conference described in this section. The conference will be held at a place and time selected by the Internal Revenue Service, but no sooner than 14 calendar days after the date by which the response must be filed with the Internal Revenue Service, unless the respondent agrees to an earlier date. An authorized representative may represent the respondent at the conference.

(f) *Suspension—*

(1) *In general.* The Commissioner, or delegate, may suspend the respondent from practice before the Internal Revenue Service by a written notice of expedited suspension immediately following:

(i) The expiration of the period within which a response to a show cause order must be filed if the respondent does not file a response as required by paragraph (d) of this section;

(ii) The conference described in paragraph (e) of this section if the Internal Revenue Service finds that the respondent is described in paragraph (b) of this section; or

(iii) The respondent's failure to appear, either personally or through an authorized representative, at a conference scheduled by the Internal Revenue Service under paragraph (e) of this section.

(2) *Duration of suspension.* A suspension under this section will commence on the date that the written notice of expedited suspension is served on the practitioner, either personally or through an authorized representative. The suspension will remain effective until the earlier of:

(i) The date the Internal Revenue Service lifts the suspension after determining that the practitioner is no longer described in paragraph (b) of this section or for any other reason; or

(ii) The date the suspension is lifted or otherwise modified by an Administrative Law Judge or the Secretary of the Treasury, or delegate deciding appeals, in a proceeding referred to in paragraph (g) of this section and instituted under §10.60.

(g) *Practitioner demand for §10.60 proceeding.* If the Internal Revenue Service suspends a practitioner under the expedited suspension procedures described in this section, the practitioner may demand that the Internal Revenue Service institute a proceeding under §10.60 and issue the complaint described in §10.62. The demand must be in writing, specifically reference the suspension action under §10.82, and be made within 2 years from the date on which the practitioner's suspension commenced. The Internal Revenue Service must issue a complaint demanded under this paragraph (g) within 60 calendar days of receiving the demand. If the Internal Revenue Service does not issue such complaint within 60 days of receiving the demand, the suspension is lifted automatically. The preceding sentence does not, however, preclude the Commissioner, or delegate, from instituting a regular proceeding under §10.60 of this part.

(h) *Effective/applicability date.* This section is generally applicable beginning June 12, 2014, except that paragraphs (b)(1) through (4) of this section are applicable beginning August 2, 2011.

Subpart E -- General Provisions

§10.90 Records.

(a) *Roster.* The Internal Revenue Service will maintain and make available for public inspection in the time and manner prescribed by the Secretary, or delegate, the following rosters —

(1) Individuals (and employers, firms, or other entities, if applicable) censured, suspended, or disbarred from practice before the Internal Revenue Service or upon whom a monetary penalty was imposed.

(2) Enrolled agents, including individuals —

(i) Granted active enrollment to practice;

(ii) Whose enrollment has been placed in inactive status for failure to meet the requirements for renewal of enrollment;

(iii) Whose enrollment has been placed in inactive retirement status; and

(iv) Whose offer of consent to resign from enrollment has been accepted by the Internal Revenue Service under §10.61.

(3) Enrolled retirement plan agents, including individuals —

(i) Granted active enrollment to practice;

(ii) Whose enrollment has been placed in inactive status for failure to meet the requirements for renewal of enrollment;

(iii) Whose enrollment has been placed in inactive retirement status; and

(iv) Whose offer of consent to resign from enrollment has been accepted under §10.61.

(4) Registered tax return preparers, including individuals —

(i) Authorized to prepare all or substantially all of a tax return or claim for refund;

(ii) Who have been placed in inactive status for failure to meet the requirements for renewal;

(iii) Who have been placed in inactive retirement status; and

(iv) Whose offer of consent to resign from their status as a registered tax return preparer has been accepted by the Internal Revenue Service under §10.61.

(5) Disqualified appraisers.

(6) Qualified continuing education providers, including providers —

(i) Who have obtained a qualifying continuing education provider number; and

(ii) Whose qualifying continuing education number has been revoked for failure to comply with the requirements of this part.

(b) *Other records.* Other records of the Director of the Office of Professional Responsibility may be disclosed upon specific request, in accordance with the applicable law.

(c) *Effective/applicability date.* This section is applicable beginning August 2, 2011.

§10.91 Saving provision.

Any proceeding instituted under this part prior to June 12, 2014, for which a final decision has not been reached or for which judicial review is still available will not be affected by these revisions. Any proceeding under this part based on conduct engaged in prior to June 12, 2014, which is instituted after that date, will apply subpart D and E or this part as revised, but the conduct engaged in prior to the effective date of these revisions will be judged by the regulations in effect at the time the conduct occurred.

§10.92 Special orders.

The Secretary of the Treasury reserves the power to issue such special orders as he or she deems proper in any cases within the purview of this part.

§10.93 Effective date.

Except as otherwise provided in each section and Subject to §10.91, Part 10 is applicable on July 26, 2002.

John Dalrymple,
Deputy Commissioner for Services and Enforcement

Approved: June 3, 2014
Christopher J. Meade,
General Counsel

[FR Doc. 2014-13739 Filed 06/09/2014 at 4:15 pm; Publication Date: 06/12/2014]

APPENDIX B
EXAM CONTENT OUTLINES WITH GLEIM CROSS-REFERENCES

This section contains the Part 3 Exam Content Outlines (ECOs) for 2021/2022.

The ECOs are subdivided into domains, and each domain has one or more topics, which are further divided into specific items. According to the IRS's *Candidate Information Bulletin* (available at www.prometric.com/irs), not every topic in the ECOs will appear on the exam, and the list of topics may not be all-inclusive. However, the ECOs are meant to reflect the knowledge needed for tasks performed by EAs.

Next to each topic, we have provided a cross-reference to the most relevant Gleim study unit(s) or subunit(s).

Domain 1: Practices and Procedures (26 Questions)

a. **Practice before the IRS**

1) What constitutes practice before the IRS – 1.1
2) Categories of individuals who may practice and extent of practice privileges – 1.1

b. **Requirements for Enrolled Agents**

1) Information to be furnished to the IRS – 1.2
2) Omission or error on return, document, or affidavit – 2.1
3) Rules for employing or accepting assistance from former IRS employees or disbarred/suspended persons – 1.2
4) Rules for restrictions on advertising, solicitation and fee information – 1.2
5) Rules regarding fees (e.g., contingent, unconscionable) – 1.2
6) Due diligence requirements – 1.2
7) Conflict of interest – 1.2
8) Rules for refund check negotiation – 1.2, 2.4
9) Standards for written advice, covered opinions, tax return positions and preparing returns – 1.4, 2.1
10) Continuing education requirements – 1.6
11) Enrollment cycle and renewal – 1.6
12) Rules for prompt disposition of matters before the IRS – 1.2
13) Rules for returning a client's records and documents – 1.2
14) PTIN requirements – 1.1
15) Practitioner supervisory responsibilities – 1.4

c. **Sanctionable Acts**

1) Incompetence and disreputable conduct – 1.5
2) Sanctions imposed by the Office of Professional Responsibility – 1.5
3) Frivolous submissions (returns and documents) – 2.2-2.4
4) Fraudulent transactions (e.g., badges of fraud) – 2.2-2.4

d. **Rules and Penalties**

1) Assessment and appeal procedures for preparer penalties – 1.5
2) Types of penalties (e.g., negligence, substantial understatement, overvaluation) – 2.2, 2.4, 4.4
3) Furnishing a copy of a return to a taxpayer – 2.1
4) Signing returns and furnishing identifying numbers – 2.1, 7.2
5) Keeping copies or lists of returns prepared – 2.1, 7.1
6) Employees engaged or employed during a return period (e.g., IRC section 6060) – 2.1, 7.1
7) Preparer due diligence penalties – 2.2

Domain 2: Representation before the IRS (25 Questions)

a. **Power of Attorney**

1) Purpose of power of attorney – 3.1
2) Signature authority (e.g., extension of assessment period, closing agreement) – 3.1
3) Authority granted by taxpayer – 3.1
4) Limitations on signing tax returns on behalf of taxpayer – 3.1
5) Proper completion of power of attorney (Form 2848) – 3.1
6) Alternate forms of power of attorney (durable) – 3.1
7) Rules for client privacy and consent to disclose – 2.2
8) Distinctions between power of attorney (Form 2848) and tax information authorization (Form 8821) – 3.1
9) Requirements to be met when changing or dropping representatives or withdrawal of representative – 3.1
10) Purpose of a Centralized Authorization File (CAF) number – 3.2
11) Conference and practice requirements (Publication 216) – 2.2, 3.1

b. **Building the Taxpayer's Case--Preliminary Work**

1) Identification of tax issue(s) with supporting details – 1.3-1.4
2) Potential for criminal aspects – 1.5, 4.4
3) Competence, expertise, and time to handle issue – 1.1-1.2
4) Conflict of interest in regards to representation – 1.2
5) Transcripts from IRS (e.g., access to and use of e-services) – 7.1

c. **Taxpayer Financial Situation**

1) Taxpayer's ability to pay the tax (e.g., installment agreements, offer in compromise, currently not collectible) – 5.1-5.2
2) General financial health (e.g., bankruptcy, lawsuits, garnishments, cash flow, assets, and insolvency) – 5.1
3) Third-party research (e.g., property assessment for taxes, asset values, state and local tax information) – 5.2-5.3
4) Discharge of the tax liability in bankruptcy – 5.3
5) IRS Collection Financial Standards – 5.1

d. **Supporting Documentation**

1) Financial documents and expense records (e.g., canceled checks or equivalent, bank statements, credit card statements, receipts, brokerage records) – 7.1
2) Legal documents (e.g., birth certificate, divorce decrees, lawsuit settlements) – 7.1
3) Prior and subsequent tax returns – 7.1
4) Other substantive and contemporaneous documentation (e.g., corporate minutes) – 7.1
5) Business entity supporting documents (e.g., partnership agreement, corporate bylaws) – 7.1

e. **Legal Authority and References**

1) Internal Revenue Code and income tax regulations – 6.1-6.2
2) Revenue rulings and revenue procedures – 6.2
3) Case law – 6.3
4) IRS forms, instructions, and publications – 6.2
5) Private letter ruling – 6.2
6) Internal Revenue Manual – 6.2
7) Authoritative versus non-authoritative source material – 6.1-6.2, 6.4
8) Tax treaties – 6.1

f. **Related Issues**

1) Statute of limitations – 2.5, 4.1, 7.1
2) Post-filing correspondence (e.g., math error notices, under-reporting notices) – 4.1
3) Deadlines and timeliness requirements – 4.2
4) Third-party correspondence (e.g., witness communications, employment records) – 2.1
5) Freedom of Information Act (FOIA) requests – 7.1
6) Tax avoidance vs. tax evasion – 2.3-2.4
7) Tax return disclosure statements – 2.2
8) Taxpayer Advocate Service (e.g., criteria for requesting assistance) – 5.3
9) Taxpayer identity Theft – 1.7
10) Judicial levels of representation beyond the scope of EA representation – 3.1, 6.3

Domain 3: Specific Areas of Representation (20 Questions)

a. **Representing a Taxpayer in the Collection Process**

1) Extension of time to pay (e.g., Form 1127) – 5.1
2) Installment agreements – 5.1
3) Offer in compromise – 5.2
4) Collection appeals program (e.g., denial of installment agreements, discharge applications) – 5.1
5) Collection appeals and due process (e.g., lien, levy, and Form 12153) – 5.3
6) Adjustments to the taxpayer's account (e.g., abatements and refund offsets) – 4.1, 5.1
7) Requesting an audit reconsideration (e.g., documents and forms) – 4.1-4.3
8) Representing a decedent – 3.1
9) Collection notice and Notice of Federal Tax Lien – 5.1, 5.3
10) Levy and seizure of taxpayer's property – 5.3
11) Currently Not Collectible (e.g., reasons and reactivation) – 5.1
12) IRS Collection Summons (e.g., purposes) – 5.1
13) Collections statute of limitations – 5.1-5.2
14) Trust fund recovery penalty – 5.4
15) Amended returns and claims for refund (e.g., Form 1040X, Form 843, effect on statute of limitations) – 4.2
16) Passport revocation – 4.4

b. **Penalties and/or Interest Abatement**

1) Penalties subject to abatement – 4.1, 4.4
2) Basis for having penalties abated or refunded – 4.1, 4.4
3) Basis for having interest abated or refunded – 4.1, 4.4
4) Interest recalculation – 4.1
5) Procedures for requesting abatement – 4.1

c. **Representing a Taxpayer in Audits/Examinations**

1) IRS authority to investigate – 4.1-4.2, 5.1
2) Limited practitioner privilege (e.g., IRC section 7525) – 1.1, 2.1-2.2, 7.1
3) Verification and substantiation of entries on the return – 4.1
4) IRS authority to fix time and place of investigation – 4.1-4.2
5) Steps in the process (e.g., initial meeting, submission of IRS requested information) – 4.1-4.2
6) Interpretation and analysis of revenue agent report (RAR) (e.g., 30-day letter) – 4.1-4.2
7) Interpretation and analysis of CP-2000 notice and correspondence audits – 4.1
8) Explanations of taxpayer options (e.g., agree or appeal) – 4.1-4.2
9) Taxpayer's burden of proof – 4.3

d. **Representing a Taxpayer before Appeals**

1) Right to appeal Revenue Agent findings – 4.2
2) Request for appeals consideration (e.g., preparation, elements contained) – 4.2
3) Enrolled Agent appearance at appeals conference – 4.2
4) Settlement function of the appeals process – 4.2, 5.2
5) Issuance of 90-day letter – 4.2

Domain 4: Filing Process (14 Questions)

a. **Accuracy**

1) Reliance on software (e.g., review of results) – 2.1
2) Miscalculations and recognition of duplicate entries – 2.1

b. **Record Maintenance**

1) Length of time to retain returns and records – 7.1
2) Data security (e.g., electronic, systems, paper) – 1.7, 2.1, 7.2

c. **Electronic Filing**

1) Application process to be an e-file provider (e.g., e-services, EFIN) – 7.2
2) E-file mandate and exceptions (Form 8948) – 7.2
3) Advertising standards – 7.2
4) Definition and responsibilities of an ERO – 7.2
5) Levels of infractions – 7.2
6) Compliance requirements to continue in program – 7.2
7) EFIN revocation appeal process – 7.2
8) E-file authorization and supporting documentation (e.g., Form 8879 and Form 8453) – 7.2
9) Rejected returns and resolution (e.g., client notification, IP PIN) – 7.2

INDEX